THE FLOATING PRISON

LOUIS GARNERAY

THE FLOATING
PRISON

The Remarkable Account of Nine Years' Captivity on the British Prison Hulks during the Napoleonic Wars

1806 to 1814

Translated from the French
with a
Foreword and Notes

by

Richard Rose

CONWAY MARITIME PRESS

© Richard Rose, 2003

First published in Great Britain in 2003 by
Conway Maritime Press
An imprint of Chrysalis Books Group plc
The Chrysalis Building
Bramley Road
London W10 6SP

An imprint of **Chrysalis** Books Group plc

www.conwaymaritime.com

ISBN 0 85177 942 5

British Library Cataloguing in Publication Data
A CIP catalogue record for this book is available from the British Library

First published in French as *Mes Pontons*
by Louis Garneray in 1851

Design and typesetting: Stephen Dent
Printed and bound in Great Britain
by Creative Print & Design, Wales

CONTENTS

ACKNOWLEDGEMENTS

THIS TRANSLATION of '*Mes Pontons*' was undertaken as part of a much larger and continuing survey of the subject of prisoners of war in Great Britain during the French Revolutionary and Napoleonic Wars. In the course of my research I have enjoyed the help of the librarians, archivists and staff of the Public Record Office, the National Maritime Museum, the Family Records Centre and the Musée national de la Marine in Paris, to all of whom I offer my sincere thanks.

Amongst the individuals who have assisted me I must particularly mention M. Bruno Ponsonnet of the Musée national de la Marine and M. Laurent Manœuvre, the author of *Louis Garneray, 1783-1857, Peintre, Écrivain, Aventurier*, the best survey of Garneray's life and art, whose advice and conversation have led me to an understanding of the complexities of Garneray's career. Very late in the production of this book I had the good fortune to meet Mr Clive Lloyd who generously shared with me his matchless knowledge of prisoner of war life in the Napoleonic period and gave me a fresh insight into Garneray's artistic achievements on the hulks. I am grateful to each of them.

Several private collectors have kindly supplied materials for the illustrations and in addition I must offer my thanks and acknowledgements to the following institutions for permission to reproduce pictures and other copyright material; to the Musée national du Château de Versailles for plates 1 and 3 (© Photo RMN-Gérard Blot); to the Musée d'histoire, Saint-Malo for plate 2 (Photo, Michel Dupuis, Ville de Saint-Malo) and plate 4 (oeuvre des collections nationales, dépôt du Musée des Beaux-Arts de La Rochelle, Photo Michel Dupuis, Ville de Saint-Malo), to the Lloyd Collection for Garneray's view of the hulks on the dust jacket and for plates 5 and 7; to the Musée des Beaux-Arts et de la Dentelle, Calais, for plate 8 (dépôt du Musée du Louvre, ©Kleinefenn) to the National Maritime Museum, Greenwich, in respect of plates 10, 11, 12 and 16; and to the Musée national de la Marine, Paris, in respect of plates 13, 14 and 19.

ILLUSTRATIONS

The illustrations in the text of *The Floating Prison* are taken from the woodcuts that appeared in *Mes Pontons* in 1851. All are by Ange-Louis Janet Lange (1816-1872) after designs by Garneray, except for the picture of Captain Rose leaving the *Crown* hulk which was both drawn and engraved by Garneray.

The capture of the Kent.

FOREWORD

I

A VIEW OF THE HULKS

BETWEEN 1793 AND 1815 tens of thousands of prisoners from France and the other nations then at war with Great Britain passed through the British prison hulks and shore establishments. Of these thousands a handful wrote accounts of their captivity and amongst such memoirs Louis Garneray's *Mes Pontons*, here translated as *The Floating Prison*, is one of the longest and most detailed.

Ambroise-Louis Garneray, always known as Louis Garneray, was born in Paris on 19th February 1783, the son of Jean-François Garnerey, a student of painting and one of the first pupils of Jacques-Louis David.[1] From 1791 onwards until 1835 Jean-François exhibited regularly at the Salon and his work during the Revolution included a portrait, now lost, of Charlotte Corday at her trial for the murder of Marat. Louis was destined by his father to follow him as an artist but the boy, though making good progress in drawing, developed an irresistible yearning for a life of adventure. At the age of thirteen he announced his intention of going to sea.

In this ambition Garneray was abetted by an older cousin, Captain Beaulieu-Leloup of the frigate *Forte*, 'a sailor body and soul, who felt the deepest pity for those who dwelt in towns'. Having obtained his father's reluctant consent to his going as an apprentice on board the *Forte*, Garneray set off for Rochefort in February 1796 to join his cousin. Garneray's father parted solemnly from his son with the following words: 'To have seen much and suffered much are two excellent things that develop both the mind and the heart in men of energy and intelligence. And yet I must confess to you my hope that a few months hence, when your imagination has been cooled by rude contact with reality, you will perhaps return, cured of your mad ideas, to ask me once more for your brushes.'[2]

Father and son were not to see each other again until 1814 and Garneray's first adult attempts at painting were done in the unpromising environment of one of the hulks in which French prisoners of war were confined in Portsmouth Harbour.

Garneray recorded his years at sea from 1796 to 1806 in his *Voyages, aventures et combats*, first published in 1851. As with most things that Garneray wrote about his life, the reader must take it on trust that he actually participated in incidents which are not recorded elsewhere, but confidence is not encouraged by the author's carelessness in dealing with events that can be independently checked and dated. The high point of Garneray's early life was his cruise on board the *Confiance*, commanded by the famous St Malo privateer, Robert Surcouf (1773-1827), which culminated on 7th October 1800 in an audacious attack on the East Indiaman *Kent* in the Bay of Bengal as she approached Calcutta. Garneray later depicted the boarding and capture of the *Kent* in one of his most spirited paintings, but even this outstanding event was oddly misdated to 7th August in *Voyages, aventures et combats*.

Surcouf then sailed for Mauritius with his prize and in January 1801 began his return voyage to France, unaccompanied by Garneray who stayed at Port Louis. During the next five years Garneray remained in the Indian Ocean and his activities are difficult to fit into a definite chronology, but amongst many other adventures he claimed to have served on board two slavers named the *Doris* and the *Union*.

After the brief period of the Peace of Amiens, war between France and Great Britain was renewed in 1803 and the task of preying on Britain's trade in the Indian Ocean was entrusted to Vice-Admiral Linois, a cautious commander who annoyed Napoleon by his failure to cause significant disruption to the East India Company's commerce.[3] The small squadron under Linois, consisting of *Atalante*, *Marengo* and the 46-gun frigate *Belle-Poule*, arrived at St Denis in the Île de Bourbon (now Réunion) in August 1805 on its return voyage to France. Garneray requested a passage home in the *Atalante* and was taken on board, but the ship foundered in a storm off the Cape of Good Hope on 6th November. All the crew, including Garneray, were saved and he was transferred to the *Belle-Poule*.

On 13th March 1806 in the Atlantic near the Cape Verde islands, Linois's remaining two ships fell in with a British fleet, consisting of seven ships of the line, two frigates and a brig, commanded by Sir John Warren. Linois badly misjudged the situation, believing the first ship that was sighted to be a single warship escorting a merchant convoy. *Marengo* and *Belle-Poule* were pursued and forced to surrender after a fierce action the next day. Garneray, slightly wounded, was sent as a prisoner on board HMS *Ramillies*, which had been severely damaged in the battle.

During the homeward voyage to England the British fleet was joined by HMS *Superb*; Pierre-Marie-Joseph de Bonnefoux, a young officer from the *Belle-Poule* who was also a prisoner in *Ramillies*, observed a succession of signals being made which were followed by a general outburst of joy. *Superb* had brought the news of Sir John Duckworth's destruction on 6th February of Admiral Leissègues' fleet at the battle of St Domingo in the West Indies.[4]

Ramillies reached Portsmouth on 14th May 1806 and at noon the following day the captives were put into a lighter and rowed out to the prison ships. Nine old warships lay anchored close together, stripped of their topmasts, bowsprits and rigging, the functional beauty of their lines and upper decks disfigured by the incongruous projection of chimneys, sentry boxes and angular sheds used as offices, kitchens and stores. A floating platform patrolled by sentries surrounded each vessel at sea level. Alternate gun-ports in the ships' sides were closed and the open ports revealed rectangular lattices made of iron bars two inches thick, behind which lay the decks where hundreds of prisoners of war both lived and slept. As they neared the *Prothee*, the hulk of a 64 captured from the French in 1780, Garneray noted with an apprehension amounting almost to dread that 'her shapeless black bulk resembled an immense sarcophagus'. A few minutes later he and his companions climbed the *Prothee*'s boarding ladder and entered their floating prison.[5]

Each officer willing to give his word of honour not to escape was briefly confined until arrangements could be made to send him to one of the small or medium-sized towns where such parole prisoners lived, subject to various regulations, in relative freedom and often in considerable harmony with the local inhabitants. De Bonnefoux was initially sent to Thame in Oxfordshire and then to Odiham in Hampshire. Officers of the highest rank were sometimes by special permission of the Admiralty exempted from living in the usual parole towns and allowed to stay elsewhere; Admiral Linois spent several years as a resident of Cheltenham and later Bath, where he was joined by his wife and daughter in 1813.[6]

For ordinary soldiers and sailors, including Garneray, life was not to be so agreeable. They were not entitled to parole. Clad in the coarse yellow clothing that identified them as prisoners of war and crowded into the shore prisons or the hulks, their only hope of freedom before the end of hostilities lay in being exchanged, invalided home as incurables or succeeding in some desperate attempt to escape.

The coins in Garneray's pockets turned out to be a little fortune by the standards of the hulks and on his first day aboard he laid out three louis to buy a healthy well-ventilated place where he could sling his hammock close to one of the *Prothee*'s gun-ports. A cobbler who helped negotiate the purchase received a generous tip and in return offered Garneray the following bleak advice:

> *Listen carefully. Remember this well; on board the hulks a prudent man never lets himself be carried away by generosity, nor by any other feeling whatsoever. You must get used to shutting your heart, your eyes and your ears to all pity. These forty sous that you've just given me, which I certainly didn't expect, represent a week's food and you will soon bitterly regret having parted with them so lightly.*

Within a few hours Garneray was initiated into the bizarre world of the hulks, where the prisoners, isolated by water and wooden walls, had evolved their own class structure, economy, manufactures, discipline and ferocious modes of punishment. Certain aspects of this world sound so unlikely that Garneray's descriptions would seem fanciful were they not corroborated by other contemporary records.

The most startling example concerns the *rafalés*, the lowest and most desperate class of prisoners, who sold or gambled away all their possessions, including their bedding and clothing, and pledged their future shares of the communally issued rations in exchange for cash or some other immediate benefit. Everything they owned or obtained was subordinated to their insane addiction to gambling and they lived, starved and scavenged about the hulk, either naked or nearly so, and slept huddled together for warmth on the bare planks of the orlop, the vessel's lowest deck.[7]

Since Napoleon's forces contained a considerable proportion of conscripts from society in general, any batch of French prisoners normally included more skilled artisans than would have been found amongst a comparable number of British prisoners. Accordingly each hulk, apart perhaps from those housing substantial numbers of *rafalés* or trouble-makers, had amongst its higher classes many tradesmen and craftsmen either serving the prisoners on board, such as the obliging cobbler encountered by Garneray, or producing a variety of goods ranging from mundane articles to delicate mechanical toys and exquisite ship models made out of bone for sale at high prices through intermediaries ashore.

At the pinnacles of hulk society there was unexpected wealth. Green Parrot, an honest, thrifty sailor, had become a millionaire in the terms of the *Vengeance* hulk through running a sort of restaurant which he had developed from a humbler business selling *ratatouille* to the prisoners. His 'scandalous profits' amounted to as much as a hundred francs, or about £4 a month. Far richer but without obvious income was Duvert, Godfather of the *Crown* hulk, in his luxurious dressing-gown and fur-lined slippers, whose wealth was derived from forging banknotes. The man described by Garneray is undoubtedly a fictional character of a type that Balzac or Dumas might well have created, but the unlikely fact remains that banknotes were forged with almost incredible ingenuity in the hulks and prisons and smuggled out into the wider world.

Garneray introduces activities on board the hulks which seem highly improbable. It is questionable whether a prize-fight was ever arranged on a hulk as he describes, but theatricals were certainly performed by prisoners in front of audiences that included visitors from ashore. On 10th July 1807 the *Theatre of Emulation* on the *Crown* hulk gave the first performance of *The Revolutionnary Philantrophist* [sic] or *The Hecatomb of Haïti*, a four-act drama written by a prisoner, 'adorned by it's Whole Shew and Spectacle fighting with Swords and Pistols', followed by Molière's 'Very Gay & Diverting Comedy' of *The Doctor a Gainst his Will*.[8] A similar performance, according to Garneray, became the opportunity for an audacious escape from the *Vengeance*. And another author records that a Masonic

Lodge was opened and conducted with all due ceremony on board the *Guildford* hulk in a little space under the orlop, illuminated by a smoky candle stuck in the neck of a beer bottle.[9]

Garneray's experiences as a prisoner of war, or rather the experiences he claimed to have undergone, can be summarised briefly. He was sent on board the *Prothee* hulk on 15th May 1806 and remained there for about three years during which time he twice attempted to escape, in the company of a Breton sailor called Bertaud, through holes secretly and laboriously cut in the ship's massive sides. On the second unsuccessful attempt on a freezing winter night Bertaud was drowned and his body was left exposed for a day on a mud-flat in view of the prisoners on board the hulk.

In 1809 Garneray was transferred to the *Crown,* where he suffered under the vicious regime of its commander, Lieutenant R____, a dwarfish brute who had lost one hand. As depicted by Garneray this ogre, 'our absolute master next to God and without a doubt the most appalling man imaginable', united the physical attributes of Captain Hook and Mr Punch with Hollywood's idea of the character of Captain Bligh. The prisoners on board the *Crown* engaged in an almost ceaseless conflict with Lieutenant R___ until they at last engineered his dismissal by smuggling a report exposing his conduct to the Board of Transport, otherwise known as the Transport Office, the department of the Admiralty that dealt with prisoners of war.

Garneray's next and final transfer, probably early in 1810, was to the *Vengeance* where he encountered the abominable Dr Weiss, part of whose duties was the selection of prisoners to be returned to France as incurable invalids but who mocked his patients and sought to destroy them by maltreatment. The influence of Colonel (later General) Louis-François Lejeune, an officer of engineers of the French army in Spain and also a painter of battle scenes, who was briefly imprisoned in the *Vengeance,* eventually secured Garneray's release from the hulks and he was sent to live on parole at Bishop's Waltham in Hampshire.

During his time in the hulks Garneray had gradually developed his talent for drawing and painting and had also become an interpreter, a position which made him to some extent an intermediary between the commanding officers and the prisoners. His paintings were readily taken by Abraham Curtis, a Jewish picture dealer from Portsea, who paid a pound each and sold them, unknown to Garneray, for many times that price. Shortly before being sent to Bishop's Waltham Garneray had been informed of Curtis's duplicity by James Smith, another dealer. Garneray declined to do any further business with Curtis and, much to Curtis's resentment, transferred his allegiance to Smith.

Following a vicious attack on two fellow-prisoners by a labourer at Bishop's Waltham, Garneray broke his parole, fled back to Portsmouth and took refuge in James Smith's house where he lived secretly for over a year, whilst working at his painting. Finally, fearful that Abraham Curtis had discovered his hiding place and was about to have him sent back to the hulks, Garneray tried to cross the Channel with three escaped French officers in a boat crewed by smugglers. Out at sea the smugglers, who had been paid £10 in advance for each passenger, tried to murder the Frenchmen in the night but were themselves killed after a struggle.

Within sight of Cherbourg the little boat was overhauled by a British ship and the four escapers were again taken prisoner. Within a couple of days Garneray was back on board the *Vengeance* where he remained, painting like a slave for Abraham Curtis, until Napoleon abdicated in the spring of 1814 and all French prisoners were repatriated.

II

GARNERAY IN PERSPECTIVE

G arneray frequently proclaimed himself to be a truthful historian but much of what he wrote reads like fiction, especially the adventures that followed his escape from Bishop's Waltham up to his recapture off Cherbourg, whilst his persecution by Abraham Curtis runs through the later narrative like a slight plot intended to give cohesion to the last few chapters.

To the modern reader the artificial elements in *Mes Pontons* seem obvious. The prisoners encountered by Garneray often talk in extended dialogues more suited to melodrama than history and are inclined to help the story along with discursive explanations such as no historian would write. The narrator's initial stance as a friendless observer tossed into the grim world of the hulks is also a contrivance, since in reality Garneray went on board with more than a hundred captives, the companions of many weeks at sea. His later position as an interpreter is most probably a convenient device to place himself at the centre of events, a confidant to the prisoners and generally the first to hear of their British captors' intentions; the few English words and phrases used in the book suggest that Garneray's knowledge of the language was in fact very limited.

Particular aspects of hulk life described by Garneray are more difficult for the modern reader to assess. His account of the *rafalés*, living and starving in their hulk-enclosed inferno, appears early in the book and though seeming far-fetched, it is in fact an accurate and almost understated description of these creatures, derived largely from another author and former prisoner, Lieutenant Mesonant. If the *rafalés* are credible then the reader can have little difficulty in accepting Garneray's lurid portrayals of certain individuals, notably Lieutenant R___ of the *Crown* and Dr Weiss, as representing real beings whose fiendish motives and conduct are equally believable.

The story as a whole raises many doubts. Were Garneray's experiences characteristic of life on board the hulks? How reliable is he as a historian? Is there any record of his attempted escapes and the drowning of Bertaud, the Breton sailor? Did the monstrous Lieutenant R___ and Dr Weiss actually exist? Was it possible for a man in the hulks to begin a career as an artist? And above all, was Garneray himself really a prisoner of war in the hulks? An attempt to answer such questions must start with a search for some record of Garneray's name amongst the Board of Transport's papers.

A prisoner going on board a hulk or being received into one of the shore prisons was allocated a number in the Board's records and had details of his name, the date of his capture, the ship or action in which he was taken, the date of his arrival and often a physical description, entered in the register of that hulk or prison. On being transferred elsewhere the date of the prisoner's departure would have been noted together with his destination. A fresh series of entries would have been made in the register of the new hulk or prison. Assuming that the appropriate registers have survived, it is usually a practicable though lengthy job to trace a named prisoner from the date of his capture to the time of his death, release or escape.[10]

In Garneray's case the registers of the *Prothee* hulk in which he was first imprisoned in 1806 and of the *Crown*, to which he said he was next transferred, have not survived for the relevant periods. However, the hulks were Royal Navy ships[11] and though they were permanently moored the usual logs were maintained, noting the daily weather, arrivals on board, the delivery of supplies and any unusual events. Garneray states that he went on board the *Prothee* on 15th May 1806 and the log records that the day was one of 'Strong Breezes & Clear Weather' on which 129 prisoners were received, followed by a further 63 the next day. The total number of prisoners in the *Prothee* was then recorded as 621.[12]

The register of the *Vengeance*, the third hulk in which Garneray claimed to have been imprisoned, has survived but although a number of men who were captured on the *Belle-Poule* on 14th March 1806 can be found amongst the hundreds of names it contains, the name of Louis Garneray is nowhere amongst them. Does this mean that Garneray's narrative is a complete invention? It seems unlikely, but if Garneray was indeed in the hulks he must have been there under an alias or assumed name. This suggestion is more plausible than might at first appear, since prisoners were frequently registered with aliases or alternative names, and identities were sometimes swapped or sold by prisoners for the purpose of obtaining a transfer elsewhere in the prison system or even gaining freedom by personating a man due to be exchanged.

A close inspection of the *Vengeance*'s register reveals an interesting entry. A seaman named Pierre Priol, alias Garnerey [sic], was received from the *Prothee* on 17th October 1807. He was twenty-six years old, five feet eleven and a half inches high and was born at Paris. He was slender, had a long fair face, brown hair and hazel eyes and was marked with the small-pox. He remained nearly seven years in the *Vengeance* and was discharged to Forton Prison, Portsmouth, presumably on his way back to France, on 15th May 1814.

Garneray's true age in 1807 would have been twenty-four, but Priol's other details, with the possible exception of the marks of the small-pox and the colour of the eyes, fit reasonably well with what is known of Garneray.[13] In the general alphabetical index maintained by the Board of Transport there are separate entries for Pierre Priol, alias Garnerey, and Pierre Garnerai, alias Priol, cross-referenced with the remark, 'Double Name'.[14] This man is the only candidate who might have been Louis Garneray and to find him on board the *Vengeance* makes the identification probable. However, to solve one difficulty with Garneray is simply to create more of them.

If Priol was Louis Garneray and had been transferred direct from the *Prothee* to the *Vengeance*, then Garneray could not have been in the *Crown* and the sufferings he claimed to have endured in that hulk must have been invented.

Even more seriously, if the *Vengeance*'s register is correct, Priol was not on board the *Belle-Poule* in the Atlantic. He was captured far away in the West Indies on board the *Alexandre* man-of-war at the battle of St Domingo on 6th February 1806 and was probably transported to England in HMS *Superb*, Sir John Duckworth's flagship.[15] Yet *Superb* encountered Admiral Warren's fleet as it sailed home to Portsmouth carrying the men taken in the battle with the *Marengo* and the *Belle-Poule*. If Priol was in *Superb* he was at that moment within sight of *Ramillies* in which Garneray claimed to have been.

There is a mystery here, which it is easier to speculate about than to solve after nearly two centuries. If the man captured at St Domingo was Louis Garneray, alias Pierre Priol, then such an identification would give the lie to the later incidents, certainly in the period 1804-05, said in *Voyages, aventures et combats* to have taken place in the Indian Ocean and to have led to Garneray's capture on board the *Belle-Poule* in 1806. Yet if Garneray was present at the battle of St Domingo, why should he have falsified even a fairly loose account of his life by pretending to have been in the *Belle-Poule*?

Confirmation that Garneray was almost certainly in the *Belle-Poule* can be gained by examining what he says about the period before his voyage from Réunion which eventually led him to the hulks. He claimed in the final chapter of *Voyages, aventures et combats* to have been the master of a little unarmed vessel named the *Pinson* which was captured when 'an English frigate, the *Terpsichore*, detached herself from the squadron blockading Île de France, came stealthily down on the anchorage of St Denis and sent her boats to cut out all the vessels moored there. Amongst them was my poor *Pinson*.' This episode can be precisely dated to 15th August 1805 when boats from HMS *Terpsichore* cut out a French merchantman from St Denis harbour. The name of this prize as written in *Terpsichore's* log appears to be *Turilurette*, but nothing is mentioned about the *Pinson* or other vessels.[16]

At first sight this seems just another episode in which Garneray's narrative does not correspond with historical facts. Yet forty years later, when Garneray was giving details to the *ministère de la Marine* to be included in his *états de service*, the official dossier of his career at sea, he mentioned that he had sailed on board a vessel named *Turlurette* at an unspecified time, which Laurent Manœuvre suggests was between May 1803 and September 1805.[17] Absolute proof is impossible, but it is hard to doubt that Garneray was at St Denis in August 1805, went on board the *Atalante* shortly afterwards, was in the *Belle-Poule* in March 1806 and accordingly could not have been at the battle of St Domingo.

But if Garneray was captured on board the *Belle-Poule*, how and why did he assume the identity of Pierre Priol? One could suggest that in the interval between his capture and the registration of his name in the Board of Transport's records Garneray encountered a man called Pierre Priol amongst prisoners from the battle of St Domingo and took his name as an alias, perhaps to cover a successful escape by Priol. An arrangement of this sort would have done Garneray credit and furnished him with additional exciting material for his book long years after the event, yet Garneray never mentions such a thing. But something must have happened for, as Laurent Manœuvre has very perceptively observed, Garneray was not a simple liar or fantasist. He may have invented parts of his narrative and misplaced real names and episodes by accident or design, but he also deliberately left no records of certain events that must obviously have occurred.[18]

Some archive may one day provide a detail to solve the puzzle of Garneray's prison identity, but for the time being it remains obscure and we are left trying to corroborate his narrative with other records that hardly ever touch on him directly.

From *Mes Pontons* it is possible to make a rough chronology of Garneray's life and a list of the persons he encountered from the time he went on board the *Prothee* until his return to France in 1814. As with almost everything to do with Garneray an attempt to match the names and dates he supplies with official records either fails or provokes fresh questions. Garneray mentions the names of twenty-four French prisoners whom he met on board the hulks or who were involved with him in attempts to escape. These include one famous man, the soldier and painter General Louis-François Lejeune; all the others, including Bertaud with whom Garneray claimed to have attempted to escape twice, are obscure individuals not one of whom can be positively identified from the registers of the Board of Transport.[19]

Apart from General Lejeune it seems that the other prisoners named by Garneray are fictitious characters introduced for narrative purposes. Even

Garneray's meeting with Lejeune on board the *Vengeance* is almost certainly fiction; if this is correct it follows that Lejeune did not then know Garneray and would have made no efforts to obtain his release on parole. Indeed, any approach by Lejeune to the Board of Transport would have been futile. Garneray, however much he later represented himself to be a lieutenant or in some way different from the other prisoners, was a common seaman and simply not entitled to parole.[20] Consequently the later experiences that occupy *Mes Pontons* from Chapter XXIII onwards, including Garneray's life at Bishop's Waltham, the breaking of his parole and subsequent adventures, are untrue.

Baffling and exasperating as Garneray is, he cannot be dismissed as utterly unreliable. Although none of the ordinary men whom he names as his companions in the hulks can be identified, when it comes to the hulks themselves and their officers he is as accurate as one could expect of a man writing from recollection more than thirty years after his release. He claims to have suffered under Lieutenant R___ on board the *Crown* hulk. He was probably never in the *Crown*, but its commander can be identified as Lieutenant James Rose and Garneray knew correctly not only that Rose had lost a hand, but also that it had been amputated following a duel. He rightly names the commander of the *Vengeance* as Lieutenant Edwards and is accurate about the date on which Edwards relinquished his command. He describes the atrocious conduct of Dr Weiss at length. There was in fact a Dr John Weir, an Inspector of Naval Hospitals, who is clearly the man Garneray had in mind, though Weir's surviving reports and papers show him to have been a highly competent physician with no discernible animosity towards his prisoner patients.

Information about such persons could easily have been obtained at second-hand from former prisoners long after 1814 and in addition one might plausibly object that to find the surname Garneray annexed to an unknown man named Pierre Priol amongst hundreds of prisoners in the *Vengeance* is no evidence that Louis Garneray the artist was ever in the hulks. However, a tiny detail in the Board of Transport's correspondence establishes that Garneray was undoubtedly a prisoner at Portsmouth, that he used his own surname, not that of Priol, and that he was also engaged in painting during his captivity as described in *Mes Pontons*.

The Board's agent at Portsmouth with responsibility for the hulks was Captain Daniel Woodriff, who may have known Garneray personally and taken some interest in his artistic work. On 12th November 1811 the Board wrote to Woodriff, 'By the Coach of this Day will be returned to you a Picture transmitted to this office by Monsr Garnerei, [query Garnern] in order that it may be delivered back to him.' Two days later they wrote, 'We have received your Letter of Yesterdays Date, and acquaint you that Mr Garnerens [sic] Picture will be sent to you by Coach this Day'.[21] The subject of Garneray's picture is unknown but it could have been an early version of his view of the Portsmouth hulks. No more of the correspondence survives, but these few words suggest that Garneray was seeking official patronage for his work. Garneray was not the only artist soliciting attention, since a similar letter dated 9th November mentions the return of a 'Drawing belonging to M. Duval ... to be delivered back to this Prisoner'.

Official co-operation and money would have been needed for an ordinary prisoner on a hulk to send a picture from Portsmouth to the Board of Transport in London. Garneray could hardly have forgotten this episode even if it turned out disappointingly for him, but inexplicably he failed to mention it in *Mes Pontons*. The reference in the Board's letter to Monsieur Duval, an unknown artist, perhaps on another hulk or in one of the Portsmouth shore prisons, also draws attention to the fact that Garneray was not unique in the work he did during his captivity and this leads on to another surprising omission on Garneray's part.

Duclos-Legris, a *timonier* or helmsman in the *Marengo*, was taken prisoner on 14th March 1806 and like Garneray was sent on board the *Prothee* at Portsmouth. Nothing is now known of him except that he was an amateur artist with a naïve but attractive style, and produced a manuscript journal illustrated by seventy-two full-page wash and ink drawings, abounding in precise details, amongst which the battle between Admiral Linois's squadron and the British fleet is depicted from various points of view. These pictures may not have been created during Garneray's time on board the *Prothee* but it seems almost impossible that during nearly eighteen months together in the same hulk Garneray did not meet Duclos-Legris and know that he was an artist. Yet Garneray makes no reference whatsoever to Duclos-Legris. [22]

Garneray's fictions tend to diminish his real achievements as a painter. He states that he continued with his painting under the easier circumstances of parole at Bishop's Waltham and whilst hiding at James Smith's house at Portsmouth, but all his work was undoubtedly produced on the hulks, probably in little cabins for which an onerous rent in cash or paintings was exacted, much as he described. Not a great deal can be deduced about Garneray's methods of work at this period or the way in which he sold his pictures, but the existence at the present day of more than a dozen views of the Portsmouth hulks, similar but by no means identical in composition and some of remarkable quality, suggests that this subject was painted in fair numbers to satisfy a recurring demand from dealers or their customers. [23]

Mysteries cluster about Garneray. What is independently known about him during his imprisonment comes down to a very few facts or probabilities. He was almost certainly captured on board the *Belle-Poule*, but the official record states that he was taken at the battle of St Domingo in the West Indies; he went under the alias of Pierre Priol for some reason now unknown; he was on board the *Prothee* and *Vengeance* hulks from 1806 to 1814; he worked at his painting in the hulks; and he was sent back to France in the general release of prisoners after Napoleon's abdication. Tiny as this information is, it is still more than would be available in the case of an ordinary prisoner who did not distinguish himself by indiscipline or escaping. And because no note of misbehaviour is attached to Garneray's name in the records, we can assume as another fact that the tales of his attempted escapes are fiction.

III

THE ARTIST AS AUTHOR

Following his release from the hulks in 1814 Garneray began a career that lasted more than forty years during which he produced a body of work that entitles him to be ranked with the foremost marine painters of the nineteenth century. Despite the calls of his artistic work he maintained, if not a literary ambition, at least a desire that some account of what he had experienced should be preserved as history. In 1821 he contributed notes and two illustrations of the hulks to Auguste-François Chomel's *Histoire du Sergent Flavigny*.[24] In 1834–36 he published in the *Revue de Rouen* a number of essays based on various episodes of his own captivity and in 1848 submitted a manuscript account of his life at sea to the *ministère de l'Instruction publique* with the idea that it should be preserved as a historic document and published in a suitably edited form at the cost of the state. The matter was referred to the *ministère de la Marine* and after nearly two years of delays and consideration by committees, the ministry declined to publish it but agreed to accept a deposit of the work. This was not what Garneray intended; he retrieved his papers in 1850 and sought publication elsewhere. *Voyages, aventures et combats*, followed by *Mes Pontons*, began to appear in the journal *La Patrie* in 1851.

Garneray was then sixty-seven years old and writing for serial publication taxed his resources. 'I was lacking in material at first, being required to supply a certain number of pages every week; my memory was frequently at fault,' he recalled in his *Scènes maritimes faisant suite aux Pontons*, posthumously published in 1863. Nevertheless he, his editors and possibly a ghost writer contrived to keep up the supply of copy.[25] Garneray's days of privateering at sea were long gone, but literary piracy was another matter and any memoirs relevant to life in the hulks were boarded and ruthlessly plundered. The most flagrant of Garneray's plagiarisms occurred when he took Lieutenant Mesonant's *Coup d'œuil rapide sur les Pontons de Chatam* [sic], his *Quick Glance at the Chatham Hulks*, one of the best short factual accounts of the floating prisons, and incorporated large parts of it, word for word, into *Mes Pontons* with the omission of references to sodomy amongst the *rafalés* and other aspects too coarse for family reading. Additions from such a reliable source did no harm whatsoever to Garneray's text.

Garneray's acquisitive approach to writing may have been reprehensible, but it was not unique nor was he the first offender as a plagiarist of hulk literature. The few popular French authors of the first half of the nineteenth century who wrote about prisoners of war had already been borrowing and cribbing from one another well before Garneray joined in. A good deal of incontrovertible truth is inevitably blended together in such derivative accounts and in Garneray's book, but the reader in search of verifiable facts needs to treat them with caution.[26]

The 'somewhat tarry style' in which Garneray wrote appealed to the readers of *La Patrie* and the serials of both *Voyages, aventures et combats* and *Mes Pontons* had an immediate success far beyond their author's expectations. They were equally popular when issued in book form, two editions of ten thousand copies being quickly sold, and have been frequently reprinted in France over the last one hundred and fifty years. Rather surprisingly, the first English translation of *Mes Pontons* appeared only in 1957 and until that date the book was known in England, if at all, through the chapters on the hulks contained in Francis Abell's *Prisoners of War in Britain, 1756-1814*, published in 1914.

Garneray's reputation as a writer and historian is a mixed one. His first publishers specifically denied that Garneray wrote fiction and for many years it was uncritically accepted that not only was he accurate in his general picture of the hulks but that he was also an eye-witness of the events he described so circumstantially. Francis Abell certainly regarded *Mes Pontons* as a primary source for the history of the hulks and accepted Garneray's stories, such as the prisoners' conflicts with the odious Lieutenant R___ of the *Crown*, which occupy eight chapters of the book, as historical events.

Recent French historians, such as Auguste Toussaint in *Les Frères Surcouf* and Philippe Masson in *Les Sépulcres Flottants*, are dismissive of Garneray. Toussaint exposes the inconsistencies between Garneray's claims to have served on board privateers in the Indian Ocean and ascertainable historical facts, whilst Masson points to Garneray's many plagiarisms and states that the *Voyages, aventures et combats* and *Mes Pontons* together 'form a singularly doubtful document'.[27] Laurent Manœuvre in his *Louis Garneray, 1783-1857, Peintre, Écrivain, Aventurier*, the only book devoted entirely to Garneray's life and art, carefully details the available evidence whilst acknowledging the problems and inconsistencies it contains.

Even without prior knowledge of the intricacies of Garneray's life the modern reader of *Mes Pontons* must be puzzled as to how the book could ever have been regarded as other than a fascinating story based on the author's imprisonment. A comparison with the memoirs of De Bonnefoux, Garneray's contemporary and fellow-prisoner from the *Belle-Poule*, makes the point clear.[28] De Bonnefoux wrote verifiable history in the form of a solid autobiography, whilst Garneray depicted characters who were for the most part imaginary, engaged in activities that were often plausible but occasionally improbable, against a well-drawn background of the hulks.

A truly accurate account of the tedium of life as a prisoner of war would have been heavy reading and accordingly Garneray enlivened his story with exciting incidents more numerous than most prisoners could ever have witnessed. His account of the prisoners' heroic opposition to Lieutenant R___ is undoubtedly fiction so far as events at Portsmouth are concerned, but probably owes much to reports of disturbances on board the *Bahama* hulk at Chatham and the shootings there on the *Sampson* in 1811 when six prisoners died in what was ever afterwards characterised as a massacre by French writers. Other dramatic episodes may have been enormously magnified from some germ of truth and throughout the book there are occasional outbursts at British maltreatment of prisoners, which seem to relate to nothing that Garneray himself saw but may have been derived from one particularly prejudiced author and ex-prisoner, Maréchal-de-Camp René Pillet.[29]

Yet, if one discounts Garneray's manifest fictions and deliberate distortions and compares his text with the more reliable printed sources that he knew and drew on, if one reads narratives of prisoner of war life that were unknown when he wrote but have since been discovered and if one consults the Board of Transport's records, it becomes apparent that *Mes Pontons* is very accurate in its general depiction of daily life, routine, rations and physical conditions on board the hulks. Furthermore, specific incidents such as punishments, duels, murders or escapes described in the book can be paralleled with exactly similar events in records and memoirs unavailable to Garneray and are in no way exaggerated.

Readers who trusted Garneray's self-proclaimed veracity and believed that he wrote nothing but the truth have been mildly deceived for more than a century whilst certain historians who incautiously relied on him have misled themselves and their own followers. Garneray himself can be accused of nothing more dishonest than hurriedly putting together a book for the popular market, a hybrid of composition and compilation, which he and his publishers certainly never imagined would still be in print in the twenty-first century.

Writing was secondary to Garneray's art, yet he was by no means a second-rate writer and his story owes its survival and continuing readership to its own merits as much as to its author's separate fame as a painter. He cannot be classed as a historian in the sense of an accurate chronicler of events, but just as Captain Marryat's fiction provides a first-hand view of life in the Royal Navy of Nelson's time, so Garneray gives a vivid eye-witness impression of what it was like to have suffered on board the hulks in the same era.

The years that Garneray spent on board the Portsmouth hulks may have been a time of relentless monotony rarely broken by startling incidents, but in *Mes Pontons* he embellished and transformed his experiences to create a remarkable book.

Paradoxically, for all Garneray's faults, for all the obscurities, concealments and mysteries surrounding his life and identity, for all his inventions, exaggerations, borrowings and plagiarisms, and to some extent because of them, he wrote the fullest and most dramatic account we shall ever have of the existence endured two centuries ago by countless captives in the floating prisons.

Richard Rose
August 2003

TRANSLATOR'S NOTE

So far as I am aware *Mes Pontons* has never before been fully translated into English; Lawrence Wood's translation, published in 1957 under the title of *The French Prisoner* is an abbreviated version of the book. Garneray's text can be read simply as a novel but it is hoped that the notes and appendices, derived largely from research amongst the Board of Transport's papers in the Public Record Office, will provide a useful historical background to some aspects of the hulks.

The text used is that of the first edition published in 1851. In translating it I have edited it lightly, whilst trying to be as faithful as possible to the original. Some redundancies have been removed and a number of inconsistencies and obvious errors of fact have been corrected. I have omitted most of the author's reminders such as 'the reader will recall…' and 'as I previously said…', which seem to have been carried over from the serial publication, together with a few unimportant allusions to Garneray's previous book, *Voyages, aventures et combats*. Three paragraphs at the end of Chapter XV, dealing with the health of the prisoners, have been moved to Chapter XVI where they seem properly to belong. When the author's knowledge of aspects of English life is clearly shaky, I have made suitable slight amendments and indicated them in the footnotes.

The hulks and other British ships (including vessels captured from the French) are given the names under which they were known in the Royal Navy; thus Garneray's *Protée*, *Couronne* and *Pégase* become *Prothee*, *Crown* and *Pegase*.

In describing the deck arrangements of a hulk Garneray refers (in ascending order from the lowest upwards) to the orlop, the twenty-four pounder deck and the eighteen pounder deck. The equivalent British names, which I have used throughout, are the orlop, the gun-deck and the upper deck. When visualising the scenes described by Garneray the reader needs only to bear in mind that the orlop and the gun-deck were the enclosed decks where the men slung their hammocks and were confined at night. The upper deck was partially open to the air by means of an oblong well in the waist of the ship and in this area, ironically called 'the Park', the prisoners took their exercise in the day-time.

The commanding officers of the hulks were always Royal Navy lieutenants and as Garneray indicates, were generally addressed as 'Captain' or 'Commander' on board. References by Garneray to *maîtres* amongst the lesser British officers on the hulks seldom make clear their precise rank or function and I have normally translated *maître* as 'mate', 'boatswain' or 'petty officer'. In translating the French naval ranks mentioned by Garneray I have used 'Ensign' for '*enseigne*' or '*enseigne de vaisseau*', the rank immediately below lieutenant.

Garneray refers throughout to his captors as 'the English' and uses the word

'British' only once in an ungallant reference to the dress-sense of the ladies of Portsmouth, who were '*parées avec ce luxe éclatant et de mauvais goût si essentiellement britannique*'.

Both French and British coinage circulated on the hulks. References to *sous, francs, livres, louis*, guineas, pounds, shillings and pence are exactly as given by Garneray, except that I have removed the word 'sterling' with which he generally qualified the pounds. A *sou* was equivalent to an old British halfpenny (½d). There were twenty *sous* to a *franc* which was worth about ten old pence (10d) or slightly less than a shilling (1s) – 5p in modern money. The *livre*, not to be confused with a British pound, was equivalent to a *franc*. Five *francs* were worth fractionally over four shillings (20p). A *louis*, depending on the date of its minting and gold content, was worth between eighteen shillings and ninepence (93p) and one pound.

I have not attempted to translate the exceedingly mild expletives, which Garneray puts into the mouths of French prisoners.

Since *Mes Pontons* begins rather abruptly with the author's arrival as a prisoner at Portsmouth the final chapter of Garneray's *Voyages, aventures et combats*, in which his voyage from Île de Bourbon and his capture are described, has been edited and included as a Preface.

CAPTIVITÉ

DE

LOUIS GARNERAY.

NEUF ANNÉES EN ANGLETERRE.

MES PONTONS

ILLUSTRÉS

PAR L'AUTEUR ET JANET-LANGE.

PRIX : **90** CENTIMES.

PARIS,

PUBLIÉ PAR GUSTAVE BARBA, LIBRAIRE-EDITEUR,

RUE DE SEINE, 31.

14.

The title page of Mes Pontons, *1851.*

AUTHOR'S PREFACE

I enter the Navy • I become a Captain • Capture of the
Pinson *• Wreck of the* Atalante *• The* Belle-Poule *• An*
ominous encounter • Battle • Capture of Admiral Linois's
squadron by a British fleet

WHEN I HAD RUN THROUGH MY PRIZE MONEY I was summoned to serve in the Navy and sent as second in command on board a cutter named the *Pinson*, which had just been purchased by the government to patrol the coasts. During a voyage in *Pinson* to Île de France her captain fell overboard and was drowned, despite all my efforts to save him. On my return to St Denis I was given command of the vessel with the rank of mate at thirty-six francs a month, a modest salary very far from the prize money I had received when I sailed under Surcouf's command, but I was at least a captain. Unfortunately, I was soon deprived of this semblance of dignity by an unlucky event.[30]

One night an English frigate, the *Terpsichore*, detached herself from the squadron blockading Île de France, came stealthily down on the anchorage of St Denis and sent her boats to cut out all the vessels moored there. Amongst them was my poor *Pinson*. Since my cutter mounted no guns, I was not overmuch troubled at having to abandon her and was only too pleased to take my crew of nine safe and sound with me to St Denis.[31]

Finding myself unemployed at St Denis, penniless, depressed in spirit and weary in body, I dreamt only of returning to France. When the frigate *Atalante*, bound for France, came into port I swiftly took the opportunity of requesting a passage home in her. My request was granted and I slung my hammock on board the *Atalante* on 30th August 1805.

I dreamt happily of my arrival in France, of my family's delight and the ease I would at last enjoy, but I reckoned without my unlucky star. What happened proved to me again how unwise it is for man to anticipate his arrival at his goal and ignore the obstacles on the path that leads him there.

A dreadful storm, a hurricane which struck us at the Cape of Good Hope, wrecked our ship on the coast and I was only saved by the greatest good fortune. Some of *Atalante*'s people were taken on board the two other vessels comprising Admiral Linois's squadron. It fell to my lot to go on board the *Belle-Poule*. In this manner, when I thought I was on my way back to France, I suddenly found myself once more on a new cruise, much against my will.

The slave trade was then flourishing and we put to sea, scouring the coast of West Africa, in the hope that English slavers would provide us with good prizes. Our crews, exhausted and ill-rewarded by infrequent and insignificant prizes, complained bitterly and all the more so since they knew that the privateers in the Indian Ocean had resumed cruising with new and astonishing successes. Their discontent increased when they saw the squadron was heading for France. A great catastrophe was soon to change these mere annoyances to despair.

During the night of 13th and 14th March, which was exceedingly dark, we perceived three vessels sailing towards us before the wind on the opposite tack. The largest vessel made signals, which were repeated by the others, and two of them shortly disappeared from our gaze into the gloom. Our Captain, Monsieur Bruillac, warned Admiral Linois that it was likely that the large vessel we had seen, which was now pursuing us, was part of an English squadron and that it would probably be wise to avoid the squadron's course and let ourselves be chased by the ship till daylight. Once we had the large vessel on her own we could then do whatever the circumstances required.

Admiral Linois took this advice very badly, maintaining that this ship of the line was only protecting a merchant convoy. The French squadron therefore held its course, led by the *Belle-Poule*, with the *Marengo* bringing up the rear.

The large ship soon began to creep up on us, tacked, followed in our wake sailing as close to the wind as possible and approached the *Marengo*, whose speed was inferior. Soon she was on her starboard quarter within small arms range and hailed her with the usual questions. The *Marengo,* recognising an enemy, loosed her starboard broadside, to which the English ship replied instantly with her larboard guns.

In less than a minute the two vessels were engaged. The *Marengo* carried 74 guns. Her opponent was none other than the three-decker *London*, carrying 104.[32] The *London* maintained the advantageous position she had taken on the *Marengo*'s starboard quarter.

The Captain of the *Belle-Poule* judged rightly that he could damage the enemy more severely by crossing her stern than by remaining broadside and manœuvred accordingly, but the Admiral immediately ordered him to station his ship in front of the Admiral's and fight there.

When fire was opened the *London* took the *Marengo* on her quarter, causing serious casualties on board. Her formidable guns and the fire from her small-arms soon swept most of the combatants from the French vessel's quarter-deck and disabled a number of guns towards the stern.

Towards seven o'clock in the morning the *Belle-Poule*'s fire had badly cut up the *London*'s forward rigging, bringing down her fore-topsail and leaving the English

The capture of the Belle-Poule.

vessel's staysails trailing in the sea. At that moment we saw the rest of the English squadron outlined clearly on the horizon. It comprised six more ships of the line, two frigates and a brig. These ships had remained astern because they had misunderstood the signals made to them by the *London* during the night. They now began an all out chase.

The damage done to the *London* meant that we could sail better than her and the *Marengo* signalled us to get away. We tried to obey but sadly it became immediately evident that all the ships of the English squadron were very much our superiors in speed.

At the start of the action Admiral Linois had been gravely wounded in one leg and obliged to quit the deck. His flag captain, Monsieur Vrignaut, also had an arm shot away and so Captain Chassériaux, being next in the hierarchy, occupied the quarter-deck.

Towards half past ten the *Belle-Poule* was about a league from the *Marengo*. At that moment the *Amazon*, the fastest ship of the English squadron, placed herself to starboard and a new fight began. At midday the 74-gun *Ramillies* joined the *Amazon*, stationed herself on our larboard quarter so that we should be caught between two fires, and prepared to devastate us with her broadside.

Events elsewhere were equally dire. The *Marengo*, surrounded by several enemy vessels, was no longer able to defend herself and struck her flag. In these circumstances the *Belle-Poule*, disadvantaged by her lack of speed and her inferiority to overwhelming force, could only surrender. We were ordered to strike.

A quarter of an hour later we were boarded by the English. The names of the ships composing the enemy squadron were, *Foudroyant*, Admiral Warren, *Ramillies*, *Hero*, *Namur*, *Repulse*, *London* and *Courageux*, all ships of the line; *Amazon* and *Resistance*, both frigates and *Locust*, a brig.

For the first time since I went to sea I was deserted by the good luck which had always been with me when under fire and I was slightly wounded. A quarter of an hour after the English had boarded us I was taken on board the *Ramillies* as a prisoner. Here ended my career at sea and now there remains one sad and final episode of my story to relate, my agony of nearly nine years' captivity in the English prison hulks.

CHAPTER I

Imprisonment • Impressions • Description of the hulks •
Equality • Rations • Work • The tribunal • Industries •
Bertaud • The rafalés

A FTER A PASSAGE OF SIX WEEKS the *Ramillies* entered Portsmouth
Harbour. The very next day, 15th May 1806, I was transferred with a
number of my companions in misfortune on board the *Prothee* hulk.[33] As
everyone knows a hulk is an old vessel of two or three decks with her masts
removed which is almost as immovable as a stone building when held in position
by anchors.

That first daunting view of the *Prothee* still oppresses me. Seen from afar,
anchored in a line with eight other floating prisons at the mouth of the Portchester
River, her shapeless black bulk resembled an immense sarcophagus. As we were
taken alongside by the Transport Office I looked despairingly at this sombre tomb
in which I was to be buried alive whilst the years of my youth ebbed away. My
imagination, piercing the thick wooden walls, conjured up the sad sunken faces of
the wretches confined within but as I realised to my dismay a few minutes later,
my vision fell far short of reality.

I sustained a fearful shock when I was led between files of soldiers on the deck
and found myself brutally tossed into the midst of the *Prothee*'s miserable and
hideous inhabitants. No description however forceful, no pen however powerful,
could describe the spectacle that suddenly met my gaze. Imagine a generation of
the dead coming forth from their graves, their eyes sunken, their faces haggard and
wan, their backs bent, their beards wild, their bodies terrifyingly thin and scarcely
covered by tattered yellow rags, and still you have no more than a feeble and
incomplete idea of how my companions in misfortune appeared.

I had scarcely set foot on the deck when the guards seized me, roughly dragged
off my clothes and forced me into a freezing bath. After this I was attired in a shirt,
a pair of trousers and a jacket of yellow-orange colour. Materials had not been
lavished on these garments for the trousers came only half-way down my legs and
the jacket, being far too narrow for my chest, could not be fastened. These two
items were stamped with a colossal black T. O., representing the initials of the
Transport Office. When this operation was over, my companions and I were led off
to have our names noted and, once classified and registered, each of us was placed
in the quarters assigned to him. My place was down on the gun-deck.

To understand what follows a full and exact description of the interior of a hulk is needed. A vessel has a forecastle and a quarter-deck which are separated by a bulkhead and a great opening down to part of the upper deck known as the well deck. This space and the forecastle were the only places where the prisoners were allowed (and that not always) to walk and get a little air. An ironic wit never fails Frenchmen in adversity and the inmates christened this place with the expansive name of *the Park*. It was about forty-four feet long and thirty-eight broad.

The forecastle, the second exercise place on board the hulks, was not nearly as large and accordingly not so well-liked as the Park. Furthermore the chimneys, which emerged here, covered the place almost constantly with a thick cloud of coal smoke, a horrible annoyance, which generally forced those taking exercise to beat a retreat.

The two extremities of the hulk were occupied by the Englishmen assigned to guard the prisoners, the stern being the quarters of the lieutenant commanding the vessel, the officers, their servants and a few soldiers, whilst the forecastle contained only soldiers.

A stout bulkhead made of particularly solid thick planks stood between the English quarters and those of the unfortunate captives. For further security this

The exterior of a hulk.

partition was studded with a great quantity of large-headed nails, so tightly crammed together as to form practically a wall of iron. In case of mutiny or riot on our part, loopholes at regular intervals allowed the English to fire on us point blank without running the least danger.

Finally, the gun-deck and the orlop were given over to the living quarters of the prisoners, each deck being about a hundred and thirty feet long by forty in width. In this confined space nearly seven hundred of us were lodged.

A ladder from the Park gave access to the lower decks without any other visible communication between them. I say 'visible' because, unknown to our gaolers, we had cut a little square hole which allowed us to pass from one deck to another. This access was so narrow that only one man at a time could use it.[34]

On the gun-deck daylight came only through the gun-ports, half of which were open, and on the orlop through very narrow scuttles specially cut for that purpose. All these openings were covered with cast iron grilles, two square inches in thickness, which our gaolers inspected every day, even though they would have been proof against any file.

All around the vessel and nearly at sea level ran a gallery, the surface of which was an open grating so that we could not slip underneath without being noticed by the sentries who patrolled ceaselessly on it. During the day two sentinels were placed there and seven were present throughout the night.

The hulk was commanded by a naval lieutenant with a master as second in command. The officers' functions were fulfilled by petty officers and the garrison consisted of forty to fifty soldiers commanded by a lieutenant of Marines.[35] The rest of the people included a score of seamen and a few lads specially allocated to the service of the Transport Office. In addition, and for greater security, the hulks were closely anchored in a line in sight of one another and kept watch on each other.

The security measures taken inside the hulks were as follows. During the day three sentinels were stationed on the gallery, one on the raft where the boarding ladder was fixed, one on the forecastle and finally one on each gangway. A further eight or ten guards stood permanently on the poop ready to take up arms at the slightest alarm.

During the night, as well as the seven sentries, of whom I spoke earlier, patrolling the gallery at sea level, there was also a guard in the Park above the hatchway down to the lower decks. An officer, a sergeant, a corporal and several sailors of the watch also made continual rounds. And every quarter of an hour we heard the sentries' monotonous cry, 'All's well!'

The hulk's boats, which we would have needed to escape, were hoisted alongside, eight or ten feet out of the water, with the exception of one, which remained floating, secured by an iron chain.

At six o'clock in the morning in summer and at eight in winter our gaolers opened the ports and the hatch covers to the lower decks. The air confined within had been breathed by such a multitude and was so tainted that the Englishmen performing this duty recoiled abruptly to avoid being nauseated by the overpowering stench that issued from our quarters. In summer the scuttles protected by iron grilles, which I previously mentioned, were left constantly open and without this precaution we should all have been stifled in a single night.

The English came at six o'clock in the evening in summer and at two in the afternoon in winter equipped with iron bars, with which they tapped all the grilles and probed the sides of the hulk to ascertain that neither had been damaged by any attempt at escape. An hour after this inspection soldiers with loaded muskets and fixed bayonets came in turn to each lower deck and made us go to the upper deck, where we were counted just like sheep, to make sure that no escape had taken place.

As my narrative proceeds I shall explain how we managed to evade this vigilance and conceal the absence of those who were lucky enough to escape, until letters informed us that they were safe.

Now I move on to our living quarters. No great effort is needed on my part to describe the furnishings of a hulk, since they consisted of no more than a bench running the length of the sides of the ship and four others placed in the middle.

The interior of a hulk.

On entering the ship each prisoner received a hammock, a very thin woollen blanket and a flock mattress weighing at most between two or three pounds. The hammocks were suspended from cleats attached to the beams of each deck.

It is needless to add that when the newcomer was an officer the English either denied his rank or took no account of it and treated him as if he were an ordinary seaman. Complete equality in suffering was the rule in these appalling prisons.[36]

Since there were nearly four hundred of us on each deck and each deck (a detail I cannot repeat too often) was only one hundred and thirty feet long by about thirty feet wide, with a height of six feet at most, the hammocks, which took up at least seven feet in length because of the cords by which they were suspended, could naturally not all be hung on one level. Half of them had to be slung beneath the others. Those prisoners who enjoyed some means constructed hanging cots for themselves which they furnished with proper mattresses and thus lay more comfortably, but they still had to endure the surrounding foul air and the vermin in common with the most miserable of us. I repeat again that our tormentors made no distinction of rank and mixed soldiers, sailors and officers together.

I now come to the subject of food and here the unstinting hatred of the English against us is revealed. Our week was divided into days on which meat was issued and meatless days,[37] five of the first and two of the latter. Each prisoner's rations consisted of a pound and a quarter of coarse bread and seven ounces of beef. It was stipulated that we were to be given soup at mid-day though most of the time this was not done and we often went without for a whole day. To make the soup we were allowed three ounces of barley and an ounce of onion or leek for four men together with some salt.

On the two meatless days, instead of meat and soup we had on Wednesdays a pound of salted herrings and a pound of potatoes and on Fridays a pound of dried cod and the same weight of potatoes. I must observe here that an English pound contains fourteen and not sixteen ounces.[38]

On a first view it would seem that our scanty diet was enough to feed a man, but because we never received the full amount it was literally only sufficient to stop us dying of hunger. The contractors, well-knowing that our complaints would not be heard, never failed to keep back a certain proportion. From this ration, already diminished by fraud, we had to retain more for the prisoners who were reduced to two thirds rations as a punishment for having tried to escape or for damaging the hulk, to pay for a newspaper which was smuggled on board (for which we were naturally made to pay three times its normal price) and to put something aside to provide some money for escapers.[39]

These deductions were made in equal proportions from the rations of the entire mass of prisoners, for we had established a religiously observed rule that in the general distribution each man should receive an identical quantity of food.

Having made these deductions, there remained for each man on the meat-ration days, nineteen ounces of bread, three ounces of meat and a pint of broth and on the meatless days, nineteen ounces of bread, thirteen ounces of cod or five herrings and thirteen ounces of potatoes.

We were divided into messes of six persons and received our rations in common. All the vessels we were allowed for our meals came down to one simple tin can, a mess-tin; spoons, forks and knives were unknown to us.[40]

When the English contractors had provisioned the hulk for the day they took no part in the distribution or preparation of the rations and left these tasks to the cooks, who were prisoners chosen from amongst us. They alone had the right to enter the galley. It is true that fifteen prisoners representing the inmates from the different decks had permission to inspect the preparation of provisions but the sentries, despite the entry tickets that were shown to them, usually repulsed them brutally with blows from musket butts, and seldom allowed them to do their job.

Our food for the day was generally divided up as follows. We breakfasted on dry bread and at mid-day had only soup in which we used to put part of our bread. Our seven ounces of meat were kept for supper. The meatless days gave us fewer expedients. The salted herrings were usually of such detestable quality that we could not bring ourselves to eat them, even when fainting with hunger. We sold them to the contractors for two sous and they kept them to serve up again the following week. I can well believe that some herrings went the rounds for ten years. With these two sous we got a bit of butter or cheese. As for the cod, though nauseating, it could be swallowed in an emergency; we let it stew in water in the great cauldron and divided it into two equal portions which we kept for two days.

After the general distribution of soup what remained at the bottom of the cauldron was divided up in rotation, so that some days we found that we had a ration and a half. This happy windfall, called a *rabiot*,[41] was usually enjoyed once a month by each mess of six prisoners.

We were often obliged to refuse the bread we were given, either because it was as heavy as lead or because our nineteen ounces were of such short measure that they scarcely exceeded the volume of a fist. We addressed our complaints to the lieutenant in command of the hulk, who passed them on to the commissary, but the latter seldom took the trouble to reply in time to satisfy our appetites. We frequently fasted until five o'clock in the evening whilst waiting for his decision. You can imagine the torments we suffered from our debilitated stomachs, deprived of all food for twenty-four hours.[42]

Water was brought from the shore in little boats used for this sole purpose. They came alongside the hulk and we were then obliged to hoist the barrels on board. Those of us who were unable to fulfil this task through weakness or age or, being officers, thought it beneath their dignity, had to pay a sou to a substitute. If they had no money they gave ten ounces of bread from their next day's ration.

Other enforced tasks abounded. Every day and in rotation we were employed in hauling up from the hold the number of barrels of water needed for the soup or filling the tank from which the drinking water was drawn.[43] And finally every night after we had gone down to our lower decks a dozen of us worked at washing down the foredeck and the Park.

Men crammed together in such considerable numbers would undoubtedly have been subject to frequent and dangerous epidemics if the greatest care had not been taken to maintain cleanliness on board the hulk. For this purpose English soldiers came on to the decks each morning to make us take down the hammocks and these were carried up to the foredeck where they remained in the fresh air all day.

Twice a week in winter the lower decks were scraped from one end to another, each man being liable to do the portion of the deck below his hammock. In summer, instead of scraping the decks, they were copiously washed down every morning.

Let me now give a preliminary idea of the discipline that had been established in our dreadful prisons. Above all, one can well imagine how such a variety of men, crowded together, exasperated by unwonted sufferings, tormented by overwhelming but unassuageable desires, embittered by misfortune and freed from the constraint of laws and authority, might degenerate and slide into depravity.

To prevent crimes and disorders as far as possible the prisoners in the *Prothee* had established amongst themselves a committee of eight nominated by the majority. Their task was firstly to issue specific rules applicable to most ordinary cases, and secondly to hear, determine and judge, without any right of appeal, in disputes that might arise amongst the prisoners. However, when it came to a crime or a serious offence, such as murder or theft, the committee had only the right to summon the gun-deck and the orlop together, for in such cases the accused was tried by all the assembled prisoners. Since no one had any right to mercy, the sentence was always executed with implacable severity.

Anarchy was the essence of our confinement but despite this fact the officers were still generally respected, enjoyed great influence and were readily listened to by the mob.

Having given these indispensable details, nothing impedes my narrative and I shall go back a little, to the point when I found myself on the *Prothee*'s gun-deck.

If anyone had told me when I was at sea with two hundred and fifty slaves in the *Doris* that it was possible to survive in an atmosphere fouler and more fetid than that on board a slaver, I would have refused to believe him; within a hulk I doubted it not at all.

The truth of what I witnessed sometimes appears so improbable that I find difficulty in describing the appalling sensation of disgust and nausea I felt when I reached the gun-deck to which I had been assigned. It seemed as though I was enveloped by a thick searing cloud which corrupted my blood with the deadly contagion of every mortal disease. A violent effort and the summoning of all my will-power were needed not to fall down in a faint.

Fortunately this distressing impression was short lived. After half an hour on the deck I felt myself, if not used to this dreadful atmosphere, at least able to endure it. I now gave all my attention to the objects that surrounded me, which my eyes, baffled by the abrupt change from light to darkness, had not yet been able to observe. The gun-deck and the orlop of the *Prothee* were an unbelievable picture, and though I know it is impossible to describe them as they then appeared to me, I cannot resist an attempt to do so, if not completely, at least in some details.

The middle of the deck lay in a gloom nearly as dark as night. Only the two sides of the vessel, illuminated by the opening of alternate gun-ports, were visible in a sad uncertain light. The prisoners' faces, lit by this wan light, were pale, corpse-like and bereft of the ordinary colours of life. They seemed to belong to some unknown subterranean race or to have the look of ghosts emerging from their graves. The incredible variety of rags in which these wretches were rigged out would be impossible to depict. All of Spain, whose tattered beggars are unequalled, could not have matched the unbelievable garb of most of my companions in misfortune.

There was great activity throughout this foul den. No one was unoccupied except for a few prisoners stretched at full length on the deck who, from their extreme pallor and the dull look in their eyes, seemed about to expire. Some with planes were engaged in carpentry; others were making fancy toys and chess sets out of bone; here model ships and frigates were being built to a perfect finish; there they were plaiting slippers or straw hats or knitting nightcaps. Every man had some different occupation.

Next to those who practised crafts and arts, for the perfection of some prisoners' work raised it to the level of art, were the tradesmen. Between a tailor and a shoemaker I saw a man deeply engaged in pounding some unwholesome black stuff. On my asking about this mixture, he informed me that it was tobacco! This prisoner was the hulk's tobacconist and God alone knows if a single leaf of the fragrant weed we owe to Christopher Columbus was ever found amongst the stock which he ground[44] from morning till night and sold to us at a fairly modest price.

Lastly, the French character was admirably displayed by the teachers of dancing, fencing and single-stick who instructed their pupils in these arts in the middle of the deck at a sou a lesson, lessons which often lasted more than an hour!

Prisoners, for the most part muffled in old greatcoats buttoned up to the neck, sat by the gun-ports in a ray of light, explaining the mysteries of algebra and geometry to their companions in misfortune. I learnt that these unfortunates were officers who had become schoolmasters to kill time as much as to better themselves. Sad to say, their lessons were rewarded at no higher rate than those of the single-stick teachers or dancing masters.

Pedlars, called *bazardeurs* by the prisoners, wandered up and down the deck endlessly calling out in monotonous, nasal voices, 'Something to sell? Who wants to sell anything? Who's buying?' Every moment some starving wretch would stop them and offer to sell his possessions, or rather his rags. The bargain was quickly over and the wretch, robbed, despoiled and shivering, for the *bazardeurs* only dealt at the lowest prices, would hurry off to another tradesman, the vendor of what was called *ratatouille,* to exchange the price of his clothes for a portion of that slop.

The roving adventurous life I had led up to that day had given me sufficient self-confidence, but despite this I found myself completely at a loss. I asked where I should sling my hammock and, being a newcomer, the darkest and most stifling part of the deck was indicated to me.

'But I could never spend a whole night there,' I replied. 'I'd be suffocated by the morning.'

'*Dame,*' replied a prisoner, 'that might well be so, since the last three people here died after a few days.'

'And you want me to destroy myself like that? Never!'

'Let me point out,' replied the prisoner, 'that it don't matter whether this place suits you or not. You've no choice but to obey. Where d'you want to sling your hammock?'

'Nowhere; I'll sleep on the floor, on the planks!'

'Impossible. The deck's no more than six foot high and the hammocks are slung in two layers from one end to the other. You wouldn't find space enough to stretch out.'

'So I'm condemned to death?'

'Of course, unless you have money…'

'Money? Unfortunately, I've so little. Between four and five louis is all I have left.'

'Five louis,' exclaimed the prisoner, eyeing me with admiration, 'but that's an utter fortune here. Mark you, I'm a shoemaker and I earn no more than seven sous by working from morning to night. And I'm one of those with no reason to grumble about his luck! Well, since you have five louis, why don't you buy yourself a good permanent place by the gun-ports?'

'Do you really believe that anyone from there would be simple enough to change places for a few francs? It's a matter of life or death.'

'Not at all, mate; just a matter of hunger, no more. Do you want me to arrange it all? I can get you properly settled in an hour. Only, since my work will be interrupted, I'll ask you to pay me for that hour. Out of the seven sous a day I get, what I charge won't ruin you!'

'Gladly. You seem like a good 'un. I'll go along with whatever you do.'

'Wait here, I'll be back soon,' answered the prisoner, moving briskly off.

Five minutes later, true to his word, he was back.

'Here we have,' said he, introducing a poor devil who seemed phenomenally lean to my eyes, 'a worthy infantryman who wants nothing better than to do business with you. He's had what is perhaps the best place on the deck for a fortnight, having waited two years for it. And since he likes it vastly he won't give it up except to a good mate who'll know how to reward his sacrifice liberally.'

'How much d'you want, soldier?' I asked.

'Three louis, comrade,' he answered in a feeble voice. Thinking I was about to protest, he continued, 'There's no point in haggling…oh, the thought of eating my fill for a couple of months…now then, take it or leave it.'

I was in a hurry to conclude the bargain, being afraid that the soldier might change his mind at the last moment, when my go-between, the officious shoemaker, spoke up once more.

'I think, Picot,' said he to the soldier, 'that your price is quite reasonable, if a bit high, but for three louis you must arrange to let him have a table, a stool and everything he needs to settle himself.'

'Done, all included,' replied the soldier, whose gaze had for some time been anxiously following the wandering course of a *ratatouille* seller.

'Well then, it's agreed; we've struck a bargain,' said the shoemaker. 'When'll it all be ready?'

'In an hour or an hour and a half. Trust me.'

And three quarters of an hour later the soldier Picot, faithful to his promise, came to tell me that all was prepared. I hurried after him and was led to the place where I was to sling my hammock. I swear that I felt my spirits rise when I saw the well-lighted and ventilated space reserved for me in a corner of the deck near to a gun-port. This place was one of the best to be found on the whole deck and well worth what it cost me. A bench to sit on, nearly long enough for me to stretch out on it, was placed in front of a table that was also mine.

'How did you go about getting this furniture?' I asked Picot.

'It wasn't very difficult for me,' he replied. 'I arranged it with my friends, which is what we do whenever we need something.'

I handed the agreed three louis to the soldier and we parted the best of friends.

'My dear comrade,' said I, addressing the obliging shoemaker to whom I was indebted for making this bargain, 'kindly take these forty sous with all my thanks for the favour you've just done me. I really owe you them for the time you've lost on my account.'

The shoemaker eagerly laid hold of the coin I offered, stowed it carefully away in his waistcoat pocket, then looked at me with a smile. 'Comrade,' said he, 'I thank you. In exchange for the generosity you've shown me let me give you some good advice. Listen carefully. Remember this well; on board the hulks a prudent man never lets himself be carried away by generosity, nor by any other feeling whatsoever. You must get used to shutting your heart, your eyes and your ears to all pity. These forty sous that you've just given me, which I certainly didn't expect, represent a week's food and you will soon bitterly regret having parted with them so lightly. Instead of that sum, for here that really is a substantial amount, you should have slipped a two sou coin into my hand and I'd have been well satisfied! Believe me, husband the two louis you still have with the greatest care and use them to shield you from the pangs of hunger for some time to come, whilst you get yourself an occupation or establish some trade. With that, thanks, and I'll get back to my shoes.'[45]

I was sitting sadly on my bench, thinking of the future that awaited me and already wondering how it might be avoided, when a joyful exclamation and a slap on my shoulder brought me suddenly back from my dreams.

'Well now! It's you, lieutenant,' said a prisoner, whom I realised was a seaman, smiling at me with an air of recognition. I looked closely at the man, but my inspection told me nothing and raised no recollection in me.

'I think you're mistaken, comrade,' I replied, 'I don't know you!'

'Nay, I'm not mistaken! It may be that you don't remember me because I was just an ordinary seaman whilst you were a lieutenant, though we've spoken together several times…'

'You're mistaken, my friend…'

'Ah, no, *sacrebleu!* You're really Garneray, aren't you? And the proof of it is that we both served under the greatest devil afloat, Surcouf! *Hein!* Now does it come back to you? It's me, Bertaud! Don't you know me? Quartermaster Bertaud, from Saint-Brieuc, good old Bertaud? Maybe my long beard makes me hard to recognise, eh?'

'Ah! *Parbleu!* Now I remember you, Bertaud. We sailed together in the *Confiance.*'

'And together we battered the English about. What a fight that was on board the *Kent!* Bullets flying around like hailstones! And the prize money… Ah! If I hadn't drunk it away like a lunatic I'd at least have had something to eat today. But, bah! The past is done with. Let's forget it. Truly, I'm vastly pleased to see you.'

There was such sincerity in the Quartermaster's voice that I felt moved and cordially shook the hand he extended. This Bertaud was one of those frank, handsome characters, simultaneously abounding in gentleness and energy, a sort that I have so often encountered in my career at sea and a credit to humanity. Meeting him was a great pleasure; I was no longer isolated amongst the crowd and I could at least rely on one friend.

'Poor Bertaud, have you[46] been long on this hulk?' said I.

'*Tiens, tu me tutoies!*' he cried joyfully. 'Well! Thank you; it means you trust me and I'm in your confidence. See here, you and me, we're friends for life!'

Again we shook hands and Bertaud continued.

'You ask me if I've been long on this villainous hulk. Sad to say, it's two years since I was taken. Since then I've been on board four hulks but only eight months in the *Prothee* and I hope I won't stay much longer.'

'How, Bertaud? What do you mean?'

'Hush, silence! Today we can be at ease; we'll talk later.'

'As you wish. And where were you caught? In the Indies?'

'Alas, my friend,' replied Bertaud with a sigh, 'I was on my way back to France…'

'Just like myself.'

'Oh! Not quite! You'll think me a bit of a fly-by-night, but what can I do about it? I can't alter the truth. I was running away from a woman. You laugh; what can I say? That's how it was. An enormous mulatto woman, my friend, name of Chapet, who wanted to wed me at all costs. Given her weight of four hundred pounds, not many men came courting. In short, she was either going to kill me or be my wife! I was afraid, I ran, I met the English on my way and here I am.'

I spent the rest of the day talking to the worthy quartermaster and his conversation initiated me further into the ways of the hulks.

'D'you want to see something very strange?' said he, after a dinner which I had made tolerable by laying out a few sous on butter, bread and vegetables.

'What is it, Bertaud?'

'I'll take you to see where the *rafalés* live. Do you know about the *rafalés*?'

This word was completely unknown to me since it originated in the hulks but had not then become widespread. I confessed my ignorance to Bertaud.

'Before I show you the *rafalés*,' he replied, 'I'll explain some things so you'll be in no doubt about them. They're well-known but not well-loved on board the hulk. Anyway, sad dogs they may be, but it has to be said for them that they don't whimper.'

'To begin with, Bertaud, tell me, where does the word *rafalé* come from?'

'*Pardi*, you don't need to be clever to guess that! At sea doesn't *rafaler* or *affaler* mean to lower away or to be caught in a squall? Well! A *rafalé* is a fellow who is completely down and under the weather. Your *rafalé* now, to return to the subject, is above all a gambler at cards, but that's nothing. What he lacks is dignity. We only have a few of them here, herded apart like filthy wild beasts. We hardly ever have dealings with them, but there's one hulk where they have about two hundred of them.

First of all the *rafalés* sell all their belongings. They have neither hammocks nor

Bertaud
recognises
Garneray.

bedclothes. To keep themselves warm they sleep huddled together, just like sardines, on the planks of the deck. They all lie down on one side and when the man at the end of the line finds himself tired of that position in the middle of the night, he sings out, "*Pare à virer!*" and everybody turns as ordered.'[47]

'You're not exaggerating, Bertaud?'

'*Dieu de Dieu!* What I've just told you's nothing. Your real *rafalé* has no breeches, coat or shirt in this world. He goes bare, stark naked! Well, would you believe it, there are folk who want to join this gang? Now, wanting to join's not enough. For a start you have to be chosen. The man who wants to get in amongst the *rafalés* starts by selling everything he owns and with the money he raises he has to treat the members of the gang with beer and bread, right down to his last farthing. Then he's recognised as a brother and they give him a great pebble to use as a pillow.'

'Bertaud, I don't believe a word of this!' I exclaimed.

CHAPTER II

*Mysterious Thomas • A robbery • A brutal punishment •
Bertaud's secret • A revelation • A lucky escape*

THE SEAMAN WAS ABOUT TO REPLY when a prisoner with a grave
and refined expression, who seemed to have overheard part of our
conversation, approached us and addressed me.

'Bertaud is exactly right in what he tells you,' he said.

'Thank you, Captain,' said Surcouf's old sailor, greeting the newcomer with
great respect.

The stranger smiled sadly, then laying his finger unaffectedly to his lips and
lowering his voice, said in a tone of mild reproof, 'Bertaud, why do you persist in
calling me *Captain*? You know well that I'm not.'

The sailor coloured. The stranger turned back to me, probably to cut short any
excuses or remarks from Bertaud, and resumed the conversation. 'No,' he said, 'your
friend doesn't exaggerate the complete nakedness of the *rafalés* in any respect. We
recently obtained new hammocks for those who had sold their own since coming
on board the hulks. Well! Would you believe it? Most were so used to sleeping for
years on bare planks that they couldn't endure the softness and comfort of a
hammock and they disposed of them for next to nothing! The moment when the
rafalé emerges resplendent in misery, if I can put it that way, is in the evening when
the roll-call of prisoners is taken. Those who are absolutely naked - a very large
number - hire an old blanket for a sou. Two or three wrap themselves in it and this
allows them to go up on deck. The sou to pay this rent comes from their next day's
rations, for I must explain that the *rafalés* are very prodigal when driven by
necessity, and deplorably ready to pledge their future rations. It's not uncommon
to see some of them starving for five or six days, having sold their food in advance.'

'Allow me, sir,' said I, interrupting the man in the buttoned-up great-coat, 'it
seems to me that you overdraw the picture. How can men go so long without food
and not perish? It appears impossible to me.'

'I don't maintain that they eat nothing at all,' replied the stranger, 'I merely say
that for five or six days, sometimes longer, they get no rations and keep a strict fast,
no more than that. Then you see them, wandering like souls in torment in the
darkest recesses of the decks, seeking the filth and rubbish rejected by the other
prisoners and greedily hurling themselves on it. In their extreme hunger they don't
despise raw potato peelings or leaves of leeks; cabbage stalks and heads of herrings

are magnificent discoveries to them. I've often seen a couple of *rafalés* after one of these expeditions, perishing of hunger, yet gambling against each other for the fish heads they've collected. These people are incorrigible.'

'But how can these wretches stand such privations and not fall ill?'

'That's a phenomenon I can't explain. Certainly, many of them do succumb; but what I can't understand is why they don't all die. At any rate, illness is a good job for them since it gets them into the hospital where they can at least have some food.'

'What singular characters these *rafalés* are,' I exclaimed. 'Thank you, sir, I've been highly interested in the details you've so kindly explained.'

'Oh! I've not done yet. So far I've only shown you one side of the coin. There's always some good mixed in with the worst things of life and I must show you the good side. The *rafalé*, despite the depths to which he has sunk, despite his gross, uncouth ways, doesn't lack a sort of bravery, even a sort of scrupulousness. It's the *rafalé* who plans and executes such marvellously daring escapes that only their success stops them being called acts of madness; it's the *rafalé* who can keep the secret of any plot that's been entrusted to him even when he's dropping dead from starvation. In the whole sad, sorry history of the hulks it would be hard to find three or four examples of betrayals done by them. After all, a man can't be totally good or ill. Without this spirit and courage these degraded creatures wouldn't belong to humanity.'[48]

The stranger had just spoken these words when the curfew bell rang, for in the hulks we were required to extinguish all lights at eight o'clock in winter and nine in summer. We were obliged to separate. Nevertheless, this prisoner's gentle, affable and dignified bearing had struck me so forcibly that I kept hold of Bertaud, who was already on his way to his hammock, and begged him to give me more details of the man.

'My dear friend,' he replied, 'I can only half satisfy your curiosity, for though I've the greatest confidence in you and we've promised friendship for life, I can't possibly break my word. I mustn't tell you the prisoner's name. I can only say that it's respected and loved by the French as much as it's dreaded by the English.'

'I respect your discretion deeply, Bertaud, and I can only praise it. At any rate, without revealing the prisoner's name, can't you at least tell me what he is? To my mind he looks like a naval officer.'

'You guess right. Though still very young, the man is already a ship's captain. After all, why should I hide part of the story? On the contrary, it's better that you should know it all. That may let you be useful to him and in any case prevent you from betraying him by mistake.'

'They're going to put the lights out: hurry, I'm listening with the greatest attention.'

'Here it is in brief. This captain was on a voyage on a ship which fell into the hands of an English frigate eighteen months ago.'

'How does he now come to be aboard this hulk? Isn't it a generally established practice that officers are kept prisoners on shore under parole?'

'Yes, and here's the story. Not wanting to give his parole he passed himself off as a common seaman. Being accepted as such he was thrown on board the *Prothee* hulk. Except for three or four persons who share the secret, no one knows him except under the name of Thomas and he's taken for a simple topman. Well, despite this, he's well-respected and has great influence. You have to believe that he's one of nature's captains and worthy of his rank. The prisoners have nominated him as president of the tribunal we established and never take an important decision without consulting him first! Poor man! It makes me rage to see the English sentries insulting him as if he were a simple caulker. For his part, always calm and grave, he seems to dismiss these annoyances and says to himself, *"This won't last for ever."*'

'Then does the captain hope…?' said I, lowering my voice.

'Quiet,' exclaimed Bertaud sharply, shaking my arm hard. 'My dear Louis, for your guidance, you must never talk when you find yourself in the dark. Left, right, all around us, there are ears you can't see.'

'English spies, of course?'

'Sadly, no, traitors. Frenchmen, brutalised by misery or broken down by suffering. They don't scruple to spill their brothers' blood so long as that blood buys a favour to bring some relief from their misery. Until tomorrow, good night. If this conversation interests you, we'll take it up again in daylight.'

After this reply Bertaud shook me heartily by the hand and we parted, he to his hammock, I to mine. Although a month and a half had passed since I became a prisoner on board the *Belle-Poule*, the first night in the hulk seemed endless. Until then, although I was a total prisoner, hope had still remained; a shipwreck, a fire or a battle might come to my aid and set me free; at any rate, until the last moment I was always able to count upon chance. Now that final consolation was withdrawn. On board the hulks could one not have written the fatal inscription set by Dante over the gates of his inferno; '*All hope abandon, ye who enter here.*'? Sadly, yes, since the number of prisoners who had succeeded in getting out again through perserverance, daring and luck were such a tiny band that it was madness to hope to be numbered amongst them. Despite this, I did nothing throughout that sleepless night but contrive plans, invent stratagems and make schemes to escape. Sleep had for a moment closed my eyes when the day surprised me.

I had just finished stowing my hammock when Bertaud came to find me. The sight of this good friend, whom I had only known as such since the previous day, for I could scarcely remember having seen him on board the *Confiance*, did me good. We resumed our conversation and might have been talking for nearly an hour about our recollections of the Indies, when a great commotion arose amongst the prisoners and groups of them gathered from all sides.

'Let's see what's happening over there,' said Bertaud. We mingled with the crowd and soon learnt that a robbery had occurred during the night.

'And who's been robbed?' asked Bertaud.

'Me, comrade,' called out a tattered wretch, whose pale face and dejected expression showed how keenly he felt the misfortune that had struck him.

'You!' I exclaimed, recognising Picot, the soldier from whom I had bought the place I occupied near the gun-port for three louis.

'Alas, yes, it's me,' he replied, 'and they got your three louis off me whilst I slept.'

Since such a sum was a very large one for the hulks, this theft caused a great stir. I was trying my best to console poor Picot, when he was approached by a prisoner whose tattered garb came horribly close to the *rafalés'* nudity.

'Friend,' said he, 'I have my suspicions about who stole your gold.'

'Suspicions!' cried Picot, flushing to his ear-lobes with excitement, 'for God's sake, speak…'

'Speak, speak! Easier said than done! My suspicions are either right or wrong. If they're wrong I'll be dragged into a duel for taking your side. Then there's the death penalty for duelling and that makes me think twice. If they're right, I'll have got back an enormous sum for you…'

'If I get it back I'll give you a magnificent reward; I'll give you five francs!'

'That's very handsome, I can't deny it. Yes, but if I'm wrong…'

'Then you'll be no use to me…'

'Which won't save me from a duel. On second thoughts, it would be wiser to hold my peace.'

After making this reply the demi-*rafalé* was going off, when Picot pulled him briskly back. The unhappy soldier could not bring himself to lose his last hope in this way.

'Come, comrade,' he implored, 'don't be awkward. Tell me plainly what you want. If it's in my power to give it, you shall have it.'

'*Dame!* To be frank, I want a huge amount.'

'Still, comrade, tell me…'

'Well, soldier, for what I know you'll have to give me – and no haggling, mind you - I'll expect two francs from you! Yes, it's a huge amount, as I say, but since it means a duel for me if I'm wrong and fifty-eight francs for you if I'm right, it seems to me that I'm not asking too much…'

'Alas!' replied the soldier, 'it'd be no skin off my nose if I had the money you want…'

'You haven't even got a sou? Nothing left at all? It wasn't worth wasting my time!' cried the ragged prisoner, marching away. The unhappy Picot's despair had touched me and I ran after the demi-*rafalé*.

'Here's the two francs you wanted,' said I, handing them over. 'Now you can speak out.'

The prisoner turned the coin I had given him over and over between his fingers and tossed it in the air with his thumbnail; being certain at last that it was of good metal, he carefully knotted it up in a rag that hung down by his legs.

'Your thief,' said he, turning back towards Picot, who was showing his gratitude by shaking my hands to the point of crushing them, 'your thief is a body-snatcher[49] from the army called Chiquet.'

'Chiquet!' exclaimed Picot in utter astonishment. 'He's my best friend, he saved my life in the hospital at Metz, where he was an orderly. He sold me a new four pound loaf when I was starving, dying of hunger. He can't be the thief. You're mistaken…'

'I don't think so. First, listen.'

Before going on the informer looked all around and seeing that no one paid us any attention, continued in a lowered voice, 'Chiquet is my neighbour; his hammock hangs just above mine. Now, last night I heard him getting up, climbing down furtively and straightaway moving off, not walking like a man who isn't afraid of being seen, but slithering on his belly like an evil snake! Well, said I to myself, I always took Chiquet for an out-and-out coward, except when it comes to fighting a duel, since he's a fencing-master and relies on his skill. But it seems that he's secretly cutting a hole and thinking of breaking out one of these days. I'd never have thought him capable of such resolution; he goes up in my estimation. I was going back to sleep when I heard a little noise. It was Chiquet coming back… Aha! I said to myself again, I'm not mistaken, Chiquet's not cutting a hole, he must have been to relieve himself, that's all.'

'Now we come to the best bit of the story. At the very moment when Chiquet was climbing back into his hammock his foot slipped and he sprawled pretty heavily on the deck. What's this? I asked myself again. God in heaven, it's raining louis! In fact I heard the sound of a gold coin bouncing on the deck and I'm sure I wasn't mistaken.'

"Are you asleep, Barrière?" asked Chiquet at once, laying his hand lightly on my arm and moving his face close to mine. Right, I thought, there's something going on and I'll ferret it out. And so I set to snoring like a serpent[50] in church.'

'Well! What does that prove?' asked Picot.

'It proves, soldier,' said Barrière, 'that if you've been robbed you deserve it, because you've certainly not got the brains you were born with.'

'After all this,' added Bertaud, 'I don't see how the orderly can be other than guilty.'

'I can't believe such a thing!' exclaimed Picot, whose indecision was plain on his perplexed face. 'Chiquet rob me! Him who sold me a four pound loaf when I was...'

'But what if this honest Chiquet really has gold on him?' said Barrière.

'Chiquet with gold! Come now! He's a *rafalé* through and through. I lent him two sous yesterday evening. Now, if he had gold on him...'

'Now, Picot, keep quiet and don't wave your arms about like that,' said Bertaud, interrupting the soldier, 'you'll draw attention to us.'

'But what can I do, comrade?'

'Go straight away to the president of the tribunal and put the matter before him.'

'Yes, you're right; that would be best. I'll go now to Monsieur Thomas... He's the man to throw light on it all.'

Five minutes later two men led the ex-orderly Chiquet in front of Thomas the pretended topman, who awaited the culprit seated on a bench between four or five prisoners, the jurors of the hulk. Since the three louis had been mine in the first place someone came to find me and warn me that the tribunal was ready for my evidence. I hurriedly obeyed and the hearing began as soon as I arrived.

Nothing could be more orderly, in form at least, than a court on board a hulk; only they dispensed justice with more than normal speed. After Thomas, the president, had listened carefully to my evidence, which lasted a minute at most, he ordered the accused to be searched. Unfortunately the fool had kept the three louis in his pocket and they were found at once.

'Where did you come by this gold?' asked the president.

Chiquet tried to talk about his family who sent him help, his winnings at cards, etc., etc., but at each excuse he was immediately shown up as a liar. In the end, with his invention exhausted and driven into a corner, Chiquet declared that he had found the money on the deck. A disapproving murmur showed him at once how misplaced such an excuse was, and he said no more about it.

'Have you anything to add?' asked the president after the defender chosen by Chiquet, a former student, had presented the case for the accused with more than enough eloquence.

'Nothing!' replied Chiquet, overwhelmed.

The president then made a rapid and impartial review of the case after which the jurors huddled together and having spoken in subdued voices for a few seconds, gave their verdict. Their judgement, against which there was no appeal, condemned Chiquet to thirty lashes to be given immediately whilst the court sat.

As soon as the judgement was pronounced twenty arms seized the unhappy Chiquet, who found himself instantly stripped of his shirt and securely triced up to one of the deck beams with his hands in the air. The punishment began without a moment's delay. The prisoners, ranged in a crowd round the sufferer, sang the

Marseillaise in chorus, to cover his cries and prevent the English from hearing them. However, this last precaution was unnecessary, for when the rope used for the punishment descended for the fifteenth time on the unfortunate victim's back he gave a great cry of pain and lost consciousness. 'Carry on! Carry on!' urged voices from all around to the man wielding the lash, who had turned towards the mob to consult them with a look. It was not until the twentieth blow, when the ex-orderly's back appeared like a single wound, that five or six compassionate souls called out timidly, 'Enough! Enough!' and sought to halt this tragedy.

Chiquet was then unloosed, his inert body rolling heavily on to the floor like a corpse, and he was thrown into a dark corner of the deck.

'He won't do that again for a while, leastways not here!' said Bertaud. *'Ma foi!* I don't pity him. He got only what he deserved. Stealing from poor devils like us is worse than a crime. But whilst it's daylight, my dear Louis, and we've no reason to fear any eavesdroppers, let's go on with the conversation we broke off at curfew-time last night.'

We both sat down on the bench near my hammock and when the sailor was satisfied that no one was observing us, he continued.

'My friend,' said he, 'I'll not ask for your word of honour concerning the secret I'll trust you with. I've noticed that people who keep pledging their honour are the least reliable. We both sailed under Surcouf and that's enough for me.'

'Speak, Bertaud, you can trust me, I'm listening.'

'First, what do you think of Monsieur Thomas?'

'His conduct shows him to be a man of determination and spirit.'

'Good. I must tell you, my dear friend, that he and I have been working for more than three months to prepare for our escape. Do you like what I'm telling you?'

'How could I not? You see how the idea of regaining my freedom affects me...'

'Pardieu, I can imagine it. Myself, I haven't slept for a fortnight. Now, to come back to the subject. We've already cut two-thirds of the hole by which we hope to get out. Do you want to help us, to join us?'

'Do I want to, Bertaud!' I cried, shaking the Breton's hand vigorously, 'I mean that I'm more obliged to you for your proposal than if you'd saved my life!'

'Then it's agreed. Let's go and find the captain, Thomas I mean, and we'll move things along.'

Needing no further invitation, I hurried after my new friend. Our search was not long, for as soon as we set out after the so-called Thomas we saw him approaching.

'I need to speak to you, Bertaud,' he said in Breton with an agitation that he could not conceal.

'What's wrong, Captain? Beg pardon, what's wrong, comrade?' asked the latter anxiously. 'Are there any hitches?'

The pretended topman cast a reproachful look at Bertaud who carried on unperturbed, 'You can speak without fear in front of this comrade. We've known one another for a long time. We sailed together under Surcouf.'

Monsieur Thomas fixed me with a questioning eye and then said with a sad smile to the Breton, 'You've committed a great indiscretion, Bertaud, but your lucky star was on your side. It's true you've found an honest man, for such I know him to be, but you could have met with a traitor.'

'No danger of that, Cap... comrade. Surcouf liked Ensign Garneray a lot, and a man who's been Surcouf's friend could never be a traitor. But what's the matter? With all respect, you seem...'

'Here, read this note which I've just received,' replied the captain, holding out a little square of paper, carefully folded, to the Breton.

'Right away, comrade,' said Bertaud, with an awkward expression, beginning to scratch his head, 'though I must confess that I only spent four days in school in my whole life, so I don't read written writing too easily... Anyway, if you insist, I'll do my best; I know A, O and C quite well...'

'Then listen,' replied the pretended topman, unable to suppress a smile at the sailor's reply.

'To tell the truth, I much prefer it that way, comrade.'

The captain, unfolding the note and glancing around to see that he was not observed, read the following to us in a low voice:

Captain, I am a wretch. To better my lot I have divulged your escape plan to the English. You and your accomplice Bertaud are both watched. However, I have respected your incognito because I was not paid any more money for that intelligence. I do not pretend that my conduct is other than base and as this warning shows I feel sincere remorse. But I have suffered so much. When I betrayed you I had eaten nothing for three days...

'*Satanée canaille!*' cried Bertaud, when the captain had finished reading. 'Well! What are we going to do now?'

'Give up our attempt, my poor Bertaud,' said the captain.

'*Pardi!* I've no wish to give the English the pleasure of shooting me point blank. So, we'll be shut up here for a long while yet.'

'No, Bertaud, I'll get out tomorrow.'

'Get out tomorrow, Captain?' repeated the sailor in amazement.

'Yes, or at least I'll make the attempt. Listen to me carefully, because I count on your co-operation. Tomorrow is the day when the little vessel comes with the *Prothee*'s water supply...'

'Yes, that's true. And I also recall that I'm on the working party for hoisting the barrels.'

'You're on the working party; that falls out wonderfully!' exclaimed the captain delightedly. 'Here's my plan. Tonight I shall slip into one of the empty barrels that the vessel will take back. I'll lie huddled in there till the middle of the following night. Then when the English crew is asleep I'll creep out and get ashore in the little rowing boat moored alongside the vessel. What do you think of this scheme?'

'I think, comrade,' exclaimed Bertaud, his face displaying simultaneous astonishment and admiration, 'I think with all respect to you, that this madness will cost you your life if you persist with the idea. It's twenty to one that you won't succeed.'

'What does it matter if it's twenty to one against? As long as that one chance remains, that'll be enough.'

'However, Captain, if you put twenty black tickets in a hat with one white one and someone said to you, draw any one out; if you get the white one you go free; if you get a black one you'll be shot. I don't think you'd take that bargain.'

'Yes, I'd take it,' said the pretended topman, his voice subdued and thoughtful, 'and for that no credit would be due to me, for I feel that my imprisonment will kill me soon if I have to endure it any longer. I must be free, d'you hear? Do you understand, Bertaud? I say I must. An *affaire de coeur* demands my presence in France.'

The captain was quiet for a few seconds then, looking upwards with a gaze in which a dull fire glowed, a look that said more than any words, continued to Bertaud and myself, 'And what about revenge? Is that nothing? Do you think that I can enjoy an untroubled rest, bearing in mind the accumulated insults I've endured for eighteen months? God created me good, the English made me cruel. I must have blood, a great deal of blood! I will be merciless to any enemy that encounters my frigate.'

Ashamed at this explosion of long concentrated anger, dragged from him through suffering, Monsieur Thomas remained silent for a few moments. 'My friend,' he began again, smiling sadly and with a calm voice, 'let's go on with a conversation which I was wrong to stray from. Above all, I thank you for the interest you display and for your advice, but I tell you again that my resolve is unchangeable. I need to know but one thing, whether or not you can and will help me?'

'Ah! Captain,' I exclaimed reproachfully, 'can you doubt our support for a moment?'

After a long conversation our plan was fixed. It was decided that during the day we would make a slight nick with a knife on the cask which the captain would choose as his hiding place. The next day, thanks to this identifying mark, we would sway it up on deck with every possible care and then lower it down into the English boat. This plan being decided upon, we very carefully went our separate ways so as not to arouse suspicion.

'My friends,' said the captain shaking us warmly by the hand, 'if I succeed in this perilous enterprise, be sure that I will neither rest nor sleep till I get you exchanged at sea for English prisoners.[51] If I perish…'

'Ah! Don't say such things, Captain,' cried Bertaud who as a Breton was full of superstition, 'it'll bring ill luck.'

I was extremely anxious all night and could not get a moment's rest. At last the fateful moment arrived. Towards ten o'clock the men were called whose turn had come round on the working party. I cannot express what I felt when, having hauled the full water casks on board, we brought up our empty ones to be lowered down into the little English vessel. I vainly tried to put on a careless look though my fear of arousing suspicion was baseless, for who would have suspected such a plan? But despite my efforts my gaze returned ceaselessly and inescapably to a cask marked with a nick, that stood near me, the one in which the captain lay hidden.

I confess that my heart beat faster than when I first came under fire when we were ordered to lower the casks into the English boat. This work was done by means of a hoist and a great hook. When most of the casks had been lowered and stowed and only the last row remained to be dealt with, the one that went on top of the others, Bertaud came up with an unconcerned air and attached the hook to the cask in which the captain was concealed. It underwent the same operation as the rest, but with such care! My heart was ready to burst when I saw it touch down in the little English vessel.

An hour later the vessel had cast off from the hulk and was on its way towards the shore. The first act of the drama had so far succeeded. I spent the rest of the day in mortal agony. Every moment I seemed to hear shots and cries and in every boat that furrowed the waters I thought I saw Monsieur Thomas trussed up and bleeding, being brought back to the *Prothee* by the English. At last, thank God, night came down and we had no reason to suppose that the intrepid captain's escape had been discovered.[52]

CHAPTER III

Ingratitude • An escape plan • Bertaud's resources • Sacrifices • My teaching • A dreadful assault • Bertaud's recovery

FOR NEARLY A WEEK Bertaud and I counted the hours, minutes and seconds. Each passing day brought us extreme happiness and redoubled our hopes.

'*Ma foi!*' said the Breton to me, 'I'm beginning to believe that comrade Thomas was right, wasn't he?'

'*Dame!* Everything supports it.'

'You think so! I've an idea! Why don't we imitate him? What stops us following his example?'

'Bertaud, you're right. We'll talk about this again.'

'Well! Agreed, we'll talk again and as soon as possible.'

Sadly though, when the little vessel bringing the water supplies arrived two days later I noticed with the keenest surprise that before the empty barrels were lowered away the English scrutinised each one with the greatest attention.

'What do you make of that, comrade?' I asked Bertaud.

'I think, my dear friend, that the game is up and they know the trick. In the joy of freedom and success I suppose the Captain may have blabbed and the spies that the English scum keep in France got wind of it and gave warning.'

'And what about us? What shall we do?'

'Let's wait a while longer! Perhaps the Captain will soon get us exchanged just as he promised.'

'Since you wish it we'll wait,' I said, 'but I warn you that if I haven't had any news in a month from now, I'll go ahead with my plans to escape.'

'*Tiens*, you talk like a fool! How can anybody think of anything else on a hulk? I've been thinking about it for two years.'

'With such determination I can't see why you haven't yet succeeded.'

'And how about traitors, my poor Garneray? Don't you know that of thirty escape plans at least twenty-nine are betrayed? Likely enough we'll see the inside of the Black Hole before we get out of here. You'll see, you'll see!'[53]

Two months went by and we heard not a single word about Monsieur Thomas.

'I don't know what to make of this silence,' said I to Bertaud one day. 'D'you think the Captain didn't succeed in reaching the French coast as we reckoned?'

'It's possible that he's still hiding in England,' replied Bertaud, 'but that would astonish me. You've seen for yourself that he's bold and resourceful. He's sharp! Now when a man like him gets clear of a hulk you can be pretty sure that he'll have known how to reach France. No, if he doesn't give us a sign of life it'll be because he's simply forgotten us.'

'That would be horrible ingratitude, Bertaud!'

'Why? Do you reckon that a captain on shore has nothing better to do than worry about two poor devils like us seamen that he knew for a while by chance on a hulk? After all, seamen are two a penny. Doubtless our Captain is busy right now applying for the command of a ship. The worse for us if he's already got one, because he'll be gunwales under in business.'

Bertaud, with his plain common sense, was not mistaken. The Captain had successfully reached France and had forgotten us. I saw him again twenty years later. He was then a man of consequence and when I was introduced as a marine painter my name did not for a moment suggest to him the unfortunate, obscure sailor whose hand he had shaken long ago on board the hulk. 'Who could have informed you of this, Monsieur?' he asked, when I had told him all the details of his escape from the *Prothee*.

'Monsieur,' I replied, 'it was I and a poor Breton sailor called Bertaud, who afterwards unhappily died, who had the honour, for we were your only associates, of hoisting the barrel in which you lay hidden and lowering it down into the English boat.'

At this reply the former Monsieur Thomas looked earnestly at me and then held out his hand. 'I was ungrateful,' he said, blushing, 'will you forgive me? Now, to prove that you don't hold a grudge, drop the *Monsieur* and treat me as a friend.'

A fortnight after this conversation, which continued for nearly an hour, Bertaud's old father, a sailor nearly blind and in misery, received a pension which allowed him to live happily and peacefully for the rest of his days. Monsieur Thomas had a bad memory but knew how to pay his debts when reminded of them.

To return to my narrative about the hulks; having finally lost all hope of receiving news of Monsieur Thomas after two months of waiting, Bertaud and I again took up our idea of escaping and were not slow in translating it into action. After having minutely examined every part of the hulk we selected the precise place that we intended to attack. We decided to cut our hole in an obscure spot beneath the orlop at water level, almost under the feet of the sentinels who mounted constant guard on the external gallery surrounding the *Prothee*.

Before doing anything else we had to fashion the tools needed to complete our project. This gave us considerable trouble but, thanks to our persistence, we succeeded in making two fairly fine stout saws from a couple of big, flat knife blades. These, with a pair of pincers, some gouges, gimlets and a mallet, completed the necessary means of attack.

As soon as we had these implements in our possession we fell to our task without delay. We began by first lifting a large piece of wood, squared and bevelled in such a way that we could replace it at the end of our day's work, thus hiding the signs of our labours from the Englishmen's vigilant eyes.

The hull of the hulk was nearly two feet thick and we reckoned that it would take us about three weeks to cut through it. From sunrise to nightfall we worked ceaselessly and without interruption. A permanent practice on board the hulk gave us great security. To avoid any surprise by our gaolers, whenever a soldier, whether a sentry or otherwise, came down to the gun-deck, he had no sooner set foot on the top of the ladder than the first prisoner who saw him was bound to cry out, 'Navire!'[54]

This word, repeated from mouth to mouth, swiftly reached the furthest limits of the deck and everyone instantly took precautions. Those who were working at forbidden trades, such as straw plaiting for example, since the English prohibited all crafts that might have competed with their own manufactures, hid the tell-tale work they had in hand and those, like Bertaud and myself, who were cutting through the hull, hurriedly replaced the square block of wood I mentioned.

About a week after the start of our great enterprise our money ran out. My accomplice and I had been living for a couple of months on my two louis and we ought to have taken better care of our slight funds and made the money last longer by denying ourselves a number of small treats.

'Look, Louis,' said the Breton when he saw my last sou spent, 'we've been too lavish. We lack restraint and foresight. Run out of cash when it's money we need above all for our escape.'

'Why do we need it?'

'For a thousand things. First of all to buy the cloth to make bags for our escape.'

'Right! At most thirty or forty sous…'

'Well! To hear you talk you'd think that thirty or forty sous would be easy to find here. That won't be enough, I can tell you. For a start, there's more to escaping than just getting ashore. Once we're on land we need to get some clothes. These yellow uniforms with their great T. O. on them can be seen a mile off. The first Englishman who claps eyes on us will grab us. We've also got to live…'

'How much do you reckon we need?'

'About thirty francs! Hold on, I've an idea. Can you write, Louis?'

'Yes, of course I can; why do you ask?'

'I mean write so that someone can read it and understand what it means?' continued Bertaud.

'To be sure, I've a pretty fair fist.'

'Good! Leave it all to me. Don't worry any more about the money. I'll deal with that. Let's break off work for today. Come with me!'

After carefully replacing the wooden cover that disguised our work I set off after Bertaud, whose carefee, confident gait showed the self-satisfaction he felt.

'Sit down there,' he said when we reached the bench next to my table. 'Take a large sheet of paper and write what I'm going to dictate in your best handwriting.'

'My dear friend,' I replied, 'there's nothing I'd rather do, but for one slight obstacle; I haven't the smallest scrap of paper.'

'Ah! *Sacrebleu!*' cried Bertaud, striking his forehead with his fist. 'I hadn't thought of that. We must buy a sheet of paper, a big 'un too, because we're going to do a notice…'

'You know as well as I do that we haven't a sou.'

'I know it too well. *Sacristi!* This is a fix. I must have it for my notice. Tell me, how much do you think a big sheet of paper will cost us?'

'*Dame*, my friend, I've no idea.'

'Well! Go and ask someone who's got a sheet.'

'I don't follow your riddles at all; never mind, I'll do as you say.'

I questioned five or six prisoners who practised drawing or mathematics. Each of them answered that since paper was very useful and hard to procure he would expect a good price. The least exacting of them asked ten sous for a sheet of drawing paper that had already been used on one side.

'Well, how much?' asked Bertaud, when he saw me from far off.

'Ten sous,' I told him, 'cash!'

'Expensive, but since we can't do without it, we'll lay it out.'

That night at supper I was highly astounded when a prisoner came and commandeered my meat ration.

'Ah! Yes,' said Bertaud, who sat at my table or to use the language of the hulks, shared my mess, 'I forgot to warn you that I'd sold our meat ration for three days at four sous a meal.'

'Are you mad? Sold our meat! The one thing that makes our soup tasty!'

'Bah! What's the use of complaining? We tighten our belts a bit for three days and in three days we'll have twelve sous. That'll be enough to buy the sheet of paper which I desperately need, as well as the pen and ink which we forgot.'

'Very well, I'll go along with it, but I'll be hanged if I understand a word of what you're up to.'

This deprivation of food, which Bertaud had independently and cavalierly imposed on me without deigning to give any explanation, was an ordeal. It was with some pleasure that I viewed the approaching end of the third day of my enforced fast. As for Bertaud, he had no sooner got his twelve sous than he hurried to give them to me, urging me to go and buy the sheet of paper, the possession of which seemed to be his heart's desire.

'Now,' said he, when I came back with my acquisition, 'trim your quill in the latest style, and write.'

Bertaud pondered for a few seconds then continued, dictating as follows:

A CHALLENGE TO THE ENGLISH!

LONG LIVE BRITTANY!

I, BERTAUD, Native of Saint-Brieuc, being vexed to hear the English bragging themselves to be the greatest Boxers in the World (which is a Falsehood) undertake

TO FIGHT ANY TWO AMONGST THEM

at one and the same Time, in all Manner of

BOXING WITH THE FISTS

(without Kicking or Use of the Feet).

The said BERTAUD, Native of Saint-Brieuc, doth further allow, the better to show his Disdain for these Impostors, that before the Fight he shall receive ten Blows from his two Opponents, such Blows to be given to the said Bertaud wherever his Opponents choose to lay them.

BERTAUD

will then

THRASH THE TWO ENGLISHMEN.

BERTAUD requires that as soon as he has received the ten Blows and before starting the Bout he will, whatever the Outcome, be given

TWO POUNDS STERLING

to compensate him for any Teeth he may have had broke.

Done on board the *Prothee* Hulk where the said BERTAUD is fretting his Life away.

'Well!' said the sailor, with an air of triumph, after I had engrossed this extraordinary proclamation, which I kept in my possession long after I had left the hulks, 'what do you think of my idea?'

'I think,' I replied with a shrug of my shoulders, 'that it wasn't worth the trouble

*Bertaud dictates
his poster.*

of suffering three days starvation to buy that sheet of paper. Upon my word, you're mad!'

'Why mad?' repeated Bertaud, not understanding my displeasure at all.

'Eh! Of course you are! Do you expect me to believe that you'll fight and get the upper hand of two English boxers?'

'Well! You're green,' cried Bertaud laughing out loud, 'don't you understand the trick?'

'I understand that the ten blows you agree to take first of all will be enough to lay you out and send you to the hospital. And that's what you call a trick.'

'Yes, exactly! *Pardieu,* I know as well as you do how the English use their fists. At the first blow I'll see three dozen candles and by the fifth I'll have already lost at least ten teeth.'

'A pretty prospect! And at the tenth and last...'

'I shall be insensible, stretched out on the deck.'

'Ah! You agree! What's happened to your clever tricks?'

'My tricks, friend, don't exactly stick out a mile, since you haven't yet guessed them. Unconscious or not, my tricks will start by letting me lay hands on two pounds, just the amount we need for our escape! There's tricks for you.'

This confession, so simply expressed, touched me more than I could say. I felt tears come to my eyes and was so moved that I could only shake the Breton vigorously by the hand.

'You understand and you agree with me now,' said he, taking no notice of my emotion, since it seemed entirely natural to him, 'let's stick our bill up on the deck.'

'No, Bertaud, I'll never let you kill yourself like this,' I cried heatedly.

'My word, you are stupid! Who the devil's going to kill himself? A fortnight in hospital and it'll be over; we'll escape afterwards.'

Breton stubbornness is proverbial and Bertaud exemplified it, for an hour later, despite all my entreaties, remonstrances and anger, the great notice was up, attached to the main-mast and drawing every gaze. The effect it produced was immense and no one spoke of anything else on board the hulk.

'Before tomorrow I'm sure my challenge will be known all over Portsmouth and Gosport,' said Bertaud. 'The English love this sort of thing; I've no doubts; we won't lack takers.'

We had for the time being left off cutting our hole, which was nearly finished, and I was busy playing chess when I heard an English soldier enquiring from the prisoners the name of the person who had written the notice. Thinking, as was highly likely, that the captain of the *Prothee* wanted to punish the offender I hastened forward in Bertaud's place. I was immediately brought before the lieutenant who commanded the hulk. The lieutenant, who was usually addressed as 'Commander', looked at me for a few seconds without uttering a word.

'Was it you who wrote the notice?' he asked.

'Yes, Captain, I did it.'

'And your name is Bertaud?'

I hesitated at that question. However, bearing in mind that any falsehood would soon be exposed, I replied in the negative.

'So you're not the man who wants to box two Englishmen?'

'Alas! Captain, I couldn't ask for more, but I lack the strength to permit myself that pleasure.'

'And this Bertaud is pretty strong?'

'Strong, Commander!' I cried, with a nicely done air of wonder and surprise, 'have you never heard tell of him? He's known throughout the whole French fleet.'

'Indeed! And this Bertaud knows how to box?'

'As to that, Captain, I must confess not. It's just that killing a man with a single blow of his fist comes easily to him and he doesn't worry about niceties. At Bourbon I've seen him with my own eyes flatten a nigger's head as if a bomb-shell had done it.'

'Really!' The Englishman thought for a moment, then turned towards me again, and changing the subject continued with, 'So it was you who wrote the bill for Bertaud?'

'Yes, Captain; Bertaud is my friend. How could I deny such a man whatever he wants? My skull isn't bomb-proof.'

'You have a very beautiful handwriting,' continued the captain. 'Would you care to give lessons to my daughter, a child of ten years of age? I'll pay you a shilling a lesson.'

This proposal, so far from my expectations, pleased and astonished me in equal measure. I need not say that I hurriedly accepted.

'Well, that's agreed,' continued the captain, 'you shall start tomorrow. So, this Bertaud kills men with a single blow; that's good to know. You may go.'

I hastened to relate this interview with the captain, at least in so far as it concerned myself, to Bertaud; he was transported.

'You see,' said he, gleefully rubbing his hands together, 'that my idea of a notice wasn't so bad and our twelve sous weren't so badly spent. If someone would just knock me insensible right now we'd be on top of everything.'

Next day the commander of the *Prothee*, faithful to his promise, sent for me and I gave his daughter her first writing lesson. I was careful to speak as gently as possible and to show myself friendly and kind to the child. My efforts to please her were not lost, and she soon responded with affection.

Contenting myself only with the miserable and insufficient rations we were given, I put all the money I received on one side for nearly six weeks without using up a single shilling. I cannot express the joy I felt as I saw our little treasure constantly increasing and twenty times a day I lovingly counted the money which represented liberty to me.

Whilst he shared my elation, Bertaud was not quite as happy as myself. A cloud lay upon his spirits. Not a single boxer had come forward and he was still waiting to be demolished. At last, when we were masters of forty-five shillings capital, we took a great decision. One Monday we fixed our escape for the following Saturday. Those five days gave us plenty of time to make our final preparations. We were able to make two bags of coarse cloth, tarred and tallowed outside to keep the water from our clothes and provisions, and at last we completed our hole. We left no more than a hair's breadth of wood at most, to prevent our work being noticed from the exterior, which would naturally have betrayed us. Five minutes would be sufficient to cut through this obstacle.

I felt such anxiety mingled with elation when that Saturday at last arrived. I could not keep still; a tremendous joy overwhelmed me, though it is true to say that doubts were mingled with it. I then congratulated myself on having let the smallest possible number of prisoners into the secret of our escape. But to give credit where it is due, I must declare that my discretion on this point was due to Bertaud's advice.

When the night came, a calm hot night, for it was already July, my friend and I stripped off all our clothes, carefully and quickly wrapped them in our well-tallowed bags and then made our way, creeping like snakes along the orlop, towards our hole which we still had to break through. It took us five minutes.

'Do you want me to go first?' whispered Bertaud in my ear.

'No,' I replied, 'it's more dangerous…'

'Too bad for you,' he replied, whispering again, 'but it strikes me that I'm your senior on board the *Prothee*, so…*au revoir!*' He was about to slide outside when he took my hand in the darkness and shook it between both of his.

'We never know what'll happen,' he said, 'let's shake hands one last time. Now, to work!'

As he finished saying these words Bertaud plunged out boldly, feet first through the hole. I was so overcome that my heart beat as if it would burst. I was just about to follow the brave Breton when a loud, 'Who goes there?' followed almost immediately by a musket shot, resounded from the gallery. I kept my nerve and throwing myself flat on the deck, put my head cautiously out of the hole in an attempt to see if Bertaud had been caught.

A deadly sight met my eyes. The ball that the English sentry had fired without aiming had only grazed my luckless friend, but despite this the poor man found himself in the worst imaginable position. The cord which bound his bag to his body was caught on a nail fixed on the outside of the hulk, the existence of which he had not suspected. He could neither get into the water nor back into the hole.

Bertaud's position made him incapable of offering the least resistance and nothing could keep back the English soldiers who, hearing the report of the sentry's musket, ran to lay hold of him. I was expecting them to do no more than seize him, but then a dull muffled sound of several blows delivered almost simultaneously came to my ears. It was a terrible onslaught, the memory of which remains with me to this day. These blows were followed by a cry of pain and rage; next I heard something like the noise of a heavy body dropping into the water and then everything fell silent again.

I cannot describe my feelings. For a moment I believed I should go mad. So great were the rage and despair I felt, so deep my outrage, that I hesitated for a few seconds over the truly insane design of going to Bertaud's help. I believe that if the idea had offered the slightest chance of success, however slim, I would have done it unhesitatingly.

Immediately after the sentry's shot the river became illuminated as if by magic. I quickly noticed several boats coming in our direction from the other hulks and at the same time a great commotion started on the *Prothee*'s deck. Self-preservation now overcame the rage and pain I felt. Seconds were vital and I scuttled swiftly back to my hammock. Thinking however, with good reason, that a minute search would shortly follow a visit by the English to our deck, I carefully and hurriedly hid the bag I had provided for our escape. Despite everything, I had enough presence of mind to remove my belongings and the money it contained.

I had just slipped noiselessly back into my hammock when, as I had foreseen, a crowd of soldiers with fixed bayonets and muskets cocked, burst on to our deck. They woke us with blows from the butt-ends of their muskets or their fists and drove us up on deck to be counted.

This operation took two hours to complete, since the English through mistake or mistrust did the counting several times over, and we were then allowed to return to our hammocks and interrupted slumbers. I should add that few of us availed ourselves of sleep. Until the next morning there was nothing but a continual volley of questions and speculations. For my part I kept to myself for the time being the fact that I was one of the two authors of the failed escape plan that had caused my fellow-prisoners to be so disagreeably and brutally disturbed.

I passed a mournful night. The reader will easily understand that my greatest reason for despair was not the thought of the liberty I so dearly desired, which I had glimpsed for a moment and lost the instant it seemed in my grasp. I could still gain my liberty, but could I save Bertaud, my brave and unfortunate accomplice? Alas, no.

His cry, the blows from sabres and musket butts and the bayonet thrusts he had received, the sound of his body falling into the water, all echoed grievously in my heart and it took all my self-control not to burst out sobbing. With the utmost impatience to get news of his fate, I waited for the hour when we were allowed on deck.

When six o'clock struck I think I was the first prisoner who rushed out from our deck. My anxiety and impatience were so great that, forgetting all caution, I immediately questioned the first English sailor I saw.

'Do you know if they've fished out the body of the poor man who tried to escape last night?' I asked.

'Rascal! What's that to you?' replied the sailor in surly tones, 'for my part I wish every Frog was at the bottom of the sea!'

We were so used to insults that this word 'Rascal', which has no equivalent in French and which Englishmen think is the worst expression they can throw at you, simply passed me by. To get news of Bertaud I would willingly have submitted to every conceivable humiliation.

'Yes, I understand your wish very well,' I replied humbly to the brutal sailor, 'but answer me, I beg you; what's happened to the prisoner?'

'I know, but I'm not telling you!'

'You know then,' I cried, joining my hands in supplication, 'Oh! Speak, I beg you. I'll give you anything…'

'Got a shilling?' interrupted the Englishman.

'Certainly, several, even…'

'Well, now, give us a shilling and I'll give you an answer.'

For fear of robbery I always carried my little treasure about me; I hurriedly brought out the coin demanded by the sailor and gave it him.

'Here you are,' said I, 'now, speak! The man's dead, isn't he?'

'Sadly not,' he replied in a disagreeable tone, 'leastways, I really hope he won't come through.'

'Ah! He's not dead?' I repeated, feeling an immense joy rising in my heart.

'By God! When I say he's not, he's not. The French dog got no more than three jabs with a bayonet, one in his side and a couple in his backside. For good measure his head was nearly split open with a sabre. Despite all that, the dog's still breathing.'

'Thank God!' I cried, 'all hope isn't lost. My friend,' I continued, addressing the sailor, 'can I rely on your goodwill to give me news of my mate every day?'

'I'm not your friend,' he retorted indignantly, 'and I do nothing out of goodwill for French dogs. However, if you want to give me a shilling every day, I'll give you news of the rascal each morning.'

'I happily accept that bargain.'

'Right, agreed. Now, to the devil with you, 'cause I'll be punished if I'm caught talking to you.'

Knowing that Bertaud was still alive I recovered some degree of calm and endured the long day better than I had expected. Next morning at six o'clock I hurried on deck. The sailor, as appointed, was waiting for me.

'Well?' I asked as soon as I saw him. He made no reply except to hold out his open palm; I laid a shilling on it as we had agreed the previous day.

'He's still raving,' he told me, 'but his condition's no worse, it grieves me to say. The surgeon's not now sure if he'll die. Till tomorrow then.'

For twenty successive days I got news of my poor friend every morning, always at the price of a shilling. Several times I was transfixed by the horrible suspicion that my friend Bertaud might be dead and that the sailor was inventing a daily bill of health to extort my money.

Nevertheless, I was not slow to note that as the reports of Bertaud's health improved, so my go-between became increasingly brusque and rude towards me. This ill-temper convinced me that I was not being deceived. Since Bertaud and I had divided the forty-five shillings we possessed at the time of our escape, I found myself unable to continue paying the English sailor after twenty days. It is scarcely worth saying that the instant I could not pay him his shilling he ceased all communication with me. It mattered little to me then. I knew that Bertaud was returning to health and unless he relapsed, which was unlikely, I should see him again soon. I remained calm and patient.

Garneray seeks news of Bertaud from an English sailor.

CHAPTER IV

My pastimes • Hope deceived • Studies • Privations •
Precautions • Bertaud's obstinacy • My first steps in painting
• Bertaud persuades me to escape

T O OCCUPY MY TIME and my over-long leisure I now settled down to study mathematics. Having heard that Surcouf had become an *armateur*[55] I hoped that some day or other his privateers would procure my release by an exchange at sea and I wrote several letters to remind him of my existence. Unfortunately such a dreaded name as that of Surcouf prevented them from reaching their destination. The English confiscated them on the way. It was, I regret to say, many years later and from the lips of Surcouf himself that I heard of these base interceptions.[56] That excellent man from St Malo first learnt of my captivity when I told him about it. If he had come to know of it through one of the many letters I addressed to him, my whole youth would not have passed by so cruelly in those hideous hulks where such a great part of my existence was consumed in torment. At any rate, hoping then that Surcouf would one day get me exchanged or that peace with England would be concluded, I worked hard at mathematics so that when the day of my liberty dawned I would be ready to take my captain's examination.[57]

Here I must note a remarkable phenomenon that appeared in the hulks. Simple ignorant seamen who had entered them some years before me, not knowing how to spell a word or form a letter of the alphabet, had in that period worked to such effect that by the time I arrived on board the *Prothee* some not only wrote their own tongue pretty well, but had also comprehensively mastered geography and mathematics. There were even those amongst them who were far more accomplished than many naval officers at that date. I cannot express the rivalry that reigned amongst the voluntary students in the *Prothee* as to who should be the most learned and adept.

Leaving aside the difficulties we experienced in obtaining the necessary books and mathematical instruments, many obstacles still hampered our studies. To work by day on deck or below was nearly impossible since the ceaseless noise in either place prevented all continuous and sustained application. We chose the night to follow our serious studies. To do so we needed a light and this was not easy to obtain. Once we had succeeded we had to find some means of hiding it, for it went hard with anyone found by the sergeant of the guard with a light after curfew. The penalty was three days in the punishment cell, deprived of a third of one's daily rations. And what a cell it was, a loathsome pit below water level, damp, cold, stinking, completely airless, a real Black Hole.

Intellectual workers were undoubtedly the poorest in the hulk. Cooks, second-hand dealers, sellers of *ratatouille* or potatoes, gamesters and fencing-masters never lacked money and looked on us with great pity and scorn. Being destitute of cash, we were obliged to overcome a great temptation and impose a hard daily sacrifice on ourselves to obtain our light for the night time. At supper each Academician (as we humorously styled ourselves) was required carefully to extract every drop of grease from his portion of meat and since that portion, including the bones, weighed at most four ounces, you will understand that I do not err in calling it a hard sacrifice.

This grease was all placed in the *pied de cheval*[58] that served as a lamp and was suspended over the great table at which we worked. When night came and the curfew had been rung we set benches around the table, which took up the space of about six or eight hammocks. Then, screening off the outer edge of this sanctuary as hermetically as possible with thick cloths, mattresses and coverlets, we isolated it with the greatest care so that the smallest glimmer of light should not be perceived by the watchful English who spied on our doings from behind the loopholes.

These breaches of the rules, which were habitual on board the hulks, were rarely discovered. However, I confess that when I was in this uneasy position the dread of discovery often caused me the keenest agonies and cruellest anxieties. It was certainly not the prospect of three days in the Black Hole that scared me. I gave not a thought to that but, with a barbarous zeal which I have always had difficulty in explaining, the English destroyed books and objects such as pens, ink, paper, slates, and the like which we used in our studies. This was done in the presence of any prisoners caught flouting such rules. At the very idea of such a misfortune, almost irreparable to us, I have seen brave men tremble and even the most philosophic turn pale.

The love of study, or more precisely the desire to absorb ourselves in an activity which would let us forget our captivity to a small extent, was remarkably strong. We submitted to so many privations and dangers to construct our hiding places and nothing can express the sufferings we had to endure in these dens. Because of the great numbers of persons in these small hiding places, the confined air was vitiated twice over by the smoke from pipes and our greasy lamp; it soon turned to an atmosphere in which I have seen Academicians (our Academicians, drawn from hardy seamen, by no means feeble, delicate or weaklings) lose consciousness. Sometimes our lamp would go out for lack of air. Many a time I have clung to the bars over the gun-ports with convulsive hands, drawing breath with pleasure from the vile mists, blowing across the mud-banks that lay all over the river at the harbour mouth, surrounding the *Prothee* on all sides. They were at least cool and damp.

Despite all this I shall never forget the hours I spent in this toil; they will always remain one of the most cherished memories of my life.

Towards the middle of September I experienced a great happiness when I expected it least. As I went up on deck one morning I saw my good friend Bertaud who had been brought back from the hospital; as soon as he caught sight of me he ran forward and threw himself into my arms.

'Well, my dear friend,' said I, noticing with a pang a great scar, newly-healed but still red, which divided his forehead, 'did you think you were going to die?'

'Not at all,' he answered, laughing.

'But a sailor from whom I got news of you for a long time...'

'Ah! Yes, I see how it is,' interrupted Bertaud. 'These English scum thought I'd die from the crack I got on my head. Fools! They reckoned without me! Break a Breton's head? They're a deal too hard for that. The soldier who took a slash at my skull broke his blade whilst he was about it. I was delighted! It'll teach him to be more careful next time...'

'Well, I'm pleased to see from your astonishing thinness that you've not changed at all.'

'Of course, I'm just the same. And on that subject, when are we going to escape?'

'I beg your pardon, what did you say?' I asked, thinking that I had not heard correctly.

'I said when are we going to escape?'

From any other person this question would have seemed either a joke or bravado, but Bertaud asked it so simply and naturally that I could not doubt for an instant that he meant it.

'Ah! *Parbleu!*' I cried, 'this is too much. If I didn't know it already I could have guessed by your stubbornness what country you come from. You're not a Breton by halves. What! Only just saved by some miracle - which by the way you must tell me about straight away – and here you are thinking of plunging into the same business in which you came off so badly the first time. It's madness!'

'Not at all, my friend, it's sanity. It's certain that if I'd got away I wouldn't think about it any more! It's only because my ill-luck let me down that I have to start again. On your side, have you given up every idea of freedom?'

'I must confess that the sad outcome of our attempt has cooled my ardour a little.'

'You must do as seems best to you, but I warn you that I want to escape and I will escape. Yes, yes, I say it and I repeat it. I want to escape. I will escape. You'll see!'

'*Dame*, what can I say, except having started this dangerous business with you, I'll follow.'

'So fear naught! I'll look after everything. We'll not be here long. We'll soon see France again.'

'So long as we aren't drowned on the way.'

'As for that, it might well happen. But, after all, what's it matter? We'd have succeeded and we wouldn't be prisoners any longer.'

A week wrought a startling alteration in Bertaud's condition. Some new change for the better in his health could be seen each hour and his strength visibly returned. However, our food and way of life were by no means favourable to a continuing convalescence. As I was complimenting him on his rapid return to health he replied simply, *'Parbleu,* it's a good thing, because I'll soon need all my strength. I must recover as soon as possible.'

I am convinced that the Breton's marvellous convalescence was produced by nothing less than the force of his will. He wanted to be cured and he cured himself. How often have I seen prisoners in the hulks or sailors at sea, the former attacked by wasting fevers, the latter by scurvy and resisting the progress of the disease with all their energy until they overcame it, whilst others of a weak constitution rapidly succumbed, though much less seriously affected.

During Bertaud's convalescence a stroke of good luck allowed me to earn some money. I have already described how my companions in misfortune occupied themselves with all sorts of work. Several of them excelled in one particular industry and carried it to perfection. I refer to designs in straw which were laid on to wooden work-boxes or boxes of every sort, though the pictures always showed the same objects, birds and flowers.

I was amusing myself one day by sketching a ship under sail on a slate, when one of these work-box makers suggested that if I would make drawings of maritime scenes he would pay me three sous each. I accepted at once. At first I saw no more in this task than the means to better my position and to help Bertaud as he recovered, but I was soon carried away and delighted by this occupation. It was congenial to my tastes and moreover it reminded me of home and my father; I ended by giving myself up to it with unequalled enthusiasm.

The work-box maker needed hints for subjects rather than finished drawings and could not be very demanding, bearing in mind the modest prices he paid me. He reproached me mildly for wasting too much trouble and time on my little designs, but I had taken the task to heart and worked more for myself than for him. Even if he had not paid me for my efforts, I would have continued with my drawings just for my own personal pleasure.

I was so absorbed and found myself so happy, relatively speaking, that whole days went by in which I thought not once about Surcouf or Monsieur Thomas. At some moments, when I had succeeded in overcoming a difficulty in my work or had made some progress, my position on board the hulk seemed fairly tolerable.

Despite myself I no longer displayed the same friendship for Bertaud as before, although my feelings towards him remained the same. I almost begrudged him the single-mindedness he showed towards recovering his freedom, that same single-mindedness which would drag me through all the agonies of a fresh escape when I was no longer so wretched as willingly to risk certain death.

Even if my captivity should last a year or two or more, I told myself, which is unlikely because the war must end at some time, won't there still be a future before me? Who would be able to prevent me from devoting any leisure left after my work as a sailor to painting? I am happy now and I shall be happy again.

'Garneray,' said Bertaud one evening after our meal, 'will you follow me? I must speak to you.'

'How serious you are! You make me afraid,' I replied with a smile, since I felt inwardly uneasy. I hoped to avoid a serious talk and turn our conversation to trifles.

'I'm serious because I must speak about serious matters. But first of all let's go to the bench near your hammock. There's no loopholes there through which we can be spied on, nor any prisoners to overhear us.'

'As you please. For myself, I've nothing to hide.'

When we were seated opposite one another and the Breton had made certain by a rapid glance that we were unobserved, he turned back to me and started to speak.

'Louis, if I hadn't sworn lifelong friendship with you, I wouldn't be here telling you what I'm about to say. Above all, before starting this conversation you must swear to answer one question truthfully. Do you swear?'

'Bertaud, you know I'm straight and true like yourself. Speak on.'

'Yes, I respect you, because without that... But all this talk is useless. Do you still want to be free?'

'Yes, I still do, only...'

'Don't forget that you've just promised to tell the truth. *Only*? Go on.'

'Only the sad outcome of our first attempt has, if not discouraged me, at least cooled me down considerably. I don't fancy dying like a dog with my throat slit. The chance must be worth the risk.'

'Yes, I understand! You want a release warrant signed by the English authorities.'

'No, you exaggerate, but I don't want to spend a month cutting a hole when it's a hundred to one it'll be betrayed to the English before it's finished.'

'I see. It'd be enough for you if some one came to fetch you in the night saying, *"Get up, Garneray, here's your bag, the hole's finished, let's be off"*.'

'Under such conditions, I confess I'd be tempted.'

'Well! If such a thing were offered, would you accept? Go on, answer, with your hand on your heart.'

'Hand on heart, I'd take it, Bertaud.'

'Yes! Well, that's agreed. Tonight I'll come and wake you at midnight, I'll bring you your bag and the hole will be ready. You'll have no more to do than to get into the water.'

'What are you saying, Bertaud?' I exclaimed in astonishment and alarm. 'What!

Are you thinking of escaping tonight?'

'Yes, my friend, this very night. *Dame,* you're surprised. What do you expect? When I get an idea I can't leave it alone. That's why I've been working to escape whilst you've been amusing yourself, scribbling on little squares of paper for a few sous.'

'What about money, Bertaud?'

'*Ma foi,* I must confess that I haven't even thought about getting any. I've a plan well worked out for that.'

'May I know what, my friend?'

'Certainly! In the two years that I've been a prisoner of the English, the villains have heaped insults on me, persecuted me, kicked me like a dog and half starved me! All this, instead of treating me with the humanity and honesty due to a poor devil whose only crime is having fought loyally for his country. Do you agree with that? Do you think it's right?'

'Your complaints are more than justified.'

'Good! Since the English treat me like a mad dog or a convict why should I show them any consideration? That would be folly, not what they deserve.'

'None of this tells me how you'll manage to get the money we need, always supposing that we're lucky enough to get ashore.'

'On the contrary! Once ashore I'll lie in ambush in a field behind a hedge, just like the *chouans*[59] do in my country, and I'll jump on the first Englishman that passes and take his money.'

'Your method seems pretty risky to me.'

'Bah! Take things as they come. At any rate I don't expect the Englishman who's unlucky enough to meet us to lend us his money. No, I'll just butt him in the pit of the stomach with my head. That'll lay him low and keep him quiet. Now, that's enough. The less we talk about it the better. Expect me about midnight tonight.'

'I'll expect you and I'll be ready.'

'Good, everything will be all right. You answered firmly and stoutly. That reassures me and puts me in good heart. Ah, my friend, the idea of seeing home again, doing as you like and living just as you please like everyone else, drives me mad with joy. Now, for safety's sake we'll not exchange another word until tonight. *Au revoir!*'

Bertaud left me after saying this, but then came back as if he had changed his mind.

'One thing,' he said, 'I forgot to warn you about an indispensable precaution that you must take. It's bitter cold at the moment and the sea won't be quite as warm as it is in the Indies, so be sure to smear yourself from head to foot with oil or grease. That'll stop you from being chilled too much by the coldness of the water. Good luck, and I'll come for you at midnight.'

This conversation with Bertaud had completely changed my ideas. The prospect

of an early escape made me look with horror on the two or three years'
imprisonment which probably faced me. Perhaps my companion had infected me
with the love of freedom that inspired him. At any rate, I was determined to hazard
anything to shake off the terrible burden of slavery.

When night came I purloined most of the grease from the lamp used by our
little Academy and rubbed it all over my body. Completely naked under my
blanket and feverish with impatience, I awaited Bertaud's arrival. Midnight struck
and, faithful to his promise, he came to warn me that he was ready. I slipped gently
down from my hammock and creeping in silence managed to get all the way along
the deck without waking a single sleeper or attracting anyone's attention.

Before continuing with my narrative I must give a short description of the
situation and surroundings of our hulk, which will be indispensable in
understanding what follows.

Facing Portsmouth was Portchester Lake which was divided into three arms by
enormous mud-flats. The hulks lay in this Lake, the *Prothee* with her bows turned
towards the port, being anchored in the middle channel known as Portchester
River. The ends of the three mud-flats stretched into Portsmouth Harbour. Facing
the mud-bank on our right on the western side lay open country; a little further
on one could see Forton Prison, also a receptacle for French prisoners of war, and
then going a little further in a line along the coast one came to the town of
Gosport. To the east of the *Prothee* and after crossing two mud-banks which
extended from one side of the river to the other, one reached open country again,
only this area was covered with forts. In a southerly direction from these forts one
came to the dockyard and the town of Portsmouth.

To resume my narrative, I repeat that after having got safely across the deck and
down into the orlop Bertaud and I reached the hole through which we were to
drop into the sea.

'Here's your bag,' said my companion, in a voice so low that I rather guessed than
heard what he said. 'Pass the cords that hold it round your right arm and your body.
The cords are only held by a knot. If need be it'll be easy to undo quickly, without
any effort.'

'What's in the bag, Bertaud?' I asked, equally quietly.

'Two biscuits, a flask of rum, a file with a sharpened end which will do as a
dagger and two pairs of boards.'

'Boards! Why do we need them?'

'So that we can walk in the shallows without sinking too far into the mud banks.
Now, stand back and let me past, I need to show you the way.'

'Oh, this time I don't agree. I'm going into the sea first or I won't escape at all.'

'I'm in a hurry and you take advantage of me to go first,' said Bertaud with mild
reproach. 'Well, I suppose I must give in. Take this rope and slide down. So, you won't

CHAPTER V

An ominous undertaking • A terrible ordeal • A hard-hearted Dane • A sad separation • Bertaud's death • His corpse maltreated

AFTER EMBRACING MY COMPANION and shaking his hand with feelings that can well be understood, I took the rope and lowered myself down into the sea. Although my body was smeared with grease the shock of cold that I felt as I touched the icy water was so extreme that for a moment I was paralysed and feared I should drown. Fortunately, after an interval of about ten seconds, I recovered somewhat. Then Bertaud joined me.

'Swim quietly and carefully,' he murmured in my ear.

As I made my first strokes I expected at every moment that the night, which was exceedingly dark, would be illuminated and I would receive a musket ball in my head. I was only reassured when a good quarter of an hour later I felt the mud with my feet.

'Bertaud,' I said in a low voice, 'are you there?'

'Yes. Courage; go on and don't talk.'

I wanted to wade, so as to save energy and not tire myself, but my leg sank completely down into the mud and I was obliged to start swimming once more. Quarter of an hour later we reached the mud-bank I mentioned on the right hand side. We wasted at least twenty minutes before we could set off again, first of all in fastening the boards to our feet and then in getting used to walking, because the ground we trod was so soft and shifting that it would have been preferable to swim.

I was so chilled with cold and exhausted by my continuous efforts to keep upright that I was forced to stop and rest for a moment. My strength returned with a gulp of rum and the joy of thinking that I was out of range of the *Prothee*'s sentries and only a step away from freedom.

After crossing the mud-bank we found ourselves again in the river, before Gosport. The night was so dark that I could not distinguish Bertaud although I was walking by his side.

'Where should we be heading?' I asked.

'I think,' he replied, 'that we've reached the point of the mud-flat, so we should go to our right in the direction of the countryside near Gosport.'

'I think so too.'

After drinking a few more gulps of rum we set off swimming again and were carried by the tide towards the mouth of the harbour. As we gradually moved onwards I felt the icy cold that had seized me as I left the hulk growing in intensity and slowing my movements so that I could only just keep afloat. I told Bertaud of my plight.

'The same goes for me, my friend,' he replied, 'do you think my body isn't flesh and bone too? I don't know why I've not sunk before now. I've an idea! Let's float on our backs.'

We turned on our backs and this change of position, with more scope for our movements, gave us a little warmth.

'You know, Louis,' said Bertaud, 'I'm beginning to fear we've gone wrong. Instead of heading for the land, we're going into the harbour, because if we hadn't missed our way we'd have been ashore long ago.'

I had already had the same idea but for fear of discouraging Bertaud, I had not dared to express it. It was soon impossible to have the least doubt on that score. It was plain that with the land to our right we were within the harbour. Our plight was becoming fearful, almost desperate. At that moment I would have willingly accepted help from the English to get back on board our hulk. The night grew darker and darker and we could see no further than an arm's length before ourselves. The cold, growing ever more bitter, numbed our limbs and deprived us, or rather myself, of all energy. Bertaud however, unshakable in his resolve, thought little of the danger he ran but only of winning through and gaining his freedom.

We continued swimming for about quarter of an hour, at the end of which I felt my strength failing and that I could not go on.

'Bertaud,' I murmured, 'can you hold me up for a bit whilst I take a gulp of rum? I'll die without it... I'll drown.'

'Put your hand on my shoulder,' he replied, moving in front of me, 'and at the same time take the flask of rum from the bag round my neck.'

'Thanks, Bertaud! You're saving my life.'

I did as the Breton said but I had only just laid my hand on his shoulder when, despite his efforts, I felt him sinking under my grasp.

'Be quick,' he exclaimed, 'the cold has got me. I can only move my limbs feebly. I think I'm going to sink...it's a pity, I know, but it's better than being taken by those English scum.'

Whilst Bertaud was saying this I managed to gulp a great mouthful of rum which at least revived some of my energy and courage, though it did not restore all my strength.

'Lean on me and do the same,' I told the Breton.

'I wish I could, but I can't... I can't move any more... *Ma foi*, it's all over. Goodbye, my friend!'

Bertaud tried to utter this reply calmly, but it betrayed his complete agony. I seized my poor friend in my arms and thrashed the water with my legs to keep myself up. 'Drink quick,' I said, 'the rum'll put you right.'

And a few seconds later Bertaud was out of danger for the moment and again swimming vigorously by my side. After a further passage of time that I reckoned at three hours, but which probably did not exceed ten minutes, the same weakness overcame me.

'This time, comrade,' I said to Bertaud, 'I think I'm really going to drown. Can you see the shore?'

'Do like me,' he replied, 'chuck the things out of your bag. Then put it round your neck. The boards'll keep you up in the water and help you to float on your back for a good while.'

'Thanks for the idea, it came just in time.'

I quickly emptied the biscuits and other things out of my bag and thus lightened I turned on my back. My weariness was so great and my blood so chilled that in the following few minutes I lost all feeling. A confused droning in the ears and a sharp pain in my temples were the only sensations which linked me painfully to the real world.

Death would have been a blessing, for I could see nothing that might save me, but despite this it dismayed me to think that in a few hours I would be no more than a corpse. How immense would have been the joy and gratitude with which I would have welcomed the idea of being transported back on board the *Prothee*. My despair was mental for I no longer had strength to express my distress aloud. Then one word from Bertaud restored my vigour and made me tremble with joy. The Breton had exclaimed, 'Land!'

At the thought that I might eventually come out alive from the freezing sea, which I already regarded as my grave, my body recovered all its energy and suppleness and I set about vigorously kicking the water with my legs to get to the land without further delay. At almost the same instant I felt a violent shock as if I had cracked my skull. I assumed that I had been thrown against a rock, but I was wrong; I soon saw that I had struck the side of a ship. Twenty seconds later I found the boarding ladder and clambered upwards, followed by Bertaud.

'Take care,' said the Breton, 'this ship could be English and it probably is. If so, we'll be caught again. Wouldn't it be better to try and take our bearings and then get back in the sea?'

'Get back in the sea? Are you mad, Bertaud? It'd be certain death!'

'What of it? Death isn't slavery.'

I made no reply and climbed the ladder as quickly as I could. It might have then been one o'clock or half past one in the morning and when we reached the deck not a single man was on watch.

A huge dog greeted our arrival with continuous howls. Stark naked and exhausted as we were, this reception was all the more disagreeable, since it put us in real danger. A handspike lay within reach; I seized it and this enabled me to hold the mastiff off and probably saved Bertaud and myself from being savaged. However, the animal became even more enraged at our resistance and redoubled its barking, which soon aroused the crew. Five or six seamen swiftly appeared on deck. Their astonishment at our appearance was indescribable. They must have taken us for a couple of ghosts.

I noticed with great joy that I could not recognise the seamen's language and this fact was not lost on Bertaud.

'They're not English,' he said, 'we're saved!'

Five minutes later we were taken before the captain.

'Who are you?' he asked in bad English.

'Frenchmen escaped from the hulks, Captain,' I replied, 'who trust your honour and humanity and seek a refuge with you.'

'Escaped from the hulks, you villains,' exclaimed the captain, 'and you dare to come on board my ship for refuge and ask me for hospitality, me, a Danish captain! You're mad!'

'But, captain,' I replied, 'I'm not aware that France and Denmark are at war. In any event, you ought to help fellow-creatures in distress. What do you intend to do? Surely you wouldn't refuse us hospitality till tomorrow?'

'Give you hospitality!' repeated the Dane with astonishment. 'Really, only Frenchmen would be capable of such impudence. When my country is England's ally do you really think that I'd take your part against the nation that supports us? I admire your boldness.'

I was so overcome with cold and exhaustion and so disheartened as a consequence that I could not treat this reply with the indignation it ought to have aroused in me.

'But, captain,' I began humbly, 'the fact that we're French has nothing to do with it. Look on us just as poor shipwrecked sailors seeking help, a mere nothing to you but everything to us. Give us a few old cast-off clothes, let us rest for an hour and lend us one of your boats to get ashore. We ask nothing more from your generosity.'

'By old clothes you mean a disguise. My boat means another escape. Really, it's all too much!' said the captain, laughing unpleasantly. 'You want to turn me into an accomplice. No, gentlemen, all I can do for you is to send you straight back on board the hulk from which you so despicably escaped.'

After these words the captain rose, doubtless to give orders to return us on board the *Prothee*. Then Bertaud, who had taken no part in the conversation, seized a knife from the table, for this scene took place in the great cabin, and hurled himself so impetuously at the Dane that I had no time to guess his intention or restrain him. He threw the man violently to the floor and placed his knee on the Dane's chest.

'One word, just one, and you'll be dead!' he said quickly in a low voice. 'Ah! You're trembling, you're pale now, aren't you? You wretch! Traitors are always damned cowards! Louis,' he continued, 'hand me the napkins from the table and I'll bind and gag this villain.'

I did as Bertaud asked and the Dane soon found himself incapable of moving or uttering a sound.

'Now, my friend, we can go,' said Bertaud.

'What are you going to do?' I asked, as we made our way back up to the deck.

'How can you ask such a question?' he replied, 'I'll throw myself back in the sea! But what about you?'

'Me! *Ma foi*, Bertaud, I tell you the trials and sufferings I've just gone through have been too much for me. I wouldn't willingly endure them again, even for my freedom. I'll stay here and let them take me back to the *Prothee*.'

'Perhaps you're right! What can you do? I may be making a mistake, but I can't help it. I can't bear the thought of finding myself a prisoner of the English again.'

'Listen to me, my dear Bertaud,' said I, seizing his hands, just as he was about to open the cabin door and step out on deck, 'listen, I implore you…'

'Go on, quick. What d'you want?'

'To beg you to give up this mad plan. Consider, it's a thousand to one that you'll succeed. Wait a bit. Even supposing you get ashore, how will you go on without clothes, food or money?'

'I'll strip the first Englishman I come across.'

'No, Bertaud, don't think about it. The first Englishman you come across will capture you. You'll be so weak and exhausted that you won't be able to offer the least resistance, not even to a child! You're hesitating, you're thinking about it! Ah! Thank God! You won't go!'

'You're mistaken,' answered Bertaud, in a firm, decisive voice, even though his teeth chattered with the cold, 'and to prove it, here I go.'

The Breton shoved open the cabin door and, still armed with his knife, appeared suddenly on the after-deck, before the astonished eyes of the surprised Danish seamen. Then, with a bound, he cleared the bulwarks and hurled himself into the sea.

Quarter of an hour later the captain, released with my help, had me taken back on board the *Prothee* but despite my pleas and supplications he obstinately refused to launch a boat to try and save Bertaud.

'The blackguard insulted me and struck me,' he said, 'why should I help him?'

It was nearly four o'clock in the morning when the Danish boat, after being recognised by the English sentries, put me on board the hulk. My return to the *Prothee* was a cruel one. The officer of the watch ordered me to be put into the Black Hole just as I was, shivering with cold and without a stitch of clothing. I shall never forget the sufferings I endured for the rest of that night. Luckily the Black Hole had been repaired a few days previously and the workmen had left a great pile of shavings amongst which I swiftly huddled myself. Without this unexpected and providential covering I should certainly have been dead before morning.

It was only during the day that I was let out and allowed to return to my place on the gun-deck.[60] There was no question of supplying me with new things. Without the charity of my companions in misfortune who, moved by my plight and the daring I had shown in the escape, lent me an old greatcoat and a pair of canvas trousers, the English would have left me completely naked even though it was winter.

After a troubled sleep that lasted scarcely an hour, I woke when I became aware of some unusual commotion on deck. Prisoners were running to all the ports on the starboard side and appeared to be anxiously gazing at some extraordinary object.

'What is it?' I asked, as I approached.

'Nothing,' was the evasive answer of the prisoner to whom I spoke.

'So why all this commotion?'

'We're looking at the crows.'

'Crows? Are you joking?' I replied, putting my forehead against the bars of one of the ports.

A terrible sight met my gaze. The shock I felt was so violent that I do not know how I found the strength to endure it without fainting. Washed up on the mudbanks surrounding the *Prothee,* which were just covered by a few inches of water, I saw a naked corpse deposited there by the tide.

'Bertaud!' I cried, in the extremity of my despair. 'Ah! Perhaps he's not yet dead!' I hurled myself up on deck and spoke to the Boatswain who was looking through his telescope.

'Ah! Sir!' I implored, 'perhaps he's not dead yet. You know that drowned men sometimes revive even after hours in the water. I beg you, in the name of all you hold dear, let the captain know at once!'

'I really think he's moving,' replied the Boatswain, pointing his telescope in the direction of the poor Breton's corpse. 'We'll find out at low tide.'

I tried to insist but the Englishman struck me a violent blow on the head with his telescope and warned me that if I dared to address another word to him he would consign me to the Black Hole.

What I suffered that day will never leave my memory. At one moment I thought I was going mad and this idea, though distressing, did not daunt me. Rather it gave me pleasure, for surely madness brings with it oblivion? It was only at slack water, nearly two hours later, when the sea was at its lowest, that we saw a boat put off from the *Veteran* hulk in the direction of the poor Breton's mortal remains.

Although, unhappily, we could have no doubt about his death, our distress was alleviated by the idea that the poor man's body was no longer to be carrion for the crows. Sadly, it was not to be.

Our eyes were fixed on the English soldiers and sailors who, having run their boat aground on the mud, made their way towards the place where our unfortunate comrade's body lay. We hoped to see them wrap him in a shroud but with unspeakable profanity they tied a long rope to one leg and dragged him over the mud. A yell of horror, a clamour for vengeance, went up from stem to stern of the *Prothee* and the prisoners began murmuring threats of the sort that generally herald mutinies.

I am certain that if some prisoner had wanted to take charge of the unrest then existing on board the *Prothee* an immediate mutiny would have broken out. The English would have taken advantage of such an act of madness to subdue it bloodily but, happily for ourselves, several officers forcefully pointed out its folly and succeeded in allaying our fury so as to keep it in reasonable bounds.

This was no easy task for them since the dreadful sight before our eyes spoke louder than reason to us. Bertaud's body, towed by the English launch and horribly disfigured, arrived alongside the hulk. We thought it would have been brought on board for burial. Nothing of the sort was done. Despite my pleas and protestations it remained in the water beside the *Prothee*, attached by the same rope that had served to tow it. It was left there till the next day when an order came to take it to the *Pegase* hospital ship and from thence to be buried.[61]

Chapter VI

Despondency • A stroke of luck • A sacrifice • Consolations of painting • Varied occupations

I SANK INTO DESPONDENCY after my poor friend's tragic end. From day to day my health grew worse and my spirits deserted me. To add to my troubles the prisoner who made work-boxes and provided me with a little employment was freed after an exchange at sea and I found myself reduced to the ordinary rations without any additional help. Now, those rations though adequate to prevent a man from starving to death for two years, or two and a half years at most, were insufficient to leave him with any strength or energy.

I was so overcome by distress that I no longer had the spirit to think of bettering my position. Instead of trying to work, to occupy myself or to employ my spare time fruitfully, I spent my days and nights sunk in a continuous state of sickly lassitude, which from time to time caused me to doubt my sanity. If chance had not taken a hand in my affairs it is highly likely that I would have ended by succumbing to the dangerous despair to which my body and soul were abandoned. Happily, as in the fable, luck came to me as I slept.[62]

As I have already said, there was a stern prohibition against bringing newspapers on board the *Prothee*, and consequently the prisoners desired nothing better than to get one. A most skilfully organised plan, pursued with rare perseverance, enabled them to bribe a sentry and obtain the public print they so ardently desired. The day it arrived on board was one of great triumph. When it was brought down to our deck it produced a real sensation. Everyone wanted to see it and touch it, but unfortunately our satisfaction was soon tempered by a simple discovery. After the first moment of enthusiasm, two things became apparent; firstly, the newspaper was written in English and secondly, no one on board knew the language well enough to read it whilst translating fluently.[63]

You may imagine the disappointment caused by this discovery. We had outwitted the gaolers' watchfulness and tyranny; troubles and shared privations had enabled us to get hold of the forbidden object; and finally it was utterly useless.

In these circumstances a prisoner who had heard me stammering a little English and knew that I had been in the Indies for a long while, thought that I might perhaps be able to fill the post of interpreter. He sought me out. I was so stupefied and in such a sad depression that I remained a long time without understanding what he wanted of me. My aversion to any mental effort made me refuse at first.

However, I was won over by the prisoners' persistent entreaties and finally I did as they wished. I followed them like a victim led to his doom by the executioner.

When it was known that I could read English tolerably and that I was to translate the newspaper aloud, my arrival in the middle of the gun-deck produced lively expectations. I was hailed and complimented by everyone. It was decided on the spot that I should be allocated a daily refresher of six sous, the money to be paid to me by means of a communal levy on their collective rations. I assumed my post at once. I must confess to the reader, and I hope my old companions on board the *Prothee* will pardon me if these lines happen to meet their eyes, that although I understood English fairly well and could easily keep up an ordinary conversation in that language, I was far from knowing it well enough to be able to translate a newspaper fluently. Nevertheless, not wanting to expose myself to the ridicule of my comrades and seeing that I could not withdraw, I went boldly ahead. I began to perform the task I had been forced to accept, if not conscientiously, at least with assurance.

I leave the reader to judge whether or not my translation was accurate and whether I allowed myself some licences and bold inventions when I occasionally encountered a text that was too difficult for me. At any rate I was never once at a loss for words and the audience who heard me were enchanted by my abilities.

The six sous that I received with absolute regularity from that day onwards allowed me to supplement my rations to some extent and thanks to this money and above all, as I firmly believe, to the distraction which the occupation provided, I gradually recovered from the brutal shock I had undergone and soon found myself in my normal state.

I was swayed by a constant urge to resume my painting. However, since I lacked money to procure the necessary paper, pencils and colours I had to defer the accomplishment of this project to better days when I would have a small amount of capital available from my savings. With that in mind I spent no more than four of my daily six sous to live upon and put the other two carefully aside.

I cannot express the joy I felt three months later when I found myself master of a fortune amounting to nine francs, but even that pleasure was nothing to the exaltation induced by the arrival of a box of colours accompanied by several sheets of drawing paper, brushes and pencils, all brought by an English tradesman one fine day. The box cost me six francs and the colours were undoubtedly poor; I did not care, being conscious only of my good fortune.

The first masterpiece I executed was a portrait. There was a particular English soldier on the *Prothee* whose absolute grotesqueness was a delight to me. I began with him. Indeed, I lacked experience but I had the happy knack of capturing faces in a striking manner. The portrait of my English soldier, even uglier than the original if that was possible, had a prodigious success. There was certainly something about it.

'*Parbleu*,' said one of my messmates, 'lend me your drawing, Garneray, I want to show it to that Goddam and see if he recognises himself.'

'Thanks, but no; he might rip it up in a moment of rage. If you like, I'll give it you when I've used the other side of the paper. Till then, I'll keep it.'

'Bah! The Goddam won't tear it up. On the contrary, he'll be flattered. And anyway, if something happens to your drawing I'll undertake to pay for your sheet of paper. You know I'm honest. I get a fair enough living from straw-hat making to be able to keep my promise. Come now, let's have your drawing.'

'In that case, here you are. But you'll answer for the sheet of paper?'

'Yes, a thousand times yes, I'll be responsible.'

This exchange took place at our mid-day meal before everybody and as soon as our miserable repast was over all the prisoners who knew what the straw-hat maker intended hurried up on deck after him to enjoy the English soldier's wrath.

Garneray draws the portrait of an English soldier.

They were greatly astonished when they saw the Goddam (as the straw-hat maker called him) utter a cry of joy and admiration as our comrade displayed the horrible portrait to him.

'Oh! Oh! My God!' said the Englishman, 'Indeed, that's pretty; I'd never've believed that a Froggy could ha' done so well. What'll you sell this likeness for?'

'Two shillings,' said I, coming forward.

'Two shillings! Indeed, it's worth far more; but since I ain't got no money, I'll give you sixpence.'

'Impossible! I can't let it go at such a low price.'

The Englishman thought for a moment.

'If you'll put into the likeness the nice new umberella that Betsy lately give me and stick my splendid mere sham pipe in my gob, why, bless me, you shall have the two bob you're asking.'

'Done. Go and get your pipe and the umbrella.'

And as agreed I added the umbrella, a vast one, and the pipe, big as a stove. These finished the caricature off in a fitting manner and I got my two shillings.

This portrait was a tremendous success. The English found that I had caught their comrade's likeness so well that they all wanted to be done by me. Thanks to this happy chance I began to do astonishing business. For each portrait I took from sixpence to a shilling; for sixpence I gave a caricature; for a shilling a true likeness. Now, since scarcely a day went by without three or four commissions, I began to find myself after a month the master of a fair amount of capital, enough to allow me to buy a cupboard, some oil-paints and canvases. I was on the pinnacle of happiness.

The end of my first year as a prisoner went by more agreeably than it had begun. Day by day I thought less of my freedom and though my plight was dreadful enough compared to that of the most wretched free men, I refused unhesitatingly to enter into several plots to escape. I must add that of all these projects only one succeeded and even then the prisoner was recaptured on shore a few days later.

My time sped by. To put all troublesome thoughts out of my mind I made it a rule not to lose a single moment of the day. The study of mathematics, my drawing and sleep occupied me in succession. In addition I took fencing and dancing lessons to exhaust myself physically and although the fencing-masters we had on board the *Prothee* had not carried their skills to the level later attained by Grisier[64] there were nevertheless men of great abilities amongst them and they made a pretty good pupil out of me.

CHAPTER VII

A duel • A calamity • A plot to save a man •
My progress in painting

WHILST ON THE SUBJECT OF FENCING I cannot do better at this point than to describe a tragic event that happened at the beginning of the second year of my captivity on board the *Prothee*. I can relate it down to the last detail since I was present at the start and finish of the business.

One day, after the evening meal, an argument broke out between two French soldiers who had been captured at the surrender of Santo Domingo,[65] concerning the possession of a meat ration. As a careful historian I cannot alter the truth, however trivial it may have been, that the cause of the quarrel was utterly futile. It was nevertheless to have terrible consequences.

At the end of this argument one of the two soldiers, an inoffensive but stubborn Alsatian named Kœller, received a vigorous slap in the face from his opponent, a man from Saintonge whose name escapes me. The Alsatian, a stickler on a point of honour, demanded immediate satisfaction, adding that if the man from Saintonge refused he would immediately murder him. This threat, though uttered in a matter of fact voice, seemed so serious that it chilled me to hear it.

I do not know if the man from Saintonge took the matter seriously or if he was moved by some old enmity of which we knew nothing and not averse to facing the Alsatian in armed combat but, whatever the facts, he swiftly accepted the challenge.

We vainly intervened between the two adversaries, pointing out the madness and danger of their scheme, since the full rigour of English law, which punished duellists by death, applied on board the hulks. Our remonstrances and pleas carried no weight against the determination of the two soldiers, who went off to find a fencing-master from whom they could borrow a pair of foils. For a moment we were able to hope that an obstacle which the adversaries had not considered might frustrate their murderous intentions and make the duel impossible.

The fencing-master whom they approached replied that he could not help them unless he was paid cash in advance, because once the buttons had been taken off the foils they would be useless to him, adding that since foils were very difficult to obtain he would be greatly prejudiced and might even have to stop giving lessons. The Alsatian and the man from Saintonge immediately went through their pockets, separately, silently and with equal haste; between them they came up with no more than seventeen sous and, needless to say, the fencing-master refused this amount.

'Very well,' said the Alsatian, 'we'll approach one of your colleagues.'

'Go on then, comrades; but I warn you in advance that not one of them will give you what you want.'

And of course not a single fencing-master would take the two opponents' seventeen sous. Since this dispute and the following events had taken a certain amount of time, they quickly became known on the gun-deck and in the orlop. Matters then took an odd turn which provided us with an insight into the nature of some of our companions.

The *rafalés* on board the *Prothee* heard of the intended duel and the impossibility of its taking place because money was lacking to hire the foils. Stirred up by the prospect of a fight that would provide them with an interesting spectacle, the *rafalés* made a collection amongst themselves to help the two combatants. Fortunately all their efforts succeeded in scraping together no more than thirty sous. Since the least exacting of the fencing-masters demanded six francs for the hire of two foils, the fight was becoming less and less feasible and we began to rejoice. But, sadly, we reckoned without the inventive genius of the *rafalés* whose poverty did not extend to their imagination. They soon provided the adversaries with the means to cut one another's throats; the blades of a couple of razors set in the ends of two flexible sticks. The fight began at once.

The memory of that sickening duel still harrows me to this day and the reader will excuse me from describing it. The two adversaries attacked each other with unspeakable fury and hideous wounds were swiftly inflicted on either side. Our desire to intervene was futile. The rage that possessed them was so great that we could not have come between them without exposing ourselves to the utmost danger. At last the unhappy Alsatian fell with a mortal wound, his carotid artery severed by his adversary's razor.

It rested with us to save the man from Saintonge from the severity of English justice and so a council was assembled at once. The first idea was to make the English believe that the Alsatian's death had been caused by an accident. Everybody agreed with this opinion, but after a moment's thought we perceived that it was utterly impracticable. How could so many wounds, which covered the dead man's wretched body, be explained by a mere accident?

The man from Saintonge could only be saved in one way. We had to get rid of the evidence, that is to say of Kœller's corpse. But how? There lay the great difficulty. Several proposals, equally disgusting and impracticable, which I refrain from relating to the reader, were made and instantly rejected. A topman from the frigate *Belle-Poule* was the first to think sensibly.

'Gentlemen,' he said, 'we can't hide this fat Alsatian or make anyone believe that he died by accident, so he'll just have to die again for the benefit of the English. Whatever death we devise for him will have to explain the wounds upon him.'

'Yes, that's it!' shouted several prisoners. 'But how?'

'Very simply, by God!' replied the topman. 'Here's my idea. Two of us take Kœller's body by the arms, whilst others lift him by the stern. We get him up on deck and lug him into the galley…'

'To give him his last drop of soup!' cried some revolting wag.

'Right,' continued the topman, 'to give him his last drop of soup. Do you understand the trick? No one here's very bright, it seems. Since I must, I'll dot the i's for you. Here's Kœller fainting from hunger. We get him to the galley to give him some broth. They let us in; well and good. But the Alsatian, all the better for a bowl of soup, comes round with such an appetite that he climbs up beside the great cauldron to shove a ladle into it. Only he does it so quick that he loses his footing. He slips, tumbles headlong…'

'Into the cauldron?' cried a prisoner.

'Exactly. Goes without saying. Well, now, a tremendous row! Desperate shouts and bawling from us; the cook drops his hook at once into the soup to fish the Alsatian out, but it takes him at least five or six minutes. And when at last he does get the body out, it's been so well clawed, slashed and ripped about with the hook that it's naturally covered with wounds. And the English are taken in.'

The topman's stratagem was received with real approval and everybody complimented him on his delicate ingenuity. But when the first enthusiasm was over, several prisoners rightly observed that the addition of Kœller's corpse to our daily rations would spoil our evening meal and send us supperless to bed. This reflection weighed heavily with most of the men on the gun-deck.

'But we can't go without eating till tomorrow!' yelled several prisoners, whose sufferings were written plainly on their thin wasted faces.

'But if you won't agree to this sacrifice,' replied the *Belle-Poule's* topman, 'then it's all up with the Saintongeais. He'll be hanged.'

'Well! Let him swing! After all, he was fighting on his own account, not for us!'

'What! You'd send a man to the gallows, when you could save him by giving up one nasty meal?'

'Nothing to do with us; that's his own business. We just don't want to go hungry till tomorrow! Let the Saintongeais sort it out as best he can.'

I shall not dwell on this scene which amply demonstrates to the reader how privation and suffering had brought the unhappy prisoners in the hulks to such a degree of brutality that they would refuse to sacrifice a miserable meal to save a comrade's life.

I must add nevertheless that after the officers added their moral authority to the debate, the topman's motion was finally adopted. However, since a fair number of prisoners still refused to agree to the sacrifice demanded of them, we were forced to take up a sort of subscription or collection to compensate them in cash for the wrongs suffered on their bellies.

All the difficulties being resolved, not without some trouble, we went on with the performance of our dark comedy which succeeded marvellously well. The man from Saintonge was not hanged.[66]

If I were to write down all the events similar to the one I have related which I saw during my long captivity my narrative would be colossal and fill volumes. I prefer to draw a veil over these dismal episodes and to recall a number of strange and singular events as they occur to me, which I hope will not be lacking in interest. Having said this, I shall, with the reader's permission, leap forward two years to the year 1809.

Those two years, filled with tedium, sufferings and studies, saw a marked improvement in my position. My rapid progress in painting in oils attracted the attention of the English and because the foul air below spoilt and changed the tone of my colours overnight, the clerk of the *Prothee* got permission from the lieutenant who commanded the hulk for me to work in a little cabin on the larboard side of the poop, with a window looking out on the after-deck. This cabin belonged to the purser, but one must not think that the English clerk's generosity was devoid of self-interest or without ulterior motives. Far from it; out of every four pictures I delivered to him, for which the Portsmouth dealers gave him a guinea apiece, or so he said, he took one as commission.

CHAPTER VIII

A great disappointment • Captain Rose • His character •
The cruel Corporal and his punishment • An officer's sad
story • Treachery of one of the Transport Board's clerks •
Duvert • The officer's escape • Start of Captain Rose's
cruelties

I WAS THEN AS HAPPY AS ONE COULD BE on a hulk when one fine
morning, without any reason being given to me, I was ordered to be ready to
leave the *Prothee* in an hour for transfer to another hulk. The news struck me
like a thunderbolt. I protested aloud and in writing but no one deigned to reply to
my words or letters and I was forced to submit. Long afterwards I learnt, and I
record it here with pain, that I had become the victim of jealousy on the part of
my comrades in misfortune. Angered by the relative wealth and well-being that I
enjoyed, they had denounced me as a leading conspirator, involved in every escape
plan and subsidising each one with my money.

An hour after I had been told to pack my things I was taken under escort in a
launch to the *Crown* hulk, which was moored in front of us. I could not have fared
worse. To this day the very name of that dreadful prison still fills me with rage and
indignation.

Lieutenant Rose, the commander of the *Crown*, was our absolute master next to
God and without a doubt the most appalling man imaginable. His appearance was
admirably well suited to his character, which was cruel, vindictive and wrathful. He
was a little man, about four feet ten inches high, enormously fat, built like a bear
and with a large monstrous neck that supported the most hideous square head
conceivable. Red hair, shifty eyes of greyish-blue, a thin hooked nose, a mouth that
stretched from ear to ear, narrow lips that were never still because of some nervous
twitch, a mahogany complexion and cheeks exceedingly pitted with the small-pox
complete Lieutenant Rose's description.[67]

In addition to all these physical attractions our ghastly gaoler lacked his right
hand. This had been amputated following a wound he had received in a duel that
had been provoked by his intolerably irritable nature.

Lieutenant Rose probably owed the honour of having been entrusted with the
command of the *Crown* hulk to his deep and well-known suspicion and detestation
of the French nation. The first offence that the *Crown*'s prisoners gave the
abominable lieutenant was to call him the *turnkey*, though such was the custom for

all the lieutenants in the hulks.

'Ah! They call me a turnkey,' said the Englishman. 'Well! I'll show these rascals just how far a turnkey's authority will go.'

This saying soon went the rounds of the various decks on board the *Crown* and seemed a bad omen to the prisoners of the fate that awaited them and the petty vexations to which they would soon be victims.

When I arrived on board the persecution by Lieutenant Rose was at its height. Under the pretext that the French in his charge had already planned several escapes Lieutenant Rose had accordingly forbidden all communication between the *Crown* and the shore. The bumboats which supplied the several hulks with the thousand and one objects needed by the prisoners for themselves and their trades, were mercilessly kept away.

I had not been above an hour in the *Crown* before all these matters were explained to me. I was also told that the English had been sent to Coventry,[68] that is to say the prisoners had agreed that all relations between themselves and their guards should be stopped, that the English should not be allowed into our quarters and that no one should speak even a word to them.

Since then not one of the English soldiers who used to come down to the tween-decks to buy our goods at wretched prices had dared to venture amongst us. Relations were severed and hostilities were openly declared. I must now, before continuing my narrative, pause for a moment to introduce the reader to a new character, Corporal Barclay, the confidant and intimate of Lieutenant Rose.

This corporal was undoubtedly the most impudent villain imaginable. With a view to gaining his superior's favours and promotion to sergeant, he acted with implacable cruelty towards the French. He did not even trouble to conceal his game from his victims.

'I want nothing to do with you, you're naught to me,' he often said to the prisoners, 'I only torment you because Lieutenant Rose likes it and I want to be in his good books. If I didn't have proper hopes of promotion I'd leave you be. I want to be made up to sergeant, that's all. As for you lot, get praying for my promotion, because when that comes you'll be shot of me.'

When it came to business Corporal Barclay was no less frank. Nothing was more revolting than to hear him bargaining with a prisoner. 'I want this for so much,' said he, 'and you'd best give it me. I know what I'm offering is well below what the thing's worth but you'd better agree, 'cause you need to keep on the right side of me. I can do you a deal of harm or at least put a lot of bad luck your way.'

And people gave in because they feared his spitefulness. After Captain Rose, Corporal Barclay was without doubt the Englishman whom the prisoners on board the *Crown* most detested.

On the same day that I arrived I was bargaining for a suitable spot to hang my hammock, when the man selling it opened his eyes wide in astonishment, gave a surprised exclamation and pointed to an English soldier who had just come down to our deck.

'It's Corporal Barclay,' he said. 'This'll be worth seeing.'

The brazen corporal, flattered by the effect that his entry on the deck had produced, or so his gait seemed to indicate, advanced with an arrogant air and swaggered towards a prisoner who was engaged in plaiting a pair of braces.

'How much d'you want for this pair?' he asked, laying hold of the most elaborate and best-made braces. The prisoner, being bound to maintain silence, did not answer. A cloud passed over Corporal Barclay's face.

'Why do you keep silent when I want to talk to you?' he demanded. After a pause for thought he continued in an offensive tone, 'Don't forget, there's nothing's easier than for me to get my own back on you. I know very well that you hate me, but I think you've brains enough to lay your hate aside for fear of the Black Hole. Now, answer me straight off, how much for these braces?'

It was easy to guess from the prisoner's knotted brow, the gleam in his eyes and the tremor of his nostrils that he was making a great effort to prevent his simmering anger from boiling over. Nevertheless, he mastered himself and kept

Corporal Barclay
bargains for braces.

silent. The corporal's pale colour suddenly changed to a deep red.

'Corporal,' said a French seaman, emerging from a tight group of prisoners who had gathered round the English soldier, 'do you want braces? If so, follow me. I've some very fine ones to sell you. Ready money is all I ask.'

'Now here's a bright lad with a head for business!' exclaimed Barclay, gratified that the rule of silence had fallen before his boldness and persistence. 'Let's see your braces, lad. I won't give you much for 'em because I don't like paying the right price. If I did, what good would it do me having you here in prison? At any rate, I'll make it up to you some other way...'

'But this sailor's bound to get a flogging from his mates for breaking silence,' I said to the prisoner with whom I was negotiating for the space to hang my hammock.

'Oh! Don't worry about him,' he answered, 'he's a good straight man who wouldn't think of cheating us. He must have some ruse behind it. Let's wait and see.'

Then I noticed that five or six Frenchmen had placed themselves at the foot of the ladder and seemed to be watching out for any Englishmen who might come down, whilst at the same time the other prisoners had formed a tight compact mass far down the gun-deck. As for Barclay, I could no longer see him.

When I mingled with the crowd I saw to my astonishment, I nearly said my delight, the overbearing and insolent corporal stripped of his uniform with his feet hobbled together by a rope a little over a foot long. They were trying him. This improvised court did not sit long. A voice shouted, 'The gauntlet!'[69] This word, flying from mouth to mouth, became the verdict.

The Englishman was wan-faced and prostrate, begging humbly on his knees for mercy in terms of the most abject self-abasement, combined with the grossest flatteries.

'Corporal,' said a prisoner, addressing him, 'you've been judged and condemned by us all to do a little dance. Our boots'll provide the music. We're kind to a fault. Nothing more's expected of you, except keeping time. Don't say you can't dance. Forget your false modesty by God! We don't mind. We're all friends here. We'll be kind to you!'

'My friends, my good friends! Noble, honourable Frenchmen! Mercy! I'll never torment you again. I like you, I respect you! I...mercy! Mercy!' cried the corporal, now a prey to one of those nameless panics felt only by braggarts and cowards. Begging and grovelling were useless. Sentence had been passed and four hundred executioners stood waiting for the victim to go by.

Firstly, the corporal's uniform was laid by the ladder to the deck so that he could recover it on his way out and then the prisoners armed themselves with rulers, canes, shoes and every object capable of giving a blow that would not be mortal. They ranged themselves in two ranks along the entire length of the deck.

'Loose the hound!' cried a voice and with that a hail of blows fell on the corporal's back. He gave a real howl of pain and threw himself towards the ladder. However, the wretch's feet were hobbled and since he was unable to stretch his legs, he could only run by hopping; in his haste he tumbled down several times and at each fall blows were laid on him in extra measure.

At last when he reached the ladder he wiped his forehead, resumed his uniform and went up on deck, but not before removing as best as he could the signs of the punishment he had suffered. The truth was that his mates disliked him and, far from condoling with him, would have rejoiced if they had come to know of his misfortune.

Since this scene of justified violence had a measure of rough humour and involved neither death nor injuries, I could only laugh heartily and feel a lively satisfaction at the sight of the well-deserved punishment so briskly visited on Corporal Barclay.

'I think we were wrong to leave that blackguard alive,' said a prisoner. 'It would have been easy enough to kill him, cut him up small and make him disappear…'

I turned round with a shudder of horror to see what sort of man could express this savage regret with such brutality. I was astonished to see a young man with a refined, handsome face. I thought I had made some mistake.

'I see you disapprove of my sentiments,' said the young man, with a wan smile,

*Corporal Barclay
runs the gauntlet.*

'I make you tremble. Well, comrade, if you were a naval officer like myself and had undergone my humiliations and sufferings, your heart would also be full of an implacable desire for revenge. Here I am, a miserable inmate on a hulk, despite having been four times exchanged at sea.'

'But that's impossible. It would mean such appalling dishonesty by the English…'

'I tell you no more than the exact truth, take my word.'

'Whose word?' I asked.

'The word of Ensign R___,' replied the prisoner, drawing himself up to his full and considerable height and casting a glance at me in which pride and sincerity were united.

His name was well-known to me and formerly celebrated. I made a respectful bow, saying, 'Permit me to ask you, sir, how does it happen that after being exchanged at sea four times you are still on board a hulk?'

'It's a sad story,' he replied, 'and one which does no credit to English honour. Listen to me.'

We sat down, Ensign R___ and myself, on the bench next to my gun-port[70] and the young man continued.

'You know,' he said, 'of the treacherous way the English put the terms of the surrender of Santo Domingo into effect. I am one of the many victims of that shameless breach of faith. It was stipulated that the French forces which surrendered at Santo Domingo should be transported to Europe, but against all the laws of nations the English brought us to their hideous hulks. Our protests, our complaints, were received with the answer that England was in Europe, as were the hulks, that they had fulfilled their promise and our grievances were groundless. I was taken prisoner on board the *Égyptienne*, then under the command of that brave Admiral Barré de Saint-Leu. But I am not complaining about this squalid trickery by an entire nation. However unjust my detention may be, I would endure it with resignation if I were treated equally with my companions in misfortune. But sadly, this is not my case. Having fallen into the hands of the English and being an officer, I was sent on parole to Bishop's Waltham. As you know these parole towns are circumscribed by boundaries within which the prisoners are allowed to move about, after first being required to give their word of honour not to attempt an escape.

'I took lodgings in the family of a protestant clergyman who, I'm pleased to recall, showed me many kind attentions. This clergyman had a daughter, sixteen years old, the cleverest little creature and pretty as an angel. She was perhaps moved by my misfortunes and soon showed herself partial to me. My life was one of such happiness that I nearly forgot France, until my unlucky star guided a clerk of the Transport Board to the clergyman's house. His name was Paterson, and he was so smitten with the charms of young Olivia - such was the name of the clergyman's daughter - that he conceived a deep aversion to me.

'I will spare you an account of our rivalry. Suffice it to say that Paterson's addresses were rejected. His bitter hatred of me was soon manifest in words and deeds. He took advantage of me because I was entirely dependent on him and one day he believed that he could treat me with utter disdain in front of Olivia. My anger was terrible. In Olivia's presence I forced the miserable clerk to his knees before me and made him apologise abjectly. This abominable humiliation did not abash the coward and when he offered to shake hands I kicked him away in disgust, like some foul beast. He made no response to my disdain except to give a sad smile. Then I knew I was lost, for a man who can grovel thus is bound to be implacable when it comes to revenge. So it proved, since a week later I was brutally seized by the authorities, accused of having tried to escape. My money and possessions were taken away and I was thrown on board this hulk, naked and destitute.

'Three years have elapsed since then. During that long martyrdom Paterson has sent his agents to me on four occasions to inform me that I have been exchanged at sea and that I was entitled to my freedom, but that since I had been so unwise as to insult him he would keep me a prisoner and oppose my release. To prove that he really wasn't deceiving me, Paterson has shown me each time the letter containing the news of my exchange. You will now doubtless understand, sir,' added Ensign R___, bringing his story to a close, 'the hatred I have for the English and this will explain the cruelty of my recent expressions.'

'Ah, sir!' I exclaimed, 'if anyone but yourself had told me such an abominable story I would not have credited it. But let me ask one question. Why have you not complained to the English government about this despicable Paterson and his doings?'

'You can well imagine that I've thought of it a thousand times and tried to do it twenty times over. But I'm under special watch and not a single one of my letters has ever left the hulk. Would you believe that the authorities at the Transport Board have never returned my money or my things, pretending that they have been used to defray the cost of my arrest? This theft has been all the harder for me because I was fined ten guineas for the supposed escape plan, which I never even contemplated. This sum is paid off by depriving me of one third of my rations, at a daily rate of five sous. And since it's an unbreakable rule in the hulks, this deprivation is borne by all the prisoners on board, by a reduction of everybody's rations. Oh! Such humiliation, such suffering!'[71]

After uttering these words Ensign R___ put his head in his hands and remained deep in thought for a while. A dark fire smouldered in his eyes as he ended with, 'If God spares me, I will have vengeance. How well I now understand the desire for revenge!'

'But I beg your pardon, sir; are you destitute? Don't you receive some money from France?'

'Yes, sir. I am destitute. All the remittances from my family have been intercepted. Without the generosity and support of a prisoner who knows of my private means and has advanced money to me, I should have been reduced to no more than the insufficient rations which the English provide. Now then, here's my banker,' added the Ensign, casting a friendly smile towards a man of about thirty-eight or forty years of age with a serious and thoughtful expression, who was passing by. The man was wrapped in a warm and handsome dressing gown and had a pair of magnificent fur-lined slippers on his feet.

'The devil,' I exclaimed, 'that's the first dressing-gown I've seen in three years. We didn't have lined dressing gowns in the *Prothee*. He must be a great capitalist to allow himself such a luxury.'

'He's an ordinary gunner called Duvert.'[72]

'An ordinary gunner, did you say?'

'Yes! But since coming on board the hulks he unexpectedly inherited an income of twenty-five or thirty thousand *livres* a year. Thanks to his income, all of which he spends, he's king of the hulk and knows how to arrange things with our gaolers. I advise you to make his acquaintance.'

After Ensign R___ had left me I concluded my bargain for the place for my hammock, stowed my things away and went up on deck. Whilst walking up and down I encountered several seamen who had served under me in the *Confiance* at the time I was in the Indies. I knew none of them well, but it was a great pleasure to meet them again. Evening came and we were going below when one took me aside, saying, 'My dear Louis, I'm sorry you're not down on the orlop. Try and get down to us through the trapdoor tonight.'

'Why tonight?'

'Because six of us are going to escape. You can be the seventh.'

'Thanks, my friend, but I've had enough of escapes for the moment.'

'Yes, I heard about your escape with poor Bertaud. I knew him well. You showed what you were made of then, which is why I'd like to have you with us.'

'I'm obliged, but I'm cured of that itch.'

'You're making a mistake. You should only take a risk if you've a great chance of success, I agree, but when after endless sacrifices and toil you've also managed to get help ashore and success is nearly certain, I tell you you'd be mad not to make the attempt. Believe me, I'm not offering you a small favour when I ask you to join us. I wouldn't even have spoken of it if one of us wasn't gravely ill and couldn't possibly come. But we now have one spare place to fill.'

'Well, why don't you offer it to one of your friends?'

'Because I can't be certain about anyone. The fact is, if I knew a dependable man, one I could rely on…'

'*Parbleu*, I think I know the man for you. Do you know Ensign R___?'

'Very well; thank you, you've given me an idea. Now then, once, twice, thrice, do you refuse?'

'Yes, I refuse, but I'm grateful to you for the offer.'

'Then I'll go and find Ensign R___. I don't think I need to advise you to keep quiet.'

'As you say, no need at all.'

He shook me firmly by the hand and strode off. A few seconds later I saw him conferring with Ensign R___, whose paleness disclosed his agitation. Then we were sent back down to the gun-deck.

I had so often been a witness to escape plans which were never put into effect that I promptly forgot the proposal that had been made to me. I fell into a deep sleep. When I awoke the next day and went up on deck I thought no more of the previous day's conversation. Ensign R___ came to mind when I failed to see him. I enquired about him from one of the prisoners on the orlop deck from where the escape was to have begun.

'Quiet!' he replied, putting his finger to his lips and lowering his voice, 'it's done; they've slung their hook.'[73] I must confess that this news caused me a sharp pang of jealousy, almost hate, a weakness which sprang from the terrible life I was leading. I bitterly reproached myself for my refusal the previous day and accused myself of cowardice.

'Are you sure?' I asked the prisoner. He was about to reply when our conversation was halted by the sight of Captain Rose who appeared on deck surrounded by all his staff. The captain, or the turnkey as we called him, was more hideous than usual that morning. A violent internal rage, which he could not conceal despite all his efforts, made him uglier than ever and lent an expression of hellish ferocity to his features.

'*Parbleu!*' said the prisoner to whom I was speaking, 'it's a good job the spies found out about this business a bit too late.'

'What! Do you think they were betrayed?'

The turnkey's face answered plainly enough, but whether he knew of the plan or of the actual escape was unclear at that moment.

'After the daily torments this butcher makes us suffer,' I continued, 'I can't believe that any Frenchman could ever… *Ma foi*, I can't find a word to describe it, could be vile enough to spy for him.'

'You forget there are men dying of hunger on the *Crown*.'

'That's nothing; it just can't be so.'

At that moment Captain Rose, as if to give me the lie, ordered his men to herd us closely together on the deck and then count us.

'Well,' said the prisoner, smiling at me mockingly, 'what do you think of that order? Don't you think my suspicions were justified a little?'

*1. **Louis Garneray** (1783-1857) by his father Jean-François Garnerey (1755-1835).*
Château de Versailles.

*2. **Robert Surcouf,** privateer of Saint-Malo, (1773-1827). Anonymous portrait,* Musée d'histoire, Saint-Malo.

Unlike most French privateers Surcouf cruised in search of prizes far beyond European waters. Whilst commanding the Confiance *with Garneray on board in 1800 he succeeded in capturing the East Indiaman* Kent *as she approached Calcutta.*

*3. **General Louis-François Lejeune,** (1775-1848). Portrait by Stéphane Baron (1830-1921) after a miniature by Jean-Urbain Guerin,* Château de Versailles.

Like Garneray, Lejeune was a talented artist. He was captured in Spain in 1811 and brought to England. Garneray claimed to have encountered him on the Vengeance *hulk, but they probably never met as prisoners. Lejeune spent only a few weeks on parole in England before escaping to France.*

4. *The Boarding of the* **Kent** *on 7th October 1800,* by *Louis Garneray. This was one of the outstanding events of the artist's early life and he painted several versions of this picture.* Musée d'histoire, Saint-Malo.

5. Prisoner of War Hulks at Portsmouth. *Oil on canvas by Louis Garneray.* Lloyd Collection.

The view is southwards with Portsmouth and its Dockyard to the left and Gosport to the right.
There appear to be seven hulks in the main line of vessels in the foreground and three to the left.
Alternate ports are open on the gun-decks and below them can be seen the scuttles cut near the

waterline to ventilate the orlops. A small sailing vessel in the foreground to the right of the hulks is characteristic of Garneray's hulk pictures. This picture was almost certainly painted on board the Vengeance *between 1808 and 1814 and the frame bears the name* Hoppey Turner, *who may have been Garneray's dealer or intermediary for the sale of paintings.*

6. Distribution of rations on a prisoner of war hulk. Illustration from the anonymous Les
Souvenirs d'un Prisonnier de Guerre. Private Collection.

'Hurry up! Bread for No. 26! Here you are No. 17! Come on No. 29! Weigh this for
me, my friend! Is that weight right? Yes, for twelve men. Here's meat for six.'
One man looks at the meat ration and says, 'Que d'os!,' 'What a lot of bones!'
This noisy scene is on the forecastle of a hulk, where a British sentry stands by a metal chimney
from which dark smoke is pouring. The prisoners were divided into messes of six men.
Representatives from the messes are receiving bread from the man in the window, whilst the
brownish bundles being handled in the background are the meat rations. The joints of meat were
uncooked when allocated and were boiled in a cauldron with a string and numbered ticket attached,
so that each mess got its correct ration. Most of the prisoners are wearing yellow canvas jackets
and trousers stencilled with the Broad Arrow and TO, the initials of the Transport Office.

7. 'Vue d'une Prison Flotante en Rivière de Ports-mouth.' *View of a Floating Prison in the Portsmouth River.* Lloyd Collection.

Oil on canvas, signed 'Marius pinxit.' Marius may have been some unknown prisoner-artist but the subject and style are strongly suggestive of Garneray's work. The sheds on stilts used as day-time stores for the prisoners' hammocks can be clearly seen.

8. Dieppe boats fishing for herring by Louis Garneray, Musée des Beaux-Arts et de la Dentelle, Calais. A fine example of one of the many varieties of fishery which Garneray depicted. The picture was exhibited at the Salon in 1831 and bought by King Louis-Philippe in the same year.

Chapter IX

Roll call • We disrupt the counting • The gaoler's fury •
A carpenter's trick • An unexpected order • More fury •
Duvert arrested as a forger • More false counts •
An unhappy end to the roll call

OUR GAOLER'S ORDER, given in a raucous, savage voice, was immediately obeyed with the utmost brutality. The English soldiers leapt furiously at us, repeatedly striking us with their musket butts and we were soon crammed into such a small space that cries of pain and distress arose from everywhere amongst us. A few prisoners, half stifled and smothered by the undue crowding, would have died if we had not come to their aid and supported them.

The roll call began at once. The Englishmen's work was doubled by the close confused mass which we formed and it is no surprise that their first attempt was not a great success. They found twelve prisoners missing. It would be difficult, if not impossible, to depict Captain Rose's fury at this news. 'Twelve men less,' said he, with a foul, violent oath, 'it can't be so, it's not possible. Do it again.'

Captain Rose was in such haste to account for the full number of his prisoners that he hurried on with the fresh roll call, railing at the sergeants who were doing it and even hurling curses at them by way of encouragement. The sergeants, as you can imagine, being thus blackguarded, set to work with such a will to escape their master's imprecations that their error rose from twelve men to seventeen.

'God damn you!'[74] cried Captain Rose, drunk with rage, hurling his hat violently on the deck, 'these brutes from the ranks can do nothing but make a muddle of things. When you want a job doing well, you'd best do it yourself. So, gentlemen,' turning to the second lieutenant and the mates, 'let's get on with the job.'

'But Captain,' observed the second lieutenant, 'we've been three hours paddling about in the cold with our feet in the snow and nothing to eat. Won't you allow us a quarter of an hour for our dinner?'

'You're a brute, King, you and your food,' exclaimed the Captain, 'to the devil with you!'

After this reply the charming Rose was preparing for another count, when he thought again and said to the lieutenant, 'To be sure, King, I don't see why we should defer our dinner for these French dogs. On the contrary, we'll dine and have the pleasure of thinking of these rascals starving in the cold whilst we're at the table.'

The insolent and inhuman captain had scarcely quitted the deck before we held a council. It was a critical position and the moment was a solemn one, since we had at all costs to gain time and allow our escaped comrades to get away safely. We had to deceive the English and make them think they still had the correct number of prisoners, a task that seemed impossible to us.

'Gentlemen,' said a master carpenter, 'I've an idea. Here it is. First of all, we have to get down into the upper deck.'

'But that's impossible,' said several voices.

'Quiet there!' rejoined the master carpenter. 'What I suggest can be done. First of all I have a few augers about me, which is a great help. To get down to the upper deck I'll pierce a hole in the decking here, above the store-room where the English don't go more than once a month. Then from the upper deck we'll get down to the gun-deck and from there into the orlop. In this way the first to reach our quarters when they count us going down will come up on deck again through the hole and make up the numbers of the missing men. Later on, once our friends are out of danger, we can hoax the English if we like and play hide and seek so as to drive 'em mad.'

The crafty master carpenter's plan was enthusiastically received and without further ado we decided to put it into effect. We were so tightly compressed in the narrow area where we were confined that we could scarcely stand upright but somehow a space was quickly cleared in the centre on which the borers went to work. In all this I cannot be sure that some prisoners did not lose consciousness.

The augers were worked in unison, attacking the deck at an angle and soon with the help of a saw made from the hoop of a barrel we detached a bevel-edged piece of planking from the middle of the deck. When the hole was big enough to admit a man the carpenters slipped rapidly down through it and into the store-room on the upper deck. The task remained to open communication between this deck and the gun-deck. It was a critical moment since the store-room door led into a passage and the least noise would have alerted the English. Fortunately, since the snow continued to fall and the cold became ever more bitter, we were able to stamp our feet on the deck with a noise louder than gunfire without arising the suspicions of our foes.

The most difficult work remained to be done by our carpenters, that is to say, piercing boards which were much thicker and harder than those of the upper deck. We were sure that it could not be done before Captain Rose returned and the thought made us desperate. Fortunately, so far as the freedom of our escaped comrades was concerned, the amiable commander of the *Crown* prolonged his meal to an extraordinary length, doubtless with inner rejoicings at the thought of us starving, exposed to uninterrupted snow and hail which swept successively and violently over the ship. Comfortably settled at an amply supplied table, it was four hours before he rose and appeared on the quarter-deck. Our position was lamentable in the extreme. Most of the prisoners were frozen and starving, incapable of moving or talking and some had lost consciousness.

It was four o'clock in the afternoon when Captain Rose appeared before us. With the first glance he cast upon us we saw him smile happily. Our plight was utterly deplorable and the hate he felt for the French must have been agreeably stimulated by the sight of our sufferings.

'Now that I've dined well, Lieutenant King,' said he, 'for I've dined capitally, we can attend to these French gentlemen who've been good enough to wait upon us. Let's make a start.'

However ironic and insolent his words may have been we felt great pleasure on hearing them since they announced the end of our day of misery. We swiftly hurried down so that the roll call could begin.

Captain Rose was counting aloud, touching each of the prisoners with his finger as they filed before him, when his second-lieutenant King came and interrupted his tally, advising him that a midshipman from the flagship desired to speak to him.

'Devil take you, King, and every midshipman in the service!' shouted Rose, furious at this interruption, since the snow had not ceased falling and the accomplishment of his self-imposed task was delayed.

'But, Captain, it's an urgent matter.'

'I am not to be distracted. The most urgent business for a *turnkey* like me,' continued Captain Rose, placing an ironical emphasis on that word, 'is to count the prisoners. Tell the midshipman to get back to his mess.'

'Pray forgive me for insisting, Captain. The midshipman comes in the name of the Admiral of the Blue.'

'Damnation and furies! You've just made me lose the number of these French blackguards,' exclaimed Rose. 'Well, inform the young gentleman, since he comes in the name of the Admiral, to get his errand over and leave me in peace.'

A few seconds later we saw the midshipman approaching, accompanied by a well-dressed gentleman and a very shabby little fat man, whose arrival excited some curiosity amongst the French.

'Who is that man?' I asked a prisoner.

'He's a potato merchant who used to sell us provisions. He traded with us and dealt in second-hand stuff before that butcher of ours stopped boats from coming to the *Crown*.'

'I think I can guess what's happening,' said I. 'The potato merchant probably has some influence with the Admiral and has come to start business again.'

'Indeed, likely enough.'

Whilst I was exchanging these few words the midshipman, the gentleman and the merchant came before Captain Rose. With a respectful touch to the edge of his hat the midshipman presented his superior with a sort of official letter done up with a large seal. The amiable Rose, still cursing, tore the cover open and read the following aloud:

ROYAL NAVY
PORTSMOUTH HARBOUR
ON BOARD HIS MAJESTY'S SHIP *QUEEN CHARLOTTE*.

Lieutenant Rose, being the Officer commanding His Britannic Majesty's Prison Ship Crown *lying in the Portchester River, will cause all Prisoners registered in his Charge to be mustered before the Officer of Police*[75] *and the Midshipman bearing this Order. The Person accompanying these two Gentlemen will likewise attend the said Muster.*

This having been done, Lieutenant Rose will cause such Prisoner or Prisoners as they shall indicate to be conducted on Shore under Escort of the said Midshipman and Officer of Police.'

'What does this order signify, sir?' exclaimed Captain Rose, his face turning crimson to such a degree that for one delicious moment we hoped to see him stricken with apoplexy.

'I don't know, Commander,' replied the midshipman.

'Could one of these French dogs that I guard for His Majesty have committed some crime?'

'I can only repeat what I said previously, Commander; I do not know.'

'Very well, sir; I can but comply with the Admiral's orders.'

At that moment the potato merchant, who until then had not uttered a single word, called out, 'No need, Captain, there's our man!' As he did so he advanced upon a French prisoner who was warmly wrapped in a magnificent dressing gown and appeared indifferent to the scene on deck.

'Is that the man I must seize?' asked the police officer.

'Aye, sir, that's the man.'

'Very well, follow me,' said the midshipman, addressing the prisoner in the handsome dressing gown, who was none other than Duvert the gunner, the man that Ensign R___ had pointed out to me the previous day as having recently inherited an unexpected fortune of between thirty and forty thousand *livres* a year.

All eyes were fixed on Duvert whose colour changed and became livid. However much he sought to display a calm untroubled countenance it was easy to guess from his haggard eyes, the convulsive tremor that shook his body, the contraction of his pupils and the twitching of his lips that he was violently agitated. In a strangled voice he asked the midshipman, 'Will you permit me to change my clothes, sir?'

'Do so, I see nothing against it.'

Duvert went straight into a little cabin on the deck in which he was allowed to live, contrary to all the regulations. As I have already said, thanks to his prodigal spending, the gunner had all our guards in his pocket. All eyes were fixed on the cabin door, waiting for the wealthy prisoner's exit, when we saw a thick cloud of smoke issuing through the chinks.

'God damn me! The rascal means to burn the hulk!' exclaimed Captain Rose, hurling himself furiously forward to open the door. His one-handed efforts were futile. The door was locked on the inside. There was something so unexpected and mysterious in Duvert's arrest, his terror and his conduct, that for a moment we forgot our enforced fast, the snow and our present state of exhaustion. We felt instinctively that something momentous was happening and that we were on the edge of some great and unexpected revelation.

'Soldiers, break in that door!' cried Captain Rose, mad with rage. At this order five or six soldiers threw themselves towards the cabin in which Duvert was locked, raised the butts of their muskets and smashed them against the door, which

Duvert emerges from his cabin.

opened half-way. The smoke had almost ceased and a few impalpable fragments of paper floated out through the cracks. The Englishmen were about to renew their efforts when the door opened and Duvert, dressed in the latest fashion, appeared on the threshold. From his blackened hands it was easy to see that he had been crushing the burnt papers and reducing them to powder. A few fragments speckled the snow that lay on the deck of the hulk.

A change had taken place not only in Duvert's dress but in his countenance. Gone was the livid pallor of his face, and his air of fear and dejection had given way to an assured and mocking expression. Captain Rose, delighted to have a plausible excuse for blackguarding a Frenchman, began hurling the most abominable epithets at Duvert.

'Coward,' replied the gunner, with an expression of supreme disdain. 'You coward, to insult a defenceless prisoner!'

'God damn you! What have you just burnt? You wretch!' exclaimed the Englishman, his rage heightened by this well-deserved reply.

'The letters from my mistress, the wife of an English lord, my dear delightful turnkey,' replied Duvert, laughing. 'Devil take it, one can't allow a lady of quality to be compromised! Not a peeress! That would be vile bad taste and unworthy of French manners...'

'Liar,' said the potato merchant entering into the conversation if such it could be called, 'they weren't letters from a mistress. You never had a mistress. You've just destroyed the false bank notes with which you've been flooding the town of Portsmouth.'

'Me, a counterfeiter!' repeated Duvert, in a tone of the deepest astonishment. '*Pardieu!* There's an accusation I'd never have expected. It displays English imagination and malice at their highest! *Ma foi,* I'm very pleased that I destroyed the letters from my dear lady, because if I'd known the nature of the accusation I might have been led to compromise the poor woman by showing them as evidence to clear myself.'

'What! You're a forger? You swindler! Scoundrel! And I thought you was rich! What! Counterfeiting bank notes in the *Crown*! This is the end for me! My God, what'll the Admiral say?' cried Lieutenant Rose in a desperate tone that gave us the most enormous pleasure. 'Soldiers,' he continued violently, 'take that man away. The sight of him turns my stomach. I feel an irresistible desire to... Away with him, and quick.'

'My friends,' said Duvert, turning to us as he was dragged away, 'I shall summon you to testify at my trial...'

'Yes, yes, go on, you summon us,' came the enthusiastic reply, since the idea of going ashore put us into transports of joy.

Night had begun to fall when the midshipman, the police officer and the potato merchant quitted the *Crown*'s deck and Captain Rose was obliged to put off his laborious roll call until the next day. Fainting with cold and hunger we were at last allowed to go down to our quarters.

Although the day had been a great ordeal for us, we were far from dissatisfied. The hapless Captain Rose had been worsted, twenty-four hours had been gained for our escaped comrades and we had the prospect of going ashore. I can only say that the day turned out well for us.

One last trouble, or rather one final affliction, awaited us before we could rest. The suppliers of provisions to the *Crown*, taking advantage of the hostilities declared between Captain Rose and his prisoners, had for some time delivered only the most abominable food, which we could not possibly have eaten but for the cruel hunger that we suffered. That evening they outdid themselves in the foul quality of their victuals. The meat was carrion, the vegetables were vile nameless rubbish, doubtless thrown into the streets by the cooks of Portsmouth, and the coarse reddish coloured bread was so doughy and sticky that it could not even be cut. When one contrived to tear a piece of it in two the halves were linked by dangling threads, like those that appear when a lump of hot pitch is pulled apart.

Despite the cruel and overpowering hunger that gnawed at me that evening, I could swallow no more than five or six mouthfuls of these dreadful rations. A quarter of an hour later I was taken with violent retchings, as were all my companions in captivity who had done the same. I shall not dwell on the sad and dreadful night I passed (one of so many that I could describe) but shall merely say that at eight o'clock next morning we were forced up on deck to resume the roll call that had been so inopportunely interrupted by Duvert's arrest the previous day.

Snow was still falling heavily and froze on the deck. If we had not been sustained by the two powerful motives of helping to ensure our friends' escape and the seductive idea of outwitting our gaoler, I am sure that most of us would have dropped down from sheer weakness. All the crew was assembled on deck, the soldiers with their muskets loaded and the petty officers ready to count us, when a boat put off from the principal vessel of the hulk establishment and came alongside.

'What the devil now?' exclaimed our furious turnkey.

The party had come to remove ten prisoners who had been denounced or mentioned by Duvert as his accomplices. At this news Rose's rage knew no bounds.

'The scum!' he shouted, shaking his fist at us, 'they've turned the *Crown* into nothing but a vast den of forgers. They'll be the ruin of me! If only I could pour grape into the whole mob!'

Our ten companions having been taken off, the counting was resumed. Thanks to the secret openings so neatly and boldly made by our carpenters the previous day it would have been easy for us to present our butcher with an exact tally of his victims. By so doing we should have been able to return to our quarters and escape the torture of the intense cold on deck, but we thirsted for revenge and rated our sufferings well below the joy of being able to exasperate the odious Rose. We resolved to drag out the deception for as long as possible.

At the first count there was a difference, not of ten or a dozen prisoners as on the previous day, but of no less than fifty according to the reckoning of those who kept the tally. On the second count the system was changed and sixty-two men too many appeared.

Rose, scarcely able to believe that he was awake and that this was not some nightmare, leapt about the deck like a demon. He cursed his crew, struck them, harassed them and seemed to be going out of his mind. We continued to play on his feelings and put him into a state of cruel uncertainty. He now had real reason to doubt his sanity. We expressly allowed an exact count to be taken on the gun-deck, but were careful to produce an enormous discrepancy in the orlop, and vice-versa. It was enough to drive anyone mad.

At each new and successful hoax on our part we raised a storm of cries, bravos and whistles. At one moment we hoped to see our detested gaoler struck down by apoplexy. It came close to that and if night had not removed us from the scene we would have succeeded. The second evening brought us no more substantial victuals than the previous day and again we went hungry to bed.

The next day, the third since our comrades' escape, we expected to be called early to go up on deck. We gathered all our strength to endure fresh sufferings but nothing happened. The hatches of our quarters remained fast shut and we heard a great noise on deck which continued till nearly mid-day. It sounded as though scaffolding was being erected. We were anxious and puzzled and then, towards one o'clock, we were ordered up. A singular spectacle met our gaze. The sight was all the more astonishing because the English had left the gun-ports shut since the previous day and so we had not been able to see what was happening outside.

When we emerged on deck we saw that the *Crown* was surrounded by a flotilla of all the boats from the other hulks. A double rank of English officers, upright and motionless, waited for us on the after-deck. Enthroned on the poop, in a vast armchair on a specially built dais, sat the Commodore of the Blue Squadron. Near to this important personage and on his left hand we saw Captain Woodriff, none other than the agent for prisoners of war. Although the matter did not concern him personally it was serious enough for him to leave Forton and come on board the *Crown*.[76]

The deck was covered with a labyrinth of narrow barriers exactly like those set up in busy theatres to contain the spectators. We were penned into these narrow spaces and before we were sent down again we were carefully counted several times in groups of ten.

Fortunately, whilst this was going on, the prisoners near our trap were able to make use of that happy device and the first count produced a figure so bizarre that the Englishmen exclaimed out loud in astonishment and rage. They had to start their task again, our blessed trap worked ceaselessly and each fresh count presented the English with some monstrously distorted number.

When night came our tyrants, afflicted with a sort of superstitious fear, had to let us go down again to our quarters. I am quite convinced that most of the Englishmen believed in the intervention of some supernatural power on our behalf.

On the third day, since the Commodore was on board and might have taken a fancy to come below and inspect our decks or the orlop, the contractors supplied fresh healthy meat, proper vegetables and bread which was undoubtedly the real article, a thing to which we were long unaccustomed.

I shall leave you to imagine how avidly we devoured our dinner and congratulated ourselves on our persistence. We were in fact ecstatic at the thought that by our firmness we were guaranteeing our comrades' escape and harrying the English. It was unanimously decided that we would keep on with our system of hoaxing.

Unfortunately we were awoken at dawn next day by a company of English soldiers who entered our quarters, roused us with blows from the butts of their muskets and ordered us instantly up on deck. We hoped we were to undergo a fresh count, but that hope was vain. We were immediately sent down into launches moored the length of the hulk and transported with a considerable escort over to the hulk of the Spanish *San Antonio*, which lay in front of us.

From that moment our ruses availed no more and we could not prevent the English from counting us and discovering that the six prisoners absent at the roll call had escaped. Fortunately, during the four days we held our gaolers at bay, our comrades lost no time and thanks to the help they had had from outside the hulk, succeeded in embarking for France where they arrived safe and sound as we later discovered.

CHAPTER X

Rose still furious • A new atrocity • The Newfoundland dog
• Murders • A perplexing trial • Foolish demands • A revolt
• Daring • A brief victory • A memorable meal

THE NEXT DAY we were returned to our hulk, the *Crown*. Even today I still recall with a shudder of outrage and anger the sad spectacle that met our gaze when we went down to the gun-deck and the orlop. There we saw, lying on the floor, the smashed remnants of our tools and utensils. In a vile act of revenge that I cannot adequately describe, Captain Rose had ordered them to be broken in our absence.

Garneray and his broken possessions.

As far as my own losses were concerned, I found the bladders containing my colours on the deck, stamped and squashed under the heels of boots, my brushes scattered about and my canvases ripped to rags. Such books as we possessed were reduced to shreds and covered the floor like a light powdering of snow.

An immense wail of anguish arose, mingled with shrieks for revenge, and there were tears and gnashing of teeth. Most of us were so overwhelmed by this misfortune that we wept like children. What joy Captain Rose must have felt!

On the same evening as this fatal disaster a huge Newfoundland dog, that our gaoler thought fit to use as a guard dog, was brought on board the hulk. At the sight of the animal kennelled at the foot of the ladder on the external gallery which encircled the *Crown* our anger erupted like a volcano. Shouts for vengeance came from every throat and we hurled ourselves towards the hatches of our quarters to smash them and get up on deck. We were dominated by our longing for revenge, heedless of English bullets and determined to kill the miserable Rose, at the sacrifice of our lives if we could only inflict bloody justice on him.

I do not know if the wretch feared for his own skin or if he was afraid that an enquiry following a mutiny would reveal his cruelties towards us, raise public opinion against him and cause him to lose his place. In any event, he neither wished nor dared to take advantage of the opportunity which we gave him to shoot us. He let us rage as much as we pleased.

For three or four days after the barbarous destruction of our books and implements we remained sunk in a sort of torpor resembling insanity. We had no idea how to employ our time and since we could not work to improve our lot we brooded in silence for most of the day. The few words we exchanged concerned our schemes for revenge.

Our indignation and rage had been roused to extremes by the addition of the Newfoundland dog to our ordinary gaolers. We turned all our ingenuity towards the death of this vigilant and ferocious animal. On the third day after its arrival we succeeded, after several vain attempts, in getting it to swallow a piece of poisoned meat and saw it die a few hours later following a painful agony. That was the first day after we were put back on board the *Crown* on which our quarters echoed to the sound of a few cheerful songs.

'You scum!' shouted Captain Rose, shaking his fist at us, 'you'll pay for this crime more dearly than you can imagine! You'll see how I settle a score.'

Our gaoler's words were greeted with a hellish chorus of whistles and he went off in a fury. From that moment the long-declared hostilities between ourselves and the English redoubled their intensity and reached extremities of hate. Two prisoners were killed, or rather murdered, by English soldiers. The first, a young apprentice from Bordeaux named Dulaure was being brutally urged down the ladder with blows from the butt of a soldier's musket. He turned to face the soldier, raised a hand to strike him and received a ball that broke his backbone. He died almost at once. The second, whose name escapes me, coming up from the orlop to the gun-deck to take a dancing lesson, was transfixed by a bayonet thrust and shot in the back. The ball came out through his stomach and he died instantly. The two murderers were made corporals. Our state of fury can be imagined.

Fortunately something happened to divert us, namely the committal of the gunner Duvert which was heard before the magistrates.[77]

Duvert had been as good as his word and had denounced two hundred prisoners from amongst us (that is to say everyone whose name he could recall) as his accomplices. Each morning a perpetual procession of boats came and went to take us ashore, and those who were summoned before the court felt an extravagant delight. The idea of leaving the hulk for a few days and setting foot on land, with the hope that an opportunity to escape might arise, made them forget their present troubles and dream of a different future.

Having succeeded with the help of a prisoner in passing a note to Duvert, in which I mentioned my acquaintance with Ensign R___, I felt extreme pleasure when my own name was called one morning.

The committal was exceedingly bizarre and made a great noise at that time in England. Having destroyed the evidence that could have hanged him, Duvert was impassive, managed matters with rare skill and mystified the magistrates with marvellous self-confidence. At one moment he seemed on the brink of confessing all and then went off down a by-way of revelations that held the magistrates' attention for hours on end, without incriminating himself at all. Then he simulated terror, looked at us with frightened eyes, hinting that his fear of becoming the victim of a formidable and mysterious gang, formed amongst ourselves, caused him to hold back the confessions that he was ready to spill.

In the last session of this memorable committal Duvert carried his hoaxing to sublime levels. Being closely examined by the chairman of the bench he first of all pretended to think deeply and then suddenly took on the part of a man overwhelmed with remorse.

'Gentlemen,' said he, standing up abruptly, 'the truth must come out at last. I know that by speaking I condemn myself to certain death, but I will not shrink from it.'

'You need fear nothing, prisoner,' interrupted the chairman, 'England's mighty arm is stretched between you and your enemies. You must understand that, far from harming you, your frankness can only gain you the support and indulgence of the jury before which we will send you.'

'Oh, sir!' exclaimed Duvert with an air of melancholy and deep sadness. 'Let us talk no more about myself. My fate is sealed and all the might of England cannot prevent what will come to pass. If you but knew…but no…'

'Speak, prisoner,' said the chairman urgently.

'No, it would be useless! That is out of the question. Let us return to our present business, to this mysterious manufactory of bank notes, to this formidable gang of counterfeiters which I alone can unmask. First of all and above all, I must declare that I myself am a stranger to this plot. I am its victim and no more.'

The chairman made a swift gesture which could have been interpreted as 'My dear friend, *you* have nothing to fear', and Duvert continued.

'Yes, gentlemen, I can untangle this strange dark web and the disclosure will strike you like a thunderbolt. But, above all, I wish you to promise me that after my revelations you will not flinch for any reason or from any expenditure to help establish the truth.'

'England is just, mighty and wealthy,' said one of the magistrates with a dignified air. 'She never flinches; speak out and fear not.'

Duvert remained sunk in deep thought for some moments and then raised his head, heavy with the weight of his pretended anxieties.

'Here,' he continued, 'is the easiest course to follow. Take me on board all the hulks and we will arrest all the culprits, since forgery has ramifications throughout the hulks. The number of culprits is about two thousand...'

At this revelation, made with admirable calm and perfect seriousness, the chairman was struck with ludicrous astonishment. This did not cause Duvert to lose his gravity.

'But this gang must have a leader,' said the magistrate. 'Do you know him?'

'Yes, certainly. No one better.'

'Then name him at once. With the leader in our power our task will be easier.'

'I ask for nothing else, gentlemen, but before doing as you desire, permit me to ask you a simple question. I am very ignorant of English law and I would not wish to worsen my position by infringing it.'

'Ask the question, prisoner,' came the reply.

'I have told you that I know the leader of the gang of forgers, but I must confess that I have never had any direct relations with him nor ever seen him making bank notes. I would find it impossible to say anything precise against him. Five hundred of his accomplices have named him to me as their leader, but that is all. Now, if I denounce this man and the law cannot convict him, might he not at a later date cause me to be sued for defamation?'

'By no means, be easy on that score.'

'Well, gentlemen, the man declared by five hundred of my companions, whom you can summon here, to be the head of the counterfeit banknote business is Lieutenant Rose, acting commander of His Britannic Majesty's Prison Ship *Crown!*' exclaimed Duvert in a ringing voice.

Such an unexpected revelation was a splendid stroke of dramatic art. The magistrate knew he had been hoaxed and we burst out with gales of Homeric laughter but many members of the public, unbelievably, took the gunner's declaration seriously.

Having produced nothing but a scandal of this sort the enquiry could go no further and was suppressed. Duvert emerged with credit from the critical position in which he had found himself and which, but for his confidence and presence of mind, might have led him to the gallows.

I leave the reader to imagine the unbelievable anger our gaoler must have felt (and did indeed feel) when he learnt a few hours later how his name had been bandied about at the hearing. He swore to avenge this insult and kept his word only too well, as will shortly appear.

This ridiculous enquiry had at least a good outcome for us since, although we were closely watched during our stay ashore, we managed to make fresh connections and get ourselves some new utensils and tools. By some means that I never discovered three prisoners also took advantage of the occasion to escape.

Let us return to the *Crown*, our floating tomb. Since the murder of our two comrades, poor Delaure and the apprentice, the hate we had felt for the infamous Rose was inadequately expressed by sending the English crew to Coventry. We decided that every time we saw Rose we would whistle ceaselessly at him.

Who would have believed it? This childish trick, for it was no more than that, hurt our gaoler more painfully than an attempted mutiny. The dreadful whistling worked horribly on his nerves and to our delight put him into transports of furious rage. He did not dare to quit his cabin and walk on deck, or receive visitors since he might have been humiliated before them, or leave the ship and go ashore since he would have had to pass in front of the gun-ports and endure our broadside. Our gaoler had become the prisoner of his prisoners.

We were enjoying this unexpected triumph to the full when one morning Captain Rose suddenly appeared on the after-deck of his ship which was separated from our Park by a high barrier. He summoned a French prisoner who acted as an interpreter on board the hulk. I need not add that the whistlers set to work with a will. However, a great silence soon came over us when we saw the interpreter coming in our direction after a fairly long conference with the captain. We immediately surrounded him.

'Comrades,' said he, 'if my job as interpreter requires me to translate the words I am ordered to pass on to you I am not obliged to approve them. Here is my message; the Captain now seeks peace with us. Although he is the one who wants a cessation of hostilities, he imposes the following conditions on us.'

A great silence immediately fell on the Park. After a short pause to give more solemnity to what he had to communicate, the interpreter continued.

'Gentlemen,' he said, 'these are the proposals that Captain Rose wishes us to accept on the understanding that if we submit completely he will remain on good terms with us. We will, firstly, agree on our honour not to attempt any more escapes, secondly, to cease all marks of disrespect when the Captain appears, thirdly, to continue to wash down the decks, fourthly, to clean the latrines[78] every morning and maintain them in good order...'

The interpreter was about to continue but at these last words his voice was interrupted by an indignant clamour of rage from all the prisoners. This typically English insult towards prisoners of war seemed so base and cowardly and exasperated us to such an extent that the soldiers on guard thought it wise to fix bayonets and interpose themselves between Captain Rose and ourselves.

'I vote for a concert of whistles with a big drum as accompaniment!' shouted one of our comrades. At that moment a chorus of whistles and ironic howls resounded from one end of the hulk to the other.

'Get those dogs back to their kennels,' stammered our butcher to the soldiers, in a voice strangled with fury. Happy to obey such an order, they hurled themselves at us and we were only able to return to our quarters after receiving a hail of blows. Our exasperation was now so deep that the ideas of mutiny which Captain Rose's dreadful oppression gave us at every instant returned more forcefully than ever.

'Be careful, my friends,' said our officers, 'you'll fall into a trap that's been set for you. Don't you see that this brute Rose wants nothing better than your disturbances to justify his cruelty? It's true that we're so miserable that death holds no terrors for us, but remember this; even if being shot doesn't matter to us, nothing would give these butchers greater pleasure than to pour a volley amongst us. Let's not give them that pleasure. Instead of letting them see by our fury that we feel their persecutions and injuries, let's remain outwardly cheerful at least. Let's mock them and laugh in their faces, but we won't stoop to self-pity. Let French spirits triumph over English cruelty! Let's whistle and sing, but we won't cry!'

We listened respectfully and took heed of this good advice, but whilst our officers were addressing us Captain Rose, drunk with rage, was busy preparing to punish us by means of the device with which we had declined to soil our hands. We soon saw, without understanding the proceeding, the ship's launch with the fire engine on board accompanied by two boats, one in front and the other behind the launch.

'That's strange!' we said, 'Why choose a cold snowy day like this to hose down the outside of the hulk?'

Our illusion was very short-lived. The launch and the accompanying boats had only gone a few fathoms from the *Crown* when Captain Rose, himself pointing the hose in our direction, ordered his men to set the pump going. A spout of water swept immediately across the ports of the gun-deck and the scuttles of the orlop, fell on us and wrapped us in its chilly embrace. Stupefied and dismayed, we tried

86 *The Floating Prison*

vainly to hide in the corners of the deck and to keep our belongings dry, but the icy water followed us and penetrated everywhere.

At last, little by little, we began to organise our resistance. Tables, benches, all the furniture we possessed, were piled against the ports and scuttles and with the help of our ingenuity we soon found ourselves sheltered. Rose, exasperated that we did not submit willingly to his shower bath, ordered his soldiers down from the upper deck into the gun-deck to destroy our barricades.

Our patience was at an end and we met force with force. We raised barricades. Armed with knives set in the ends of long sticks and sheltered behind our benches, we waited firmly for the English soldiers, determined not to give an inch.

'Take aim!' ordered a sergeant, who did not dare to charge us at the head of his men and found it much more convenient and less dangerous to shoot us from a distance. The Englishmen raised their muskets and were only waiting for the word to fire, when one of our comrades, a privateer captain, abandoning a corner in which he had taken cover, leapt between them and us.

'Soldiers!' he said, turning to face them and swiftly ripping open the rough jacket that covered his chest, 'if you are murderers, get on with your bloody work! If you are brave soldiers, ground arms!'

The Englishmen were surprised and abashed by the privateer's commanding presence. They seemed to hesitate and looked at their sergeant but he also, with a downcast gaze, appeared to be extremely out of countenance. The privateer, perceiving that the advantage was on his side slowly advanced a few paces, fixing the Englishmen with a cold imperious stare of the sort that common natures cannot endure. With a commanding and disdainful expression he put a finger to the barrel of a musket that nearly touched his chest and repeated, 'Ground arms!' in a ringing voice that resounded throughout the gun-deck.

The Englishmen obeyed. 'But, sir,' said the sergeant, 'we've been ordered to destroy the barricades you set up at the gun-ports to keep out the water. We have to obey.'

'Obey!' exclaimed the privateer, 'What! You, soldiers, and you let yourselves be used as an executioner's lackeys? You know that the freezing water they're pumping on us will be fatal. I can never believe that you would thus disgrace your uniform.'

'I don't say that the Captain's wrong or that he hasn't gone a bit too far,' interrupted the sergeant, 'that's none of our business. We've got to obey orders. So get back, or else...'

'Or else you'll shoot us! Will you? Well, I defy you,' shouted the intrepid privateer.

'Ah! Take care, prisoners...'

'My friends,' said the privateer turning towards us, 'throw down your arms, come out of hiding and stand boldly here with your jackets undone in front of these soldiers. We'll see if they dare to dishonour English arms.'

We hurriedly obeyed this invitation and placed ourselves, unarmed and inoffensive, a few paces from the Englishmen.

'Now,' continued the privateer, 'I warn you that my comrades will not let you get to the ports, unless you use your arms and massacre us all! Since there are nearly four hundred of us here, prepared to die without trying to defend ourselves, not a single one of you will be harmed. As a result it will be clear to the whole world, even if not one of us survives this monstrous slaughter, that we were not mutineers and that you butchered us for the mere pleasure of shedding our blood! Who knows? Are you afraid of meeting us one day, face to face on some battlefield? Fire if you dare! I defy you!'

This short speech imprinted itself so deeply on my memory that I believe I have given it verbatim. It utterly disconcerted the English sergeant.

'You stubborn rascals,' he exclaimed, 'it's not worth talking to you! Do as you please! I hope Captain Rose will make you regret obstructing his orders.'

After delivering himself of this, away went the sergeant with his men, leaving us masters of the battlefield. We thought we were safe and were considering making good the damage caused by the Captain's hose, but we counted without our opponent. Another detachment of armed soldiers and seamen invaded the gun-deck and the orlop and soon forced us up on deck.

Then the crews of the two boats stationed ahead and astern of the launch rowed towards the hulk and with their boathooks broke up the obstacles we had placed in front of the ports. The pumping was started again, the stream of water playing alternatively over the upper deck and into the gun-deck, so as to soak both ourselves and our possessions.

A comic episode then occurred. Exasperated by Captain Rose's taunts and cries of joy one of our comrades seized a cooked potato from a huge pile on the deck, dipped it in a tub of pitch and hurled it with such good aim as to strike our persecutor full in the face. French humour being what it is, no sooner had the projectile struck Captain Rose's ugly face than an immense burst of laughter and frantic jeering went up to the heavens. We immediately forgot our sufferings and the losses we had just experienced and leapt at the pile of potatoes. The tub of tar was turned upside down on them and armed with these novel missiles we began pelting our gaoler. In less than two minutes his body was tarred all over.

Cruelly battered, blinded and speechless, Captain Rose was sublime in his resistance. Ten times the hosepipe fell from his hands; ten times he retrieved it and tried to play it on us. At last, defeated, he gestured to the seamen to pull again for the hulk, which he boarded a few seconds later. The reader must imagine the monstrous uproar that greeted our gaoler when he set foot on board. It was like a chorus directed by Aeolus and performed by his children. If Rose had dared to shoot us at that moment I am positive that not a single one of us would have escaped his fury. He must certainly have thought of loosing a few shots, the English government being very tolerant of that sort of thing, but he doubtless feared that the ensuing inquest, however mild and lenient it might be, would cast too harsh a light on what had gone before and hasten his dismissal. This fear saved us from a bloody vengeance.

We thought that our victory would allow us to return to our quarters, but we were mistaken. Captain Rose was not a man to give up the struggle like that. He had to have the upper hand. It must have been about three o'clock in the afternoon. Thick snow came driving down, simultaneously blinding and numbing us, and there were several prisoners, worn down by fever and scarcely covered by their miserable rags, who were shivering with cold and could hardly stand. When we saw sentries being posted by the narrow ladders that led to the gun-deck and the orlop we understood that our stay in the teeth of the wind was to be a lasting one and tried to encourage one another to be patient. Sadly, we did not guess how far our vindictive turnkey's anger would go.

I cannot express the despair we felt when we saw the English soldiers and seamen, who had gone down to our quarters, coming up again bent beneath the loads of our bedding, clothing and the new tools and utensils which we had managed to obtain ashore at the time of Duvert's trial. Thrown into a dreadful heap on the poop deck, exposed to the snow and rain, lay our beds, belongings and utensils! This time we were cowed by such barbarity and subdued by our poverty. We begged for mercy.

A prisoner was dispatched to treat with the Captain, but his return soon deprived us of all hope. Rose remained pitiless and before entering into any negotiations with us demanded that we should first accept the conditions that he had expressed through the interpreter, namely that we should give our word of honour not to escape and that we should help the English in swabbing and cleaning the ship.

Instead of causing us to submit, these demands revived all our indignation and courage. We unanimously resolved not to submit and began to arrange matters as best as we could to resist the sufferings that awaited us. The prisoners who had the warmest clothing gave up part of their garments in favour of those who were ill and then, having swept away the snow that encumbered the deck, we lay down. We huddled together, one against another, *rafalé*-fashion, so as to resist the cold which began to affect us so severely that we could not move ourselves or our limbs.

The sight of our belongings which the English continued to pile up in a sort of pyramid on the poop caused us pangs of agony but we were determined that our sufferings should not give our tormentors any satisfaction. In the face of this heartrending spectacle we affected a profound indifference which we were far from feeling. We sang the *Marseillaise* in chorus several times. Most of the English seamen, touched by our courage and our terrible plight, did not conceal the fact that they were on our side. They were outraged by their Captain's conduct.

At four o'clock, since the winter days are short in England, night began to fall. The distribution of rations had not taken place and except for a token breakfast which could not reasonably pass for a meal, we had fasted since the previous day.

To recollect some scenes is as painful as having endured them and I shall pass over in silence the time that elapsed till the moment when we were told that the soup was about to be distributed. Midnight was then struck on the bell and so we had been fourteen hours on the open deck exposed to all the rigours of winter. We were so weak and numb that, despite the hunger gnawing at our bowels, we had to be forced to our feet to descend to the gun-deck and the orlop to take our meal. Most of us, being soaked from head to foot by water from the hose, had our clothes completely frozen and experienced the greatest difficulty in standing upright.

At last, when we had shaken off our lethargy, nature reasserted herself and, elbowing one another aside, we rushed down to our quarters where our supper awaited us. And here is a trite detail, almost grotesque at first sight to those who have never lacked for anything, which aptly ends the tale of our sufferings. Everything had been taken away or broken by the English and we did not have a single spoon. Since the vile soup we were given was burning hot we had no idea of how to eat it.

The profound gloom of our quarters served greatly to increase our confusion and prevented us from organising our messes. On all sides names were called out, persons sought one another, cans and tins were knocked over and there were cries, curses and blows. What a spectacle it would have been for our friends in France if they could have seen us, throwing ourselves flat on the floor in the darkness to devour the spilled and filthy contents of our tins. It was dreadful. At last, having stayed the worst pangs of hunger, we lay down on the wet planks of the deck and the orlop and tried to go to sleep.

This time our officers, pushed to the brink by so much cruelty, shared our indignation and far from opposing our plans to mutiny, encouraged our resistance. I knew that unless some unexpected happening came between Rose and ourselves I would soon be the witness of an outstandingly bloody catastrophe.

I was so disgusted with life that it pains me to confess that the thought of killing Englishmen was at that moment all that brought some relief to my sufferings. There were some terrible hours during my captivity, the memory of which still pursues me; I feel an invincible repugnance against putting them before the reader and I excuse myself for not dwelling on the seven days that followed. I must however record that our belongings remained on the poop for that entire week, exposed to the ceaseless rain and snow, and when Captain Rose allowed us to take them back they were all so spoiled that we were obliged to throw most of them into the sea.

The notion of a mutiny of which I have spoken was by no means extinct amongst us. On the contrary, most of us assembled for a council in which we deliberated how we might best conduct such a dangerous enterprise and we agreed a plan so that if things went badly for us, as was unfortunately highly likely, then our defeat would also cost the English dear. Above all what we longed for beyond anything else was not so much the hour of freedom as that of revenge.

Our plans were nearly ready and we were only waiting for a favourable occasion to strike a decisive blow when there happened an event, which at first seemed to have nothing to do with us, that halted us on the edge of the abyss.

CHAPTER XI

A transformation • Rose's humanity • Duvert's treachery • A murder • Failure of an escape plot • I am made interpreter

CAPTAIN ROSE was engaged in a dispute with the victualling contractors who had apparently refused to agree to certain of his demands. Even whilst we were being so ill-used the Captain wanted to see the matter taken to a higher authority and accordingly he suddenly came down on our side, pretending the deepest indignation and feigning to be revolted by the barbarous manner in which we were treated.

We only discovered the true cause of this change of conduct long afterwards but it was enough to make us abandon our plans. After the nameless sufferings we had had to endure up to that time the new life before us seemed like bliss.

The bumboats came to the *Crown* again, we were allowed to make straw hats (which was forbidden) and to revive our relations with the shore. Captain Rose, in an excess of generosity, caused ten of us to be brought before him and asked if we were content with our rations. Our reply can easily be imagined.

'Well, my friends,' said Captain Rose, in the most affable manner, 'send a petition signed by you all to the Transport Office. Set down all the villanies of those thieving contractors and enter into great detail about the scandalous way they have used you. In a word, draw up a long statement of the facts with which you can tax them and then bring the record to me. I will see that it reaches the proper authorities.'

We were delighted with this proposal and debated how we might manage the business to our greatest advantage. This discussion led us to a stratagem which, if successful, would give us our revenge over both Captain Rose and the contractors. Firstly, and most importantly, we swiftly fell in with the wishes of our old enemy (and new ally) and set down a highly circumstantial report of all our complaints against the contractors. They were many, as the reader can imagine.

This long list of our sufferings ended with a pompous testimonial praising the manner in which Captain Rose, commanding His Britannic Majesty's Prison Ship *Crown*, had behaved towards the prisoners committed to his care and supervision. I must confess that this encomium was troublesome to write. With each word we wrote the memory of some cruelty or arbitrary act caused the pen to fall from our hands, but with the prospect of revenge before us we contrived to finish it as best as we could.

As soon as this report was duly signed by us all we proceeded to a second version in a much more congenial form, a narrative of the numberless cruelties and infamies which Rose had made us suffer. Nothing was omitted and our indignation heightened its style immeasurably.

Then we chose a detestable loaf (not a difficult choice) from the loaves that had been distributed that morning, hollowed out part of the crumb and slipped the compromising report inside. The loaf was then carefully adjusted and put in a small, unsealed box which we took to Captain Rose. After reading the report concerning the contractors with great approval our gaoler threw a glance at the sample loaf that accompanied it and burst out with a great oath, damning the rogues who could impose so meanly and impudently on poor French prisoners. Then he had the box sealed in our presence and dismissed us with the promise that the report and the box would be sent off within the hour. Our joy can be imagined when we saw his own launch leaving the hulk, carrying with it our two denunciations.

During the next two or three days our gaoler's generosity increased rather than diminished. Communication with the shore was allowed and compared to our previous state we enjoyed excessive freedom. Captain Rose was waiting for the end of the enquiry which would be provoked by our petition against the contractors before taking revenge for his irksome generosity and returning to his former cruelty.

'My friends,' said Duvert the gunner, who enjoyed great esteem on board the hulk after his trial, 'we mustn't be lulled by the turnkey's smooth hypocritical ways. We must take advantage of them. Listen carefully. Thanks to the opportunities we now have of communicating with the shore I've arranged to make use of certain go-betweens and agents. But, before I go on, I'd like a few men to stand guard by the ladder to make sure the English don't overhear and to warn us if they're coming.'

Two seamen immediately detached themselves from the crowd and stood guard. Duvert continued: 'My friends,' he said, 'you may think my plan mad. But remember well that desperate diseases need desperate remedies, otherwise we shall be hopelessly lost. The ordinary means of escape are well known, so we must invent something new and unexpected. This is what I suggest. We shall finish cutting all the holes that are being worked on at present. There are many more of them since Rose softened towards us, because no one has thought of anything except escaping from his oppression. In five or six days when the work is done, we shall escape *en masse*.'

'What do you mean *en masse*?' asked a prisoner.

'By *en masse* I mean that instead of slipping furtively into the water with care to avoid the attention of the sentries, we shall all plunge in just as if the English weren't there. What the devil do you think the sentries will do when they see men coming down as thick as hail? They'll be so surprised by the sight that they'll think they're dreaming and by the time they've collected their wits we'll already be out of range. And even if they let off a few shots, what harm will there be? Two or three wounded or killed, the rest escaped. It will be a magnificent affair.'

'I don't like to look a gift horse in the mouth, Monsieur Duvert,' interrupted a seaman, 'but I'd like to ask you a question. Once we're in the water, what'll happen to us? Won't we be grabbed at once by the boats they'll send after us?'

'Certainly we would be, but for the agents on shore that I told you about. Thanks to them four yawls will be waiting a few fathoms from the hulk for the whole of the night we choose for our escape.'

'Ah! With four yawls waiting, that's an entirely different matter. I reckon we ought to finish cutting our holes as quick as possible.'

All the prisoners, especially those who could swim, swiftly gave their support to the plan and it was decided that the work should proceed. This conversation, or rather conspiracy, happened about four o'clock in the afternoon. So as not to raise our gaolers' suspicions we went back up on deck, even though the weather was foul.

'Aren't you going down?' I said an hour later to a seaman, whose hammock was next to mine, when it was time to return to our quarters according to the rules.

'I'm staying up, comrade,' replied the seaman, whose name was Duboscq.

'Are you keeping watch tonight to protect our escape holes?'

'Not at all. I'm waiting for Corporal Barclay to come and open the door. We've a little business to do together and we agreed to meet tonight.'

'That's strange. With the freedom we've now got what stops you finishing your business with the corporal during the day?'

'Oh, Barclay's a crafty villain. He knows that though our turnkey seems to favour us he still hates us, probably more than ever, and that he's taking note of those amongst his men who deal with us and show us pity so that he can pay them out later. Now, Barclay wants to be made a sergeant. To get his promotion and keep in his superiors' good books he pretends to treat us very harshly and only does business with us secretly and on the quiet.'

'Now I understand your rendezvous tonight. But, come to think of it, wasn't it you who lured that damned Barclay with a pair of braces into the trap which cost him such a good flogging?'

'That was me! Don't you think he well deserved the honour of running the gauntlet?'

'He deserved the gallows. But aren't you afraid that he might bear a grudge for the flogging? Surely his meeting with you might be an opportunity for revenge?'

'What sort of revenge? I don't understand.'

'It's very simple. Why shouldn't Barclay take you in charge for breaking the rules? That'd get you a week in the Black Hole.'

'Abetted by him? Would he charge himself as well?'

'You're right, I hadn't thought of that. Despite that, if I were you I'd have nothing to do with that man. He can't have forgotten what you made him suffer. Believe me, in one way or another he'll find some way of making you regret it.'

'Perhaps you're right. Yes, on second thoughts, I'd better break completely with him. Only, since he owes me five shillings, I'll see him again tonight, but this will be the last time.'

'My dear Duboscq, I'm glad to see you following my advice. Good luck!'

Without any further thought on the matter I went to my hammock and lay down. Perhaps two hours later, when I was in a deep sleep, I was abruptly woken by a loud explosion. I leapt out of my hammock. Almost immediately I heard a cry of pain.

'Who's wounded? What's happening? Who fired?' clamoured prisoners everywhere as they jostled in the darkness.

We did not have to wait long for an answer. There were groans from the bulkhead near the aftermost part of the deck. We rushed to where the unfortunate Duboscq lay, covered in blood and nearly lifeless. We were about to try and staunch the blood that spurted from a dreadful wound which he had received full in his chest, when the English crowded down on to our deck, with dark lanterns and cocked muskets, and seized him.

'My friends,' said Duboscq in a faint voice, 'revenge me... Barclay did it...'

The reader will well understand the outrage that this tragic event caused. For us the rest of the night was a sleepless one.

The next morning our gaoler, the dreadful Rose, told us that our poor comrade was dead. He then rebuked us with unaccustomed mildness, which must have cost him dear, concerning our repeated attempts to escape. It was futile to reply that Duboscq had never had any such idea, that his death was not an act of discipline but a truly horrible murder and that we were able to prove our assertion. We vainly asked him to have the villain Barclay arrested. He remained deaf to our accusations and entreaties and merely advised us to abandon our plans for escape. Since our petitions were rebuffed, we swore to take revenge on the murderer of our unhappy friend.

Four days later the preparations for the great escape we had planned were finished and we agreed to attempt our perilous enterprise on the following night. I cannot express the despair felt by the prisoners who could not swim at the thought that they would be unable to share our dangers and hopes. I must also confess that many of our comrades were frightened by the boldness of our enterprise and stated plainly that they wanted nothing to do with it. However they all begged us, if we were lucky enough to get back to France, not to forget them, to send them some assistance and to secure their exchange.

Alert expressions were seen and lively voices heard all day on board the *Crown*. I could not understand how such unusual animation could escape the watchful gaze of our guards and midnight, the time fixed for our escape, was a long time coming.

Then I bitterly regretted having refused to join the previous escape, which had succeeded so well. How I envied Ensign R___ his freedom! 'Who knows?' I said to myself, 'If he hadn't accepted the place that I was offered, perhaps I would have found the resolution to go.'

Suffering made me unreasonable and I also cursed Bertaud's memory, good brave Bertaud, whose tragic death had so affected me and deprived me of all my spirit. In the end I was determined not to hang back this time nor to be daunted by any obstacle or peril.

Towards the middle of that memorable and fateful day we saw the villainous Barclay appear on deck, wearing his sergeant's stripes. I cannot express the fury that this sight aroused in us. This reward for such a cowardly and treacherous shedding of noble blood inflamed us immeasurably and increased, if that were possible, not only our hatred for the English, but our desire to escape from their vile oppression.

Curfew time arrived and we went down to our hammocks and undressed. A profound silence broken by a few whisperings soon reigned on our deck and the orlop, but our hearts were beating as if they would burst.

With each minute as the solemn moment approached our anxiety increased. The time went both too slowly and too swiftly; we earnestly wished to have another twenty-four hours before us and at the same time we longed for the signal to escape without further delay. As for Duvert, the soul and leader of our plot, he slid and crept from hammock to hammock, and all over with orders and encouragement.

I passed the time until the fulfilment of our enterprise between extremes of mad hope and despair. At last the English rang midnight on the bell up on deck and we arose as one man. Each stroke on the bell echoed in my heart and I recall what I felt as if it were yesterday. In a few seconds the die would be cast, for good or ill. Then, suddenly, the door to the orlop opened and Captain Rose appeared at the head of a strong company of soldiers.

'Let no one move,' he shouted as he entered, 'or I'll have you all shot!'

At his words and the sight of him we were seized with terror and dismay. Dumbstruck and appalled, we lost our heads. Despite his orders we scurried to our hammocks, or to be more truthful, into the nearest hammocks within reach.

'Frenchmen!' bellowed Captain Rose in the midst of a deep silence, 'you have done wrong to presume on my kindness. Have I not treated you more like a brother and a friend than a commander? And instead of rewarding my generosity by exemplary conduct, you try to evade my vigilance and escape! I would be within my rights if I punished you severely, as my duty requires. But on the other hand, taking into the account the daily vexations you suffer from the contractors' shameful conduct, I pity you and incline to mercy.'

After this pretty speech Rose, whose moderation must have concealed suppressed anger, was silent for a moment and then continued menacingly, 'It was the contractors, wasn't it, whose ill treatment led you to hatch this vast plot which was to come to a head tonight? Answer me!'

Since everyone understood that Captain Rose attached great importance to the answer we all hurriedly cried out, 'Yes!' it being vital above all to avoid the punishments to which we were liable.

'Very well,' said the Captain, 'I forgive you. However, you shall declare in a statement signed by you all that the sole motive for this enormous conspiracy was to get away from the contractors' cruelty and that if your rations had been wholesome and of full weight, as they used to be, you would never have dreamt of this escape. Do you agree to sign this declaration?'

We were only too happy to get off so cheaply and hurriedly declared that not only would we sign the statement but that we would also thank the Captain for allowing us this opportunity to establish the truth.

It seemed that the English had received good intelligence and that the traitor who had betrayed us had not kept anything back, since our gaolers knew the existence of every hole we had pierced. They spent the rest of the night and until the morning in repairing and blocking up our holes and quitted us only when certain that we had no further means of escape.

I cannot tell if the despair caused by the abortion of our plan was equal to our rage at the betrayal we had suffered. On the gun-deck and in the orlop a single thought absorbed all the prisoners, that of finding the culprit and inflicting on him the punishment he so well deserved.

On the morning after our setback I was walking alone on deck, sad and disheartened, when I was told that the Captain wished to speak to me. I was as much surprised as I was annoyed, because I hated Rose to the extent that the sight of him made me feel sick, but I had to obey his order.

'Sir,' said he, when the English soldiers ordered to bring me before him had shown me into his cabin, 'my warders have told me that of all the French you are the one who best speaks and understands English. Since my interpreter is at present in the hospital, I ask you to replace him for the time being. In that period you shall have a salary of twelve sous a day.'[79]

My first idea was to refuse but since, all in all, the interpreter's position was a neutral one which might allow me to be useful to my comrades, I changed my mind and accepted. My friends congratulated me on this good luck and I took up my duties at once. I had resumed my walk on the deck when my attention was drawn to the arrival of a launch alongside, carrying an English officer in full uniform and a Negro clad in magnificent livery.

CHAPTER XII

*Lieutenant Rose, the Colonel and his Negro • Impudence
and cruelty • Robert and his countrymen • A bargain •
Planning an entertainment*

WE HAD BEEN SO LONG without any distraction that the smallest happening was enough to excite our curiosity, and so every eye was fixed on the English officer, a Colonel, as soon as he set foot on the exterior gallery. However, when we caught sight of the black servant who accompanied him we paid no more attention to the Colonel. The Negro was far more worthy of attention than his master.

He was of gigantic stature, at least six feet tall, of a Herculean build suggestive of superhuman strength, with a head as big as that of a bull and hideously ugly. His face was deeply pocked by some skin disease and bore an expression of mingled ferocity and insolence such as the brush might depict but the pen cannot describe.

Stationing himself on the after-deck and staring at us with a provocative effrontery the colossal Negro soon attracted our dislike and aroused our anger. Catcalls and whistles were heard from everywhere and the gesture of utter scorn with which he responded turned the catcalls to furious jeers. The black seemed delighted to have put us into such a state and let loose an immense and echoing roar of laughter, accompanied by scornful and derisive shrugs of his shoulders.

At that moment Captain Rose summoned me to attend him and I was obliged to leave the deck and the commotion that was bound to ensue. When I entered the great cabin I found him with the English Colonel at a table covered with a variety of bottles. Both officers seemed merry.

Briefly described, the Colonel was from one of the greatest families in England, his name was very well known and at that time he was said to enjoy an income estimated at a million francs a year. He was reckoned to hold a high place in *the fashion*. He was famous for his betting, his horses, his extravagance and his eccentricities, and employed his enormous wealth as a substitute for the brains he lacked. A glance was sufficient to sum him up and guess that immense self-importance and stupidity replaced all other qualities and alone motivated his actions.

'Young man,' said he, toying with his gold-headed cane, an inevitable and almost obligatory adjunct of his class, 'I have an errand for you. There'll be something in it for you if you manage to perform it with a little intelligence.'

I felt a flush of indignation rising to my face. 'Colonel,' I replied, 'I am a French sailor, a prisoner of war, and not a servant. Accordingly, I take neither orders nor wages from you.'

The Englishman shrugged his shoulders insolently and leant back in his chair.

'For a beggar like yourself, you appear mighty proud,' he replied. 'The rags on your back show that you wouldn't turn your nose up at a few shillings. Never mind, being French you think you must answer arrogantly. You're a fool, young man!'

Faced with such rudeness I regretted that I was a prisoner and would at that moment have cheerfully given a few years of my life for one hour of freedom. But what could I do? Nothing, for I had no means of retaliation. Not wishing to expose myself to further humiliation, I was about to withdraw when Captain Rose detained me.

'Stay, sir,' he said, 'I have something to say.'

Then, turning towards the Colonel whom he appeared to treat with profound respect, he added, 'Do not be offended by this prisoner's behaviour, my lord. It can be explained by the sufferings inflicted by the contractors which these wretches have had to endure for some time. I shall deal with the business you have in hand.'

Our gaoler then drank a glass of grog and continued.

'Were you up on deck just now?' he asked.

'Yes, Captain, I was.'

'Well, you must have seen a splendid Negro who came with his lordship when he did us the honour of coming on board?'

'A Negro whose bones I'd happily break. Yes, Captain.'

'You'd break my nigger's bones?' exclaimed the Colonel, bursting into laughter, 'Ah! By God! That I'd like to see! In any event, that's the only reason I came to visit the hulk...'

'I don't understand you, Colonel. If you mean you'd like to have your black knocked about, nothing would be easier. Send him down to the gun-deck or the orlop and I promise you he won't come out alive.'

'Ah, bah! Why?'

'Because since that brute came on board he hasn't stopped insulting my comrades and if the soldiers hadn't held them back they'd have chucked him in the sea long ago.'

'You are an uneducated ignoramus,' replied the Colonel coldly, 'or you would know that the ugliness, strength and insolence of Little White, as my nigger is called, are of inestimable worth. But why talk of things that are above your capacity and understanding? All you need do, interpreter, is what Captain Rose asks you to do and no more.'

The turnkey spoke again.

'Sir,' he said, 'the Colonel is at present diverting himself with a tour of the hulks to find opponents for his nigger. Ask your comrades if there are any boxers amongst them willing to be matched against the glorious Little White. Anyone coming forward shall have a purse of twenty pounds from his lordship and keep it whatever the outcome of the fight. If the Frenchman dies, his heirs shall have the money.'

Incensed at such a proposal, I was about to refuse disdainfully to translate it, when it occurred to me that someone might be found amongst our wrestlers and strong-arm men[80] to avenge this insult to France. I changed my mind.

'I shall do as you bid, Captain,' said I as I went. On deck I found the colossal Negro engrossed in putting out his tongue at the prisoners, whose exasperation had reached its height.

'Silence, my friends,' I said, 'I have a serious and important matter to communicate.' The catcalls ceased at once and I recounted the conversation I had just had with the Colonel. The end of my speech was greeted with a cry of fury when the Negro shouted out in his outlandish jargon that his master was very kind to take the trouble to seek an opponent amongst the French who were too cowardly to accept. I am certain that not a single prisoner would have refused to meet Little White with any weapon, including hatchets and knives, but the African's athletic appearance proclaimed such extraordinary and invincible strength that not one Frenchman took up the challenge.

'Very well,' said I with a sigh, 'I shall go back and tell the Colonel that the French refuse since they don't wish to make an exhibition of themselves or pander to his pleasures.'

'Wait a moment, mate,' said a sailor whose square face, broad round shoulders, short height and long hair clearly indicated his Breton origins, 'maybe you'll find your man if you'll come with me.'

I did as the sailor asked and followed him to the back of the orlop near to the bulkhead pierced with loopholes which served as a barrier for the English soldiers. When I arrived at the Bretons' corner[81] I found some of its occupants smoking their pipes, others lying or sitting on narrow benches they had made themselves, and all perfectly calm and quiet. Such were the men to whom the sailor had led me.

'Robert Lange,' said my conductor, addressing a young man aged about twenty-seven or thirty, who was walking silently up and down with his arms folded and his pipe in his mouth, 'the English say we are cowards.'

'And the English know well that they're liars when they say so,' replied Robert Lange calmly. 'We've knocked them about often enough and hard enough for them to have no doubts on the matter.'

'Comrade,' said the Breton sailor, 'could you tell my countrymen a bit of what you've just been giving out to the crew?'

'Of course, comrade,' I replied and quickly recounted the English Colonel's proposal.

'Well! Robert,' said one of the young man's friends, 'what d'you think of that?'

'I don't envy rich folks their wealth if that's the way they amuse themselves.'

'That's true; but what about the black?'

'Well, what of him?'

'Are you, the best lad whoever attended a *pardon*,[82] going to let us be mocked by a black? You must maintain the honour of the parish, comrade, and make the African dance a step or two. Your friends at home will be glad when we tell them about it.'

The young Breton appeared surprised by the suggestion.

'But I've never seen this black,' he replied, 'why should I want to do him any harm?'

'*Ma foi*, if you'd seen him, comrade,' said I, 'you wouldn't need to worry about that. He's tall enough to break you over his knee.'

At this reply all the Bretons started laughing.

'Ah! Break Robert Lange! That's not possible!'

'Well, Robert,' I continued, 'think about it, but remember that the Captain's waiting for me, and I'm waiting for your answer.'

'Tell the turnkey to leave me be.'

I was going away with some satisfaction because the Breton had not accepted the Negro's challenge for, although his comrades appeared to regard him as a redoubtable athlete, he did not seem to have anything like the build needed to oppose the African.

I felt a hand on my arm, turned round and saw Robert.

'Well, my friend,' said I, 'have you changed your mind?'

'It's not me,' he replied, 'it's my countrymen who say that Brittany will be dishonoured if we let this little black go. They want me to fight him.'

'But how about yourself? Do you accept?'

'Since my countrymen want it, so do I.'

'Very well, come with me to the Captain.'

A minute later I led Robert before our gaoler, saying, 'Captain, here's a man who accepts the Colonel's challenge.'

At this news the Colonel could not hide a smile of satisfaction and triumph, and with the close attention of a connoisseur he fell to inspecting the champion prepared to fight his Little White. A nearly imperceptible shrug of Robert's shoulders showed that he did not relish the inspection.

'Have you seen my nigger?' asked the Colonel.

'*Ma foi*, no Colonel, but that's of no account to me.'

'On the contrary, you must be introduced. Follow me.'

We went from the cabin to the after-deck where our appearance attracted every eye.

'Now, my lad,' said the Colonel introducing the colossal African to Robert Lange, 'here's your opponent. What do you think of him?'

'I think he's monstrous ugly!' replied the Breton artlessly, looking at the Negro with an air of utter indifference.

'His beauty lies in his ugliness; but I mean his appearance and his build. What do you say to them?'

'I think he's monstrous big,' replied the Breton equally calmly.

'And you're willing to be matched against him?'

'That I am, since my countrymen will have it so. But after all, I don't see why such a bother should be made about a simple wrestling bout.'

'Wrestling! What! You're thinking of wrestling? Put that out of your mind. I mean a mill, a proper boxing match.'

'Ah! A boxing match is it, Colonel?'

'Certainly. Don't you understand what that means?'

'*Ma foi*, I'm not sure, I never tried before. But boxing and wrestling are near enough the same. Neither's a matter of life or death.'

'You think so?' exclaimed the Colonel, beaming. 'Well, you're mistaken. Little White has already killed three Frenchmen.'

'Ah! Bah! Really?' cried Robert, a faint blush suffusing his cheeks. 'Ah! This black's already killed three Frenchmen? Then you and this black are both a pair of villains. Well then, yes, put me down for a boxing match and whatever goes with it. My countrymen were right, honour's at stake here.'

Though Robert Lange pronounced these words quite moderately and calmly, I knew from a glint in his eyes and the way his chest heaved that he was aroused and in a real passion.

'And when do you want to box?' asked the Colonel, 'for to tell you the truth you appear to me far too lean and feeble to stand up to Little White, and I wouldn't wish to take any advantage of you.'

'I'm ready now, Colonel! Your black who kills Frenchmen with his fists for sport makes me so angry that all the strength I've lost in five years' imprisonment comes back to me,' replied Robert Lange.

'No, my lad, the mill can't come off today. Here, take two guineas of the twenty I shall give you. Build yourself up for a week and get yourself into a state to make a proper showing when you come up to scratch.'

The Colonel gave the two promised gold coins to Robert who took them without thanking him, and pocketed them, murmuring contentedly, 'That's for my countrymen.'

'Captain,' said the Colonel as he took leave of our gaoler, 'this day week I will, with your permission, bring along the prettiest women in Portsmouth and we'll make the battle into a great occasion.'

'My lord, the day will be a proper triumph for myself and England, since I cannot doubt that your Little White will be victorious. When you come again you will find the deck adorned and everything set up ready for the fight.'

After swapping a few pleasantries on the presumed defeat of Robert Lange the two Englishmen parted, having made their appointment for the following week.

Robert Lange's acceptance of the challenge by the terrible Little White caused me simultaneous pleasure and fear. On the one hand I was happy to think that there was a chance that French honour, so insolently provoked, might have its revenge; on the other I was afraid that the Bretons might have a mistaken idea of their comrade's merits and that their exaggerated opinion of him would end in a shameful defeat. I was preoccupied by these thoughts and wishing to know more about the Breton, I seized the first excuse to get into his company.

'Now, tell me, Robert Lange,' I asked after a few minutes' conversation that had been trifling and I might also say monosyllabic, since Robert was no great talker and generally answered with a simple yea or nay when questioned, 'is it true that you had great success at home at assemblies or *pardons*?'

At the word *'pardon'* which brought Brittany back to him, the Breton's wan and sallow cheeks took on a little colour.

'Ah, yes!' he replied with a sigh, 'it's true that I used to amuse myself in my youth. I was a good lad then…'

'And more than that, the best wrestler in the parish, weren't you?'

'True, I really liked wrestling.'

'And I'm sure you always carried off the prize?'

'Yes, I had to, you understand. It concerned the honour of the parish.'

'In my view it now concerns the honour of the *Crown* hulk. Can I tell you something, Robert?'

'Don't feel awkward, mate. I'm all right, I'm not at all vain, I can hear the truth.'

'Well, I fear that this colossal African is endowed with greater strength than yours and you won't be able to resist him.'

'I think you're mistaken, comrade,' he replied. 'This Little White is an overfed insolent lump. He seems to me to make a lot of empty noise. But he knows how to box and I know nothing about that business.'

'Sad to say, that's right. It makes one more reason…'

'Yes, but he's killed three Frenchmen in his cowardly fashion,' continued Robert, interrupting me, 'whilst I'm an honest man that never harmed anybody on purpose. Now, since the Lord ought not to be on the side of villains, I don't see why I shouldn't give the black a thrashing.'

'I like to see your confidence, Robert, but let's be reasonable. If you don't know how to box, Little White will give you twenty blows for each one you lay on him.'

'That's all I ask for. As long as I can just smite him with one shrewd blow then, with God's help, I hope the villain will have had enough.'

'You really are strong!' I exclaimed, looking at the Breton's frame with more attention than before.

'So they said in my parish,' he replied affably, 'I never really thought about it, but I believe it must be so.'

I was doubly prejudiced in favour of Robert Lange, firstly because of national partiality and secondly on account of his modesty, but with all my goodwill towards him I could find nothing in his appearance to suggest more than natural strength. Robert was about five feet five inches high. His slightly rounded shoulders were large, it is true, but his limbs exhibited no extraordinary development and as for his thin bony hands, they were rather small than large.

'I'm not saying, Robert,' said I after my inspection, 'that you've no chance at all. From your paleness and sickly look anyone would judge that privations and imprisonment had lain heavily on you. I think you'd do well to use the two guineas the English Colonel gave you to get a better diet.'

'It's a fact that our daily rations are pretty poor, comrade, but that's not what makes me ill. If I could only breathe the air of home for an hour...'

'Yes, but since that's not possible...'

'Well then, when it comes to the fight I'll imagine that amongst the three Frenchmen Little White has killed there was perhaps a Breton and that'll amount to the same thing.'

'As you wish. So, farewell and good luck, comrade. Don't forget that as the interpreter I'm able to do you some small services and I'll always be at your command.'

The Breton thanked me heartily and we went our separate ways.

CHAPTER XIII

Disagreeable business of Sergeant Barclay • A denunciation •
Betrayed by Duvert • An intervention • An endless
punishment • A catastrophe

I HAD JUST LEFT ROBERT LANGE when a prisoner whom I knew pretty well came seeking me urgently. 'I've been looking everywhere for you, Garneray,' said he, 'come quick, we need you!'

'Who's *we*?' I asked.

'The men in the orlop. Hurry.'

The prisoner seemed very agitated. I was going to question him but he gave me no time and set off in such haste that I could only postpone my enquiries and follow him. Our arrival in the orlop caused a great stir from which I gathered, as the prisoner had told me, that I was anxiously awaited. Something unusual was happening, but what could it be? I soon knew.

Several of my comrades surrounded me. 'Interpreter,' they said, 'Sergeant Barclay, who murdered poor Duboscq, was unwise enough to come down here. We overpowered him and have got him securely trussed up. We were waiting for you before questioning him. We're so anxious to do away with the villain that if you'd come a bit later you'd only have found a corpse.'

'But, my friends!' I exclaimed, shocked at this information.

'Not a word from you,' replied one prisoner, 'our minds are made up. Nothing will change them. We just want to know one way or the other if you'll interpret for the Sergeant to help him make his defence.'

'I'm at your service. Take me to him.'

In one of the darkest corners of the orlop Sergeant Barclay was being held, tightly lashed to a beam.

'Interpreter,' said a prisoner, 'tell him that we're going to take out his gag and question him. If he tries to take advantage of that and cries out, he'll get stabbed straight away, ten times in the chest. Be quick.'

I swiftly translated this to the Sergeant though, to tell the truth, the dumb show of a seaman next to him with a sharpened file in his hand ready to stab him if he tried to cry for help, was clear enough and said as much as any words. With this precaution the piece of thick rag with which Barclay was gagged was removed and his interrogation began.

'Do you confess that you did the foul murder of Duboscq?'

'Aye, I confess it; it's true.'

'And so that you could strike him down with impunity, you led him first into an ambush?'

'I agree that I was crafty about it.'

'You owed five shillings to Duboscq and under pretence of paying him the money, did you lure him into your trap?'

'I never meant to pay them five shillings.'

'Did you kill Duboscq after an argument or did you do it without even being provoked?'

'I might refuse to answer that question, but I'm not afraid of you. I know perfectly well you won't do me no harm. I admit it; I shot Duboscq before he had time to say a single word.'

Sergeant Barclay's cynical effrontery aroused a long murmur of indignation amongst his audience and I reckoned that he was a dead man.

'Have you nothing else to say in your defence?' continued the prisoner who acted as president of this improvised and secret court.

'There's nothing that I can add in my defence, since no one's defending me,' replied Barclay calmly, 'only before you condemn me, listen to me a while. First of all, I must tell you that you couldn't have chosen a worse time to be rid of me. If you'd killed me whilst I was just a corporal and making you suffer so that I could

Sergeant Barclay is condemned.

get my sergeant's stripes, I'd have understood it. But it's not clever to kill me now, when I've got what I wanted and I've no more interest in you.'

'That has nothing to do with the case,' interrupted the president, 'I shall pronounce your sentence.'

'Wait, my friend,' exclaimed Barclay, now turning pale, 'please to wait, or you might regret your haste. Yes, I confess I murdered your mate. I killed him for revenge. I led him into an ambush. I kept the five shillings I owed him. I confess to anything you want. I just add that if you stab me now you'll never know the name of the man who lately betrayed you. The one who prevented your great escape. Only two people know his name, Captain Rose and myself. Now, once you've done away with me I doubt that Captain Rose will let you know who it was.'

Barclay's reply caused a hubbub amongst his hearers, including the president himself. The thought that we might at last learn the name of the traitor who was still amongst us and capable of betraying us again was too great a temptation to be resisted.

'If we pardon you, will you promise to reveal the traitor's name?' continued the president to Barclay, after rapidly gathering the opinions of the spectators.

'I swear it.'

'And what's to prove you're not deceiving us?'

'The culprit's behaviour.'

'So you agree to confront the spy?'

'If you want to kill him at once, yes. If not, no, because that would get me into trouble with the Captain. And what about you? Do you swear on the honour of France that when I've declared the traitor's name you'll let me go and do me no harm?'

'Yes, we swear!' we cried with one voice.

'And that afterwards you'll never hound me over your mate's death…that you won't attempt anything against me?'

'We swear it! Come now, speak!'

Sergeant Barclay thought for a moment and continued, 'And you'll sell me your goods at the same prices as before?'

'Of course! But talk quick.'

Sergeant Barclay's shifty, frightened gaze traversed our ranks and then, lowering his voice, he said at last, 'The traitor who betrayed you is Duvert, the gunner.'

Such an unexpected revelation provoked a murmur of indignation and astonishment amongst us. We could not believe our ears. Duvert, our leader, the soul and contriver of the plot; Duvert who had done us such good services during his memorable trial; Duvert a traitor! No, it was impossible. Clearly Barclay was lying and wanted to deceive us. However, on the other hand, if the gunner was not guilty what advantage could Barclay gain from denouncing him? None. A simple confrontation would be enough to confound him.

A Norman seaman called Millet who had been five years on board the *Crown* and was fairly intimate with Duvert said, 'My friends, I'm inclined to believe what the Englishman says. I've known Duvert more than anyone else and been in his company a lot. Well, I've never been able to form a fixed idea about him. He seems all right, but I suspect that at bottom he's otherwise. At any rate there's not a minute to lose. We can't keep this villain Barclay here any longer without attracting suspicion. Let's get Duvert before us.'

Millet's proposal was unanimously agreed and a prisoner was dispatched at once to fetch Duvert who was then on deck.

Two minutes later the gunner made his entrance into the orlop. We had taken care to hide the English sergeant and since Duvert saw all eyes turned towards himself, he must have surmised that he had some important part to play. He began by smiling at us most agreeably.

'What is it, comrades?' he asked in a patronising manner, for I repeat that, since his trial, the gunner enjoyed great esteem on board. 'Is Captain Rose up to his tricks again? Are we planning a new escape? Tell me, I'm at your service.'

'Duvert,' said Millet, coming out of the circle that had formed round the accused, 'you're a traitor and a villain. You betrayed us and we intend to kill you! No shamming; that won't do. I'm certain of the facts. What have you to say for yourself?'

This accusation was so forcefully delivered and so far from what Duvert expected to hear that he went pale as if he were about to faint. He lowered his head and was silent.

'Your confusion proves that you're not as vile as I thought,' continued the seaman Millet, 'because some traitors exist who have the brass face to defend themselves. You know you deserve to die and you're resigned to death. Just as well. We won't keep you long.'

Our furious indignation and our determination to be revenged could be guessed from a significant murmur that ran through the crowd of prisoners. Before pronouncing a single word Duvert was already irrevocably condemned. I knew that nothing could save the wretch.

There then took place in lowered voices a hideous, horrible debate, the memory of which haunts me to this day, although I had no part in it. The subject was the way of killing Duvert so as not to attract the suspicions of the authorities. Some prisoners proposed stabbing him and then cutting his body into pieces that could be thrown into the sea; others wanted him to be smothered between a couple of mattresses, so that his death could be put down to apoplexy. It was a master tailor from the infantry, who had been brought to the hulks after the breach of the surrender terms of Santo Domingo, whose suggestion gained the common consent of this dreadful assembly.

'Comrades,' he cried, 'we must give Duvert some means of retrieving himself a little in our eyes. He shall write that he no longer has the courage to endure the ill-treatment of the English, utterly despairs of life and hangs himself of his own free will. That way there'll be no inquiry and if the letter's published in the newspapers it'll maybe help to improve our lot.'

'I'll never write that letter!' shouted Duvert, who until that moment had not uttered a word. 'What! You want me to bring about my own death? Are you mad?'

'Miserable scum,' said the master tailor, 'we judge you as better than you are, that's all. Since you refuse the chance we're good enough to offer you to retrieve yourself in our sight, well, so much the worse for you. Your punishment will be all the more terrible and you'll soon long for the rope that would have ended your cowardly existence without too much suffering.'

'Comrades, good friends!' said Duvert, who had almost recovered his composure though he understood only too well the full horror of his position, 'must you sink to murder, become murderers, just because I was overcome and broken by long captivity and went the wrong way about getting my freedom? In the end, who was hurt by my disclosures? No one, not a single one of you has had any action taken against him…'

'Silence, traitor!' shrieked a voice, interrupting the hapless Duvert.

'Kill him, kill him!' bayed the prisoners.

Duvert understood our resolve not to allow him to continue and that throwing himself on our mercy offered no chance of salvation. He gathered all his strength, leapt towards us at the moment we least expected it, with his head lowered to ram his way through the crowd, and began screaming for help. The instant he moved he was lost. The reader will know how wild and irresistible is the strength unleashed by an angry mob when the first act of violence occurs. Nothing can restrain it. The line between man and beast is crossed and each individual in the crowd is transformed into a ravening tiger. So it was in Duvert's case.

He had scarcely uttered his first cry for help before twenty arms, each fortified by fury, battered him and he rolled bleeding on the floor of the orlop. A horrible scene followed, the dreadful details of which I refrain from relating. It was chaos, a ghastly scrimmage in which everyone tried to strike the traitor and everyone succeeded.

Nothing revolts my nature and temperament more than scenes of violence. When I could no longer stand seeing the doomed gunner stretched out on the deck, motionless as a corpse, the object of every man's savage brutality, I made haste to get away. A prisoner held me back.

'Where are you off to, comrade?' he asked.

'To get some air on deck. I'm stifled here.'

'That's as may be, but you don't leave the orlop till the spy's been punished.'

'And who'll stop me going?' I exclaimed, feeling rage mounting within me.

'I will. Everybody will. I don't suppose that you're other than all right. I don't suspect you and you look like one of us, but with so much treachery around no one's to be trusted. Duvert must die and I tell you, no one goes out of the orlop till he's dead.'

My argument with the prisoner had attracted the attention of several persons who were not slow to express their agreement with him. Despite myself I had to give up my intention and remain an unwilling spectator of this drama, whose swift and terrible end I foresaw only too well.

The unconsciousness into which Duvert had lapsed at least gave him the benefit of no longer hearing the arguments about how he was to be put to death. Aroused by the violent scene that had just occurred, the prisoners had lost all human feelings and restraint. The most abominable and cruel suggestions, far from stimulating disgust, were furiously applauded. It was no longer a question of finding a way to murder the hapless Duvert without later being brought to justice, but simply of inflicting the utmost suffering. They were like a band of crazed savages.

At that moment I would have gladly sacrificed all my small savings not to witness the approaching bloody and inevitable end, but the ladder was guarded by prisoners with files and sharpened pieces of foils and it would have been certain death to try and get past them to go up on deck.

I wanted to close my eyes and stop my ears, but a fatal and invincible curiosity, stronger than my will, prevented me and overcame my feelings and loathing. I remained amongst the outermost rows of spectators, with my chest constricted, scarcely able to breathe.

The ghastly debate was soon over. It was unanimously decided that Duvert should be beaten to death. He had already been stripped of his clothes and tied tightly to a stanchion; his extempore executioners stood with their cudgels raised, waiting for the signal, when a prisoner who had up to that point been notable for his ferocity, emerged from the throng and delayed the slaughter.

'Comrades,' he cried, 'when Duvert betrayed us he was in his right mind and had his reason. Now we're about to punish a thing that's no better than a corpse. For justice to be done the punishment must match the crime. Before we beat the spy, let's bring him round and make him conscious again.'

This refinement of cruelty was agreed by nearly all and the very same men who like brute beasts had hurled themselves unmercifully at Duvert a little while before, now rushed to attend him. These attentions worked only too well. Painfully stretching out his bruised arms and opening his swollen eyes with difficulty, the wretch gazed at us for a few moments with a stupid, wild expression. Little by little his senses returned and with a terrible cry of fear, for his gag had been removed, he suddenly covered his eyes with his hands.

'Mercy, my friends,' he implored, 'mercy! In the name of your honour, don't murder me...'

'Traitors aren't murdered, they're punished,' exclaimed a prisoner.

'Yes, my friends,' continued Duvert, in a state of terror close to madness, 'I know I'm vile, a traitor, a coward, unworthy to be amongst you, I deserve to die! Give me a respite and I'll do justice myself...I'll kill myself later...I promise...I swear it... But first of all, let me write to my poor old mother, to prepare her for the news of my death.'

'No mother mourns for a son who's a spy!' replied a prisoner.

'Duvert's trying to fool us, comrades, by bringing in his mother's name,' interrupted the seaman Millet, 'when she's been dead these ten years.'

At this revelation a howl of rage resounded from one end of the orlop to the other and I felt my whole body quiver, for this wild, spontaneous howl was the end of all hope.

'Well, yes, friends, I lied...my mother's dead,' continued Duvert, hurriedly speaking up to gain time, 'what do you expect? I'm afraid...'

A fearsome torrent of abuse followed, with the vilest and basest execrations hurled from every direction. Then a phenomenon occurred, a mysterious happening, scarcely explicable or comprehensible. Duvert had until then hung his head, crushed by unspeakable terror. Suddenly he now seemed to recover his energy and dignity.

'Gentlemen,' he said, turning an assured gaze on us, whilst his face changed completely, as if by magic, 'I was wrong and I bitterly repent having sunk to begging. Yes, I'm a traitor. Yes, the love of freedom made me forget my obligations. But a coward I am not. Some of my old comrades, prisoners here as I am, have seen me in the face of the enemy. They know that I've never been unworthy of the uniform I once wore and that I never flinched or ducked my head under fire. When it came to a point of honour and I had a sword in my hand, I never gave an inch and won every duel I ever fought. Take the bravest, the most fearless man and set him down at his lowest ebb in front of five hundred madmen, all howling for his death, and you'll see him weaken as I weakened. Be patient. I've nearly done. One last word. You want vengeance and to make an example of me. So be it. I submit to your justice. Only I hold that when five hundred men set on a single man they become cowards and remain murderers. Don't dishonour yourselves by every one of you beating me. You're right to condemn me, but don't spoil your cause. Let just one of you stab me and make an end of me.'

After Duvert had pronounced these words forcefully and, it must be confessed, with a singular dignity, he folded his arms, raised his head and said in a calm and assured tone, 'I'm waiting, I'm ready, gentlemen.'

A great silence reigned in the orlop. The change which had overtaken Duvert was so unexpected and extraordinary and caused such an impression on the mob, that for a moment I hoped his boldness had saved him.

'What do you think of this wretch, Garneray?' asked a naval lieutenant, Monsieur S___, who was standing near me.

'I think he's no ordinary man, sir,' I replied.

'I share your view. There's something about him. He lacks one thing. Integrity. With some morals he could have gone far. Poor devil! The staunchness he's just showed makes me angry, because he grows in my opinion and that will make the spectacle of his death more distressing to me.'

'Couldn't you save him, lieutenant?' said I eagerly to Monsieur S___.

'I? Are you mad, Garneray?'

'But, lieutenant, why should it be impossible? Your rank and the general respect you have on board the *Crown* make you able to bring it about more than anyone else. I don't say that you'll succeed in the attempt, only I believe that no one's better placed than you to manage it. Look, the moment couldn't be better. The shouting's stopped. Our fellow-prisoners seem more ashamed than angry, Duvert's on his knees praying. No one's going to interrupt him. Try, lieutenant, I beg you.'

'It's just this calm that makes me fear for Duvert,' replied Monsieur S___, 'because it shows me, far more than all their recent shouting, how fixed and unshakeable their decision really is.'

'Hurry, sir, there's not much time. Look, Duvert's stirring…'

Monsieur S___ remained for a few seconds in a deep abstraction, as could easily be guessed from his serious, reflective expression, and then spoke again.

'I didn't think you'd ask me to save this wretch,' he said emphatically, 'but sadly I can only think of one way, and that's worse than death.'

'What is that terrible way?'

Monsieur S___ was about to reply when we saw a prisoner, pale but determined, emerge from the mob and approach Duvert with a knife in his hand. This was the man who had accepted the job of executioner.

'*Ma foi*, his time's up! I can't let this poor devil have his throat slit in cold blood,' said the lieutenant. 'God knows my heart. He'll forgive the dreadful thing I must do. There's no other way to prevent this crime.'

Monsieur S___ thrust his way violently through the crowd and sprang between the condemned man and his executioner.

'Pardon, lieutenant,' said the latter, trying to thrust him back, 'we've delayed too long. The English could arrive at any moment.'

'One second's enough to stab a man,' exclaimed Monsieur S___ to the astonished crowd, 'and Duvert can't get away, so let me speak!'

The prisoners had not expected the lieutenant's intervention and in my view it seemed to make a disagreeable impression on most of them. Fortunately there were a few persons, moved by pity like myself but not daring to show it, who applauded S___'s action and shouted for him to be allowed to speak. Supported by this minority, Monsieur S___ continued in a clear, assured voice.

'Friends,' he said, 'any fears that my conduct seems to make you feel are unfounded. You are well enough acquainted with me, both from my past service and from our lives together, to know that I'd never support spying and treachery.'

Three cheers greeted these words and Duvert, whose hopes appeared to have revived at the sight of the lieutenant's intervention, lapsed into his previous apathy.

'Friends,' continued Monsieur S___, when silence fell again, 'I repeat that not only do I not excuse this wretch's crime but that it outrages me even more than it does you. In proof of this, I dismiss the death you want to inflict on him as too easy! A pretty thing, a stab to the heart! What a revenge! A pain so quick and fleeting that it can scarcely be called pain, followed by eternal rest. Where's the revenge in that? Where's the example? It does no more than encourage treason!'

The isolated murmurs which greeted these words were soon drowned by a noisy, forceful endorsement. The murmurs came from a few petty officers held on board the *Crown,* who could not view without pain one of their colleagues exciting the mob's deplorable instincts and advocating murder. Monsieur S___ seemed to notice neither this disapproval nor the others' encouragement and continued in the same angry tone.

'What's needed,' he exclaimed, 'is a terrible punishment, something fearful, something worthy of the crime, a punishment the sight and memory of which will freeze with dread any wretch who may be tempted to imitate Duvert! Do you agree, comrades?'

'Yes, yes, Lieutenant!' replied almost all the prisoners crowded in the orlop, 'you're right! What'll we do?'

'Do as our brothers did on board the *Sampson* hulk. We must stamp the seal of infamy on Duvert so that his life – and I wish him to live - becomes an unbearable torment, an endless punishment. Don't interrupt me! Hear me out! We shall write, we shall tattoo, these words on the traitor's forehead, in letters that can never be erased, *I betrayed my brothers to the English on board the Crown hulk, the 10th March 1809.* Then, after that, we'll give him fifty lashes on his bare back and make a show of him on deck with our verdict written in English about his neck for our enemies to read, *Thus in future will we treat all spies whom we discover amongst us.* There, my friends, that's what I suggest. To give Duvert credit he looked death bravely in the face before, but now his paleness and his proper fear are proof that I'm right.'[83]

Thanks to his rare shrewdness and presence of mind Duvert understood that support for Lieutenant S___'s generous proposition would depend upon his appearing deeply affected by it and although he would have preferred to be stabbed rather than tattooed, his features nevertheless became hideously discoloured and took on a livid pallor. This finally decided the prisoners.

'Yes, yes, tattoo him!' they exclaimed enthusiastically. Twenty arms seized Duvert and slung him to the floor again.

'I've saved the man's life as you see, Garneray,' said Lieutenant S___, coming back to me, 'but I had to use dreadful means to do it. God forgive me! I could only prevent a great crime by putting a great punishment in its place. I had to let them do something vile.'

Few readers can fail to have seen crude, simple designs in black, dirty red or pale blue on the chests and arms of old soldiers and labourers, representing flaming hearts pierced by arrows, women's faces, or republican emblems. These are produced by tattooing. Nothing can be simpler than the requirements for this work. A few fine needles tied together and a little gunpowder, indigo or vermilion are all that is needed for such small masterpieces. The inscriptions below these eloquent vignettes – 'Caroline My Love', 'Thomas and Pierre, Friends for Ever', 'Liberty or Death' – are all done in the same way. The operation causes a little discomfort to the patient and demands no great talent from the artist.

A hundred prisoners could have tattooed Duvert, but they needed gunpowder to do it, of which we had not a single grain. It was Barclay who procured us a cartridge in exchange for our swearing to keep what he had told us as an inviolable secret.

Five minutes later a great dark swarm of prisoners who were tattooing Duvert or jostling to watch the operation could be dimly seen in one of the obscurest corners of the hulk. Such were my feelings that I got as far away as possible and turned my back.

An hour afterwards an immense yell of joy and triumph signalled the end of the execution and at almost the same instant I saw the unfortunate Duvert pass by close to me. He was horribly disfigured and a hundred arms were shoving him towards the hatch. The tattooing which covered his forehead and cheeks rendered him hideous. He seemed to understand the full extent of the misfortune that had just overtaken him and to realise his awful position, since he staggered as he walked, as though his legs wilted under the weight of his body. His head drooped in humiliation and great tears escaped from his eyes. It made me sick to see him.

He had scarcely got up on deck before the vast placard attached to his neck attracted the attention of the English who surrounded him, keenly curious, and read the contents of the judgement and the warning given by us to future traitors.

As may be supposed, this event was too grave to be passed over in silence and Captain Rose, being informed of what had happened, hurried down to our Park.

I shall never forget the comical expression on our gaoler's face when he had taken stock of the threats set out on the placard. In his usual way he was, on the one hand, furious and exasperated with the French dogs who had thus dared to treat his spy. On the other hand, he was restrained by the fear that if he renewed hostilities we would abandon him in his dispute with the contractors at the critical point of the forthcoming enquiry. He was uncertain whether to abuse us or smile at us. If I can be forgiven an apt comparison, he was like the crater of a volcano throwing out pretty little Roman candles. We burst out laughing.

Torn by such opposite feelings Captain Rose sought to get out of this fix by a middle way and began loading Duvert with goodwill and kindness.

'Come with me,' said he, taking Duvert by the arm, a rare honour, 'bearing in mind what you have suffered in England's service I have no doubt that the Transport Office will compensate you amply for this indignity. England never abandons those whom she employs.'[84]

After these words of encouragement to future spies the Captain was moving away with Duvert when the latter threw off his partner's arm with a sudden jerk, made a leap, cleared the netting and hurled himself overboard. A dreadful scream followed, accompanied by the sound of splintering wood and we realised that instead of dropping into the water, the poor man's fall had been broken by the outside gallery that encircled the hulk. Five minutes later Duvert was carried bleeding back on deck. Despite the great height from which he had thrown himself he was not dead. Both his legs were broken.

'A warning to future spies and traitors!' said a deep sonorous voice. All the prisoners clapped and clamoured, 'Bravo!' Our gaoler scuttled off to his cabin.

In this tale of my imprisonment it is hardly to be expected that I can do more than give partial endings, and to conclude Duvert's story I must add that we later learnt that he recovered from his injuries and enlisted in the English army. I do not know his fate, though he may still be alive, which is by no means impossible since he was not much older than myself when I saw him on board the *Crown*.

To return to my narrative; after our exploit we expected to be severely punished but fortunately our fears were not realised. A week elapsed in which the sullen Captain Rose seemed not to think of revenge for the way we had treated his spy. His hostilities with the contractors to the hulk protected us, he needed our testimony and he prudently deferred the explosion of his wrath to a later date.

CHAPTER XIV

A wager • A meal • The Colonel's fresh impudence •
Robert's resignation • An unexpected triumph •
Disappointment of a select audience • Devouring a dog

I HAD JUST COME UP ON DECK one morning when I was surprised to
see carpenters at work building a tier of benches in the space between the
mainmast and the poop. These benches, rising upwards, decorated with flags
of every colour and shaded with an awning had an unaccountably festive
appearance. It was all like a theatre in the open air.

'What are these preparations for?' I asked a carpenter.

'By God! It's for all the pretty ladies and the quality of Portsmouth and Gosport,'
he replied. 'Have you forgotten that the boxing match between one of your mates
and the pugilist Little White is fixed for today?'

'Ah! My God! It's true, I hadn't thought of it,' I exclaimed sadly.

'It seems to dismay you,' said the Englishman cheerily. 'If the Frenchman gets off
he'll be able to call himself lucky.'

'I don't agree,' I replied coldly. 'On the contrary, it'll be a miracle if Little White
doesn't have his back broken.'

'Indeed!' exclaimed the Englishman, 'so your mate knows about boxing?'

'In that business, he's supreme!'

'Indeed! Indeed! So much the better! The fight'll be all the more interesting. The
fancy in Portsmouth, where they speak of naught else, were afraid that Little White
might kill your man too quick. Some pretty steep bets have been laid.'

'What, bets laid! I don't understand. Explain yourself.'

'Nothing easier. The bets ain't on the Frenchman's death or defeat. That's not in
doubt. They're betting simply on the number of blows he takes before he's knocked
down for good. Some are laying three to one on a single blow, others two to one
on two and most evens on three. Since you say your mate knows how to box, I'll
wager on five. Ought I? Don't humbug me now.'

'Here's a guinea,' I replied, taking a gold coin from my pocket, 'which I'm saving
for my comrade. I'm backing him to win. Will you take the bet?'

'Bless me, but I ain't got money like that,' said the carpenter, 'but if I had I'd take
your offer with all my heart. But, wait a bit, perhaps my mates will help.'

The Englishman then explained the business to his companions and the guinea
was made up at once.

'It's agreed. Good-bye for now,' said the workmen mockingly, 'and don't you go a-spending your money, 'cause we're counting on it to drink a barrel of ale to toast Little White's triumph.'

'Never fear, my lads, a Frenchman's as good as his word,' I replied as I went away, 'but be warned; if you expect to drink ale after my comrade's defeat your throats'll be dry till doomsday.'

My confidence in the Breton, loudly proclaimed though I did not feel it, made the Englishmen laugh heartily. I hurried to meet Robert Lange and found him still asleep in the orlop.

'Well, comrade,' said I, gently shaking his arm, 'the great day has come.'

The Breton looked at me wide-eyed with astonishment and then replied in a tone of mild rebuke, 'Ah, sir, it was unkind in you to wake me like that. I was dreaming that I was at one of our festivals at home.'

'It's all very well dreaming, my dear Robert! Now then, I repeat, this is the great day. The English workmen are just this minute finishing the preparations. They tell me that throughout all Portsmouth there's nothing being talked about except your fight with Little White.'

'The fools!' said Robert Lange softly, accompanying the exclamation with a dismissive shrug of the shoulders, 'they must have time to waste if they trouble themselves with such a dull subject. For my part I'd nearly forgotten it.'

'Robert, I mustn't keep from you the fact that the English regard your defeat as a sure thing. I've just bet a guinea on you. Now, do you think you can win it for me and that we'll have a treat out of it?'

'I think, comrade,' replied the Breton, his frankness tinged with sadness, 'that you haven't dealt honestly in this business. Let the English bet on my death and bank on it, that's only to be expected, since a poor French prisoner isn't even worth a horse or a cock in their eyes. But that you, one of my countrymen, should lay money on how many blows more or less I might give or take... well, frankly, between the two of us and in perfect friendship, I don't take it kindly on your part.'

There was such gentleness and good nature in the way the Breton reproached me that it struck me to the heart.

'My dear Robert,' I replied, shaking him warmly by the hand, 'you have completely misunderstood my conduct. If I've backed you it's certainly not from greed or self-interest because, if I can also speak frankly, I daren't believe in your victory and I only behaved as I did out of love for my country and so as not to be shown up in front of the English.'

'Yes, I understand now,' said the Breton happily. 'And I didn't explain myself! How foolish of me to have had such an idea. Do you forgive me, sir? I'm truly ashamed of myself. I owe you my thanks.'

'Let's say no more about it, Robert, and get back to your fight. How do you hope to escape from this awkward position? If you were to cry off with the excuse of your debility, which after all is sadly no more than the truth, wouldn't that be better than…'

'Being knocked out!' exclaimed the Breton with such spirit that I scarcely recognised him. 'No, sir, that would not be better. I'm as good a Christian as I can be and mean no harm to anyone. As God's my witness, I've often cracked a few lads' ribs when I wrestled at our *pardons* and gatherings, but it was never out of spite. It was just a friendly pastime to uphold the honour of my parish. It's nothing like that today. A few Englishmen, butchers and devils that they are, want to divert themselves with the pleasure of seeing a good honest Breton destroyed by a black heathen cur. Hold hard, you mustn't believe that because a Breton's good-natured that he's a fool, that in his simplicity he'll let himself be thrashed without defending himself, and thrashed, I say it again, by a heathen black in a flunkey's coat. That'd be a sight, and do you think it wouldn't enrage my countrymen? They'd treat me like a wastrel and they wouldn't want to speak Breton to me any more. *Mille nom de noms!* Now these ideas are in my head, this morning's going to seem devilish long.'

As he said these words Robert Lange was no longer recognisable. A complete change had overtaken him. His eyes sparkled and were bloodshot, his fists were clenched, his upper lip rigid with an expression of implacable ferocity. He leapt to his feet with one bound, pulled himself up to his full height and appeared to be gazing at an opponent. For the first time I saw that his mates were perhaps right to trust him and I no longer despaired of the outcome of the fight. I had learnt a little while before that given ten nuts he could normally break eight or nine of them between his fingers.

Being deprived of all distractions as we were on board the *Crown*, the reader can imagine the sensation caused in the hulk by that day's great event. Robert Lange, the hero of the moment, was surrounded, complimented and questioned by all the prisoners. I should add that this noisy popularity appealed only slightly to the Breton; at any rate, since he was good nature personified, he tried his best to conceal his impatience at being the object of this irksome general attention.

Unusually, the weather that day was magnificent, with not a single cloud in the blue sky. As soon as our scanty dinner was over we went up on deck. For my part, although my confidence in Robert had increased since my morning's conversation with him, I was still far from untroubled. I was considering how I might be useful to him when I had an idea which I hurriedly put into execution. Taking advantage of the freedom given by my position as interpreter, I sought out Captain Rose on some slight pretext and then broached the real reason for my visit.

'May I ask, Captain,' I said, 'at what time ought Little White to be here?'

'Ahah!' he replied, with a malicious smile, 'is your comrade having second thoughts? Is he afraid? I must tell you, and this you shall repeat to him, that if he repents of his rashness and wants to withdraw from his engagement with Little White, he can no longer do so. Your countryman has already received two guineas as earnest-money and that deposit binds him. At this stage a refusal on his part would be considered exactly like a fraud and punished as such. Let him think on that.'

'But, Captain, you're completely mistaken about Robert's intentions. He's given me no message for you. I come of my own free will to make a request without letting him suspect my intention.'

'Let's have your request, interpreter. Speak out, you know my generous nature.'

'I appeal to your justice, Captain. No one knows better than you how shabbily we have been used by the contractors. We are literally dying of hunger. Robert is now in a state of utter exhaustion and I'm afraid his debility will undermine his courage and willingness to fight. Couldn't you, being generosity and justice all in one, order him to be given a good dinner?'

'I can't comply. That would be to betray the good faith and friendship between myself and the Colonel.'

'Not at all, Captain. By restoring his spirits and giving him his strength back for a while, the proper meal that I request for Robert can only make Little White's triumph all the more complete and brilliant. If my comrade falls at the first blow, there's no doubt that he'll take all the spectators' sympathies with him and his defeat will be put down to his sad state of exhaustion.'

Captain Rose pondered for a moment before answering and then turned towards me, smiling with the most agreeable expression of which he was capable, that is to say a hideous grimace.

'Well, I see no great inconvenience in agreeing to your request,' he said. 'To be sure, I should be horribly put out if the boxing were to end with the first round. Yes, you're right. For the occasion to pass off well your countryman must at least make a show of resistance. Go and fetch him here at once.'

There was no need to repeat that order. I hastily sought out Robert Lange and broke the good news of what awaited him.

'Confounded English,' said he, shrugging his shoulders in his usual way, 'they refuse to give the bare necessities to poor devils who are dying for lack of them, yet they offer good dinners to the ones who amuse 'em with boxing matches. Precious rascals they are! Never mind! I haven't had what could be called a meal these seven years and I don't mind sitting down to a few good things. It'll be another prize taken from the enemy.'

Five minutes later the Breton, seated in front of a sumptuous dinner, was eating like four men and drinking like six.

'Be careful,' said I, 'you'll make yourself ill. Beware of that port wine most of all.'

'It's too good to be insulted like that, comrade.'

'Yes, I'm sure it's to your taste, but don't forget that you're not used to strong

Robert Lange's dinner.

drink and so it's bound to have a great effect on you. Get your strength up, but don't get fuddled.'

'Fear naught, comrade. Before I came to the hulks I drank half a litre of brandy every day and I can assure you without bragging that I still don't know what it is to be drunk.'

'Very well then, I'll say no more; carry on as you like.'

Robert Lange availed himself so freely of this permission that in the end the waiter who served him was utterly stupefied. In all his working life the Englishman had never seen the like.

'All done,' said the Breton at last, rising calmly from the table, 'no score to settle, no host to thank, nothing could be better. Shall we go?'

Robert Lange, whose least movements I scrutinised with uneasy curiosity, took me by the arm and walked calmly and firmly away.

'Don't you feel the fumes of the port rising to your brain?' I asked when we were once more on deck in the open air.

'Very droll,' he answered with a laugh, for he thought I was joking, 'port's a light refreshing wine, a bit weak perhaps but not to be despised. It's nearly equal to cider.'

'*Ma foi*,' I thought, 'if Robert's as good a boxer as he is a boozer, I might well win my guinea bet. He's an uncommon young man and I'm almost tempted to believe that his comrades are by no means wrong in backing him.'

Towards two o'clock in the afternoon a boat was sighted approaching the *Crown*, containing several English ladies rigged out with the startling splendour and vile taste that are so essentially British. Captain Rose bustled about welcoming his guests with all the gallantry he could muster and settled them on the best seats in the tiers. We supposed that the time for the fight was drawing near and at almost the same moment about ten boats carrying all the fashionables of both sexes from Portsmouth and Gosport reached our hulk, whose deck soon displayed a lively and picturesque scene.

Soon cheers and shouts of joy resounded, announcing the arrival of the exhibition's arranger and of its hero, that is to say, the splendid Colonel and the renowned Little White.

'What's Robert Lange doing?' I asked of one of his friends, a Breton who passed close by to me at that moment.

'Robert's playing at *drogue*,' he replied.[85]

'What's he thinking about? What does he say about it all?'

'He thinks all these folk are very stupid to go to such trouble just to see two poor devils hammer each other. He wants to be left to his game in peace and to be called just when they need him.'

'*Ma foi*, his confidence is starting to win me over. I begin to believe that he'll come through this with credit.'

'Comrade,' replied the Breton, chewing his quid with a slight air of mockery, 'you're talking about one of my countrymen. You know nothing, just like a blind man discussing colours. I say only this, which will have to do for the moment. You'll learn soon enough from your own eyes that Bretons aren't to be knocked about by darkies for nothing. I'm expecting a farce. We'll all split our sides at it.'

My conversation with Robert's friend was interrupted by the arrival of the English Colonel, Lord S___, who immediately attracted every gaze when he appeared on deck, followed by his pet Little White and a magnificent Great Dane dog. Captain Rose hurried to greet the Colonel and after shaking him respectfully by the hand led him to the place of honour set aside for him.

'Well, my dear Captain,' said his lordship, 'is the Frenchman still ready to hazard the venture?'

'However badly brought up the French may be, they still know enough of the world to understand that no one incommodes a person such as your lordship without reason,' replied Captain Rose, with a deep bow to the Colonel.

'In that case, my dear Captain, pray let him know that Little White is at his command and awaits him.'

'The celebrated Little White wasn't born to wait for a French dog,' replied our gaoler gallantly. 'Hallo there, interpreter, off with you, quick, and fetch your countryman.'

We were powerless and all too accustomed to such abuse for any idea to occur to me of retorting to this insult. I contented myself with a disdainful shrug of the shoulders and obeyed.

'Robert,' I said, coming upon the Breton calmly engaged in his game of *drogue*, 'the black has sent me to ask if you're mocking him, since you've not come to pay him your respects.'

'Certainly, I do mock him', replied the Breton in a manner that was calm and placid, but belied by the blood that rose to his cheeks. 'Tell him I've a few more tricks to win and that he'll have to wait for me. Waiting's his job.'

I was overjoyed at this reply which allowed me to take my revenge on the Captain for his gratuitous insolence. I hastily returned to him and announced loudly and clearly before all the quality, 'Captain, Robert, the seaman, is playing cards and he instructs me to reply to the invitation by Little White, the lackey, that he'll come as soon as the game's over.'

As I had expected, these words produced uproar. A chorus of curses damned the French and their impertinence. Captain Rose, giving way to his brutal headstrong nature, was all for throwing Robert Lange into the Black Hole. The Colonel had the greatest difficulty in calming him.

'I'm told that it's the custom in France, Captain,' he said, 'to satisfy any whims of a condemned man in his last hour. Let this man finish his last game of cards. As for you, Little White,' added his lordship, 'strip and make ready.'

Little White immediately put off the rich elaborate livery in which he was garbed and a murmur of admiration, almost terror, ran round the tiers when his naked, Herculean torso was disclosed. His arms were in fact bigger than normal thighs and

Little White.

the volume of his chest was greater than that of two men standing face to face. Little White was truly phenomenal, a man of incredible and indeterminable strength.

The flattering murmur lasted until in his turn Robert Lange appeared. The Breton with his peaceful expression, slightly rounded shoulders, hands in his pockets, quid in his cheek and his cotton cap on his head, presented such a striking contrast to the superb bearing and theatrical attitude of his adversary that the English were instantly disappointed.

'But that fellow could never stand so much as a nudge from the handsome black,' said the ladies peevishly, 'this fight's a jest…'twas scarce worth the trouble of coming for such a trifle…I'll wager 'tis one of Lord S___'s hoaxes; we should have known it.'

As for Little White, he remained for a few seconds sunk in the deepest astonishment and then delivered himself of a peal of laughter so long and loud that it sounded like the braying of a trumpet.

'My God! My God!' he exclaimed when he had at last succeeded in stemming his mirth, 'this is rich!'

Robert, who had maintained all his coolness and composure whilst this scene was acting, asked me calmly, 'Now then, sir, what's the matter with that animal? Does he really think that I've left my game of *drogue* to watch him pull faces? If he's afraid of boxing, let him say so. I'm by no means bothered about knocking him down. It's all one to me, and I'll go back now and finish my game of cards.'

Like the greater part of the English aristocracy Colonel S___ understood the French language and spoke it pretty well. He immediately addressed Robert Lange. 'My friend,' he said, 'your sorry appearance justifies my black's merriment. But a bet's a bet, so let's be done with words and proceed to action. Who are your *parrains*?'[86]

'I'm a Christian and I have but one *parrain*, Colonel,' replied the Breton, misunderstanding the question.

The Colonel could not refrain from smiling with an expression of pity, since such ignorance of the manners and customs of the ring increased his ill opinion of Robert. However, being anxious for the fight to take place, he deigned to explain civilly enough to the Breton that the combatants were always attended by two seconds or *parrains*, who were charged with looking after the opponents' interests.

'Such a to-do about it all!' said Robert calmly. 'At any rate, I suppose I have to comply because it's the custom. Who'll be my seconds?'

'At your service!' I exclaimed, running forward.

'Thank you, sir, I accept without ceremony. Now then, do you come also, Jean,' added the Breton, beckoning one of his countrymen. 'Now that's out of the way, we can get on with the dance.'

The Colonel then asked, 'Have you a watch, interpreter?'

'Why do you ask such a question, Colonel?'

'This is incredible,' exclaimed Lord S___, addressing his compatriots. 'Really, the extent to which French education is neglected. Nowhere have I ever seen such ignorance! Here, take my watch,' he continued, presenting me with a magnificent pocket watch which told the seconds. 'This will be indispensable for settling how long your man is *hors de combat* each time he's floored. If the time exceeds half a minute he can no longer rejoin the fight and will be deemed beaten.'[87]

'What a rigmarole, just to give someone a hiding. I pity 'em,' said Robert. 'I really can't conceive how such stupid folk can sometimes be good seamen. Put the watch in your pocket and let me get on.'

As he said these words Robert Lange drew off his shirt and put himself in a fighting posture. A spontaneous roar of mocking laughter resounded along the tiers of benches. I understood that the attitude assumed by the simple Breton was against the rules of the ring and ridiculous to the spectators.

'Anger is taking hold of me,' said Lange.

'Robert,' said I sharply 'when these people make sport of you they insult both Brittany and France. Listen to me; you must thrash the black at all costs. Fail, and I warn you that we'll be a laughing-stock.'

A slight colour tinged Robert's pale countenance.

'Ah! So you think those villains want to ridicule Brittany,' he replied fervently. 'Never fear, I know how to defend my country's honour! Ah! God! What a pity that you can't butt with your head when it comes to boxing! Without bragging, I can say that I excel in head-butting. If I could just give the darkie a single butt, you'd soon see him laid out unconscious on the deck with his four hooves in the air.'

'Colonel,' I then said to Lord S___, 'my man is ready. Can we start?'

'With pleasure, sir; but there remains one formality to be observed by the contestants. They must shake hands as a sign of goodwill. Little White,' continued the Colonel, 'do the Frenchman the honour of offering him your hand.'

Obedient to his master's orders the Negro strutted forward, proudly and contemptuously. Then, standing before the Breton in a theatrical attitude which showed off his awesome and powerful torso, he held out his arm to his opponent, saying, 'Shake my hand with respect. It has already laid several Frenchmen low and killed them.'

At this characteristically churlish insult, which the English received with prolonged applause, a quiver of anger shook the crowd of prisoners.

'What's the black saying?' asked Robert.

'He says, my friend, that you must touch his hand with respect because it has already laid low and killed several Bretons.'

These words wrought a miraculous effect on Robert. A gleam shone in his eyes, his brows contracted, his nostrils flared, his raised upper lip displayed his gritted teeth and his face assumed an expression of indescribable rage and savagery. At that moment the man, normally so mild and gentle, had something of the tiger about him.

Despite the prodigious strength with which he was endowed and which had never before betrayed him, the foolhardy Little White could not stand unmoved before the fixed glare of his opponent. We could easily surmise from his awkward countenance that he was oppressed and abashed by that gaze. A deep silence reigned on the deck. The English seemed to anticipate that a proper drama was about to be played. I saw that Robert Lange had opened their eyes.

My agitation was such that the few seconds which the Breton employed to check the immense rage seething within him seemed to me like hours. A feverish impatience heated my blood; I longed to see battle joined and have the catastrophe over and done with. At last Robert Lange, with a motion imbued with an inexpressibly sublime energy and grandeur, extended his arm and seized the Negro's hand. With their clasped hands, their staring eyes, their incensed faces thrust together and only a tiny chink between them, the two motionless and impassive opponents appeared like a group sculpted in marble.

Gradually it seemed to me that an expression of anguish crept across Little White's face. I was not mistaken. All of a sudden, the Negro let loose a terrible moan which he must have sought to suppress for a long while, bit his lips, half-closed his eyes, threw his head back and, raising his shoulders which shook convulsively, appeared about to lose consciousness. The Breton by contrast remained calm and impassive to outward appearance and not one of his muscles moved. He was like a statue. What was happening was so extraordinary and unexpected that we knew not what to think. Robert Lange himself gave us the clue to the mystery.

'Scoundrel!' he cried in a resounding voice, 'soon no one, not even a child, will dread the hand that has murdered so many Bretons!'

I can vouch on my honour for this prodigious display of strength, but if I had not witnessed it myself I should never have credited what took place. The Breton's hand had gripped that of his opponent with such violence that blood spurted from the Negro's fingers.

'Mercy! Mercy!' cried Little White a moment later, unable to endure the fearful torture of that terrible grasp. 'Mercy! I give in!'

But Robert, insensible to these pleas and deaf to all groans, only released the hand that he was crushing when the Negro had dropped to his knees. It was a hideous sight. We saw the hand dangling, limp and bleeding. It had been literally squashed.

Our ecstasy and frantic joy could not possibly be described. Delirious cries of *'Vive la France! Vive la Bretagne! Vive Robert!'* greeted the brave Breton's triumph. We were insane with glee. As for Robert Lange, he had lost none of his composure.

'Colonel,' he said, with the sly, bantering, sham peasant simplicity that he must

Robert Lange crushes Little White's hand.

have retained from his days in the countryside, 'now that the little formality of the handshake is over, I think we can get on with the boxing. What do you think?'

Lord S___ was above all a man of the world and affected not to understand this sarcasm. He addressed Little White as if nothing unusual had taken place.

'Are you ready?' he asked.

The Negro was suffering such agony that he was incapable of speech. He answered the question with a shake of his head.

'Do you concede the fight?' continued Lord S___, with the same gravity.

'Yes.'

'Then as umpire I declare you beaten. Monsieur Robert,' continued the Colonel with great civility, 'here are the twenty guineas I owe you. I acknowledge that you have a grip of extraordinary power, despite which I'm sure that if Little White had stood up with you in the ring he'd have killed you.'

Instead of immediately taking the four five-pound banknotes that Lord S___ offered, Robert Lange fell back a step, then changed his mind and seized them without a word of thanks.

'I'd be a fool to leave this money in English hands!' he exclaimed, putting the notes in his pocket. 'There's another prize taken from the enemy.'

The Breton rejoined us, and the reader can imagine the welcome we gave him.

He was carried off in triumph.

'Ladies and gentlemen,' said Lord S___, addressing his compatriots who had come to attend Robert's defeat, 'pray accept my apologies for the needless trouble I have caused you. I am at the same time both embarrassed and innocent for, reasonably speaking, I could not have foreseen what has occurred. I think that the best we can now do is to go and leave the French gentlemen to recover quietly from their transports of joy.'

Captain Rose's face was crimson with rage, an ominous sign of cruelties to come typical of those we knew from past experience. Lord S___ gave him his hand, motioned to Little White to follow, whistled to his handsome Great Dane dog and prepared to step into the launch that waited for him by the side of the hulk. Little White did not need to be told twice and fell in behind his master with a sheepish, confused expression. But the handsome Great Dane was not so obedient. The Colonel whistled and whistled again, yet the dog was nowhere to be seen.

'Would you be kind enough, Captain,' said he to our lord and master, 'to have someone look for my dog? He must be straying about down below.'

'Down below!' repeated our gaoler, his florid hue shifting to a tinge of the deepest blood red. 'Your dog's gone below, Colonel! Then your lordship will never see him again. The animal's lost.'

'Lost! And why so? The lower decks aren't a desert and my dog is hardly so microscopic as not to be found.'

'It's just because the poor animal was so big and fat, my lord, that I repeat, you've lost him.'

'How's that? *Was*, did you say? So, d'you think he's no more?'

'I do more than think, my lord, I'm sure of it. Believe me, I don't deceive myself when I say that the wretched beast is now reduced to a couple of joints, a few dishes of stew and more beefsteaks than you could count.'

'Horror!' exclaimed the Colonel, in an accent of incredulity and disgust. 'This is impossible. What! Would these Frenchmen have devoured my dog?'

'Nothing can be more certain, my lord.'

Our gaoler was not deceived in his supposition. The *rafalés* on board the *Crown*, tempted by the Great Dane's appetising plumpness, had treacherously coaxed the over-trusting animal on to the gun-deck. Once within their power, they had all persuaded themselves that the dog was a sheep and had proceeded accordingly.

The Colonel had only just embarked in his launch when he caught sight of the skin of his favourite Great Dane dangling from one of the gun-ports. This ghastly spectacle drew from him an oath to which we replied with a chorus of whistles. It was a decidedly unhappy day for Lord S___, with his big Negro crippled, his dog eaten and Robert in rude health whilst the richer by twenty guineas. France had won on all fronts![88]

CHAPTER XV

A terrible conflict • The prisoners' resolution •
A narrow escape • Our complaints considered •
Captain Rose's removal

A S WE SAW THE LAST GUEST DEPARTING we rightly thought that the kindly Rose would turn his attention to us and we were not mistaken.

'Drive this rabble back to their quarters,' he shouted furiously to the soldiers, 'and if they don't obey quick enough, beat 'em with the butt-end of your firelocks.'

In fairness to the English soldiers, I have to say that each time such an order was given they fell to work with the utmost eagerness. Hurling themselves at us furiously, they began to knock us about and drive us before them with extraordinary zeal. Some of them, doubtless absent-mindedly, confused the butts of their muskets with the barrel ends and wounded several Frenchmen quite severely with their bayonets.

'Death to the English! Revenge!' screamed one seaman as he was struck down. At this shout we stopped, took up the cry, 'Death to the English! Revenge!' and in less than half a minute the deck of the *Crown* was a bloody battlefield. Arming ourselves with a few muskets wrenched from English hands, we quickly took the offensive against them in a tremendous mêlée, a proper battle, with loud curses and howls of rage and pain.

The English soldiers behind the barricades did not dare to shoot since their men and ours were so mixed together that their fire would have struck both. They hurriedly hoisted the flag used to signal a mutiny.

Only when the soldiers who had begun by treating us so barbarously had taken flight did we go back to our quarters, amidst confused shouts of '*Vive la France!*' and '*À bas les Anglais!*'

I must confess that once our anger had cooled we soon regretted having been so impetuous. We knew Captain Rose too well not to be certain that he would swiftly seize this outburst as an excuse to renew hostilities against us. We had already suffered so much from his cruelty and knew his capabilities so well that the prospect frightened us.

What were we to do? Since blood had been shed it was too late to go back. We decided to resist the inevitable persecutions to our utmost and not to give an inch. We had just finished conferring when the Captain sent for the interpreter.

'I can already hear the thunder rolling,' I said to my comrades. 'Never fear, friends, I'll be equal to the event. I won't weaken.'

I found Captain Rose rapidly pacing the quarter-deck, talking loudly to his second in command. 'Interpreter,' he said, 'go and warn your comrades that unless within the hour they send a deputation to beg my pardon and give me the names of twenty of the ringleaders I will shoot every man of them.'

'Captain,' I replied coldly, 'my duty obliges me to obey, but I must warn you that the errand you charge me with is utterly useless and will be fruitless.'

'Do you think these wretches will dare to refuse my conditions?'

'I'm sure of it, Captain, for two reasons. Firstly, they were within their rights to repulse a vile and unjustified attack; secondly, they will not believe your threat since it would exceed your powers. You will allow me to observe that you have no right to do it. You don't shoot seven hundred men for the sole reason that you're angry and feel the need to vent your fury.'

'Ah! So you think I wouldn't shoot them. You're completely wrong. If I've not received the deputation and the names of twenty of the ringleaders within the hour I shall pretend there's a mutiny and you'll see how earnest I am. My soldiers want nothing better than their revenge and, I repeat, I will see that they shoot you. I don't claim that I'll destroy you all. That would be impossible, but you will grant that more than one of you will die under a sustained fire, point blank through the loopholes. Be silent!' added Captain Rose, seeing me about to reply, 'not another word. I've done with you. Get out! Don't forget, I give you just an hour.'

The one-handed commander then gave me a violent shove and I went off to accomplish my sad errand. The rage and fear induced by my message can be imagined. We knew Rose was capable of going to any lengths and we trembled to think that he might carry out his threat. But on the other hand, to yield would have meant grovelling and betraying our brethren. That could not be done.

'Friends,' exclaimed an officer, 'I know that what I suggest is insane and impossible, but we must choose the lesser of two evils. Let's arm ourselves as best we can and drive back force with force! It's better to die fighting than to let our throats be cut like cowards without defending ourselves.'

'Yes, yes!' we clamoured enthusiastically, 'to arms! Death to the English!'

The reader can only have a slight idea of the resources we discovered in our despair. We took advantage of everything, our tools, our fencing foils, pairs of compasses and table legs. In less than half an hour we were armed in a way that was doubtless decidedly irregular but which at least allowed us to defend ourselves. We then began hurriedly making barricades or obstacles with our furniture and beds to block the English loopholes.

The fateful hour was about to expire when, we noticed through the ports a magnificent launch full of high-ranking naval officers, apparently making its way towards our hulk. A few minutes later this boat came alongside the *Crown*. The joy that this unexpected arrival brought us can be imagined for it was unlikely that Captain Rose would put his bloody threats into effect before these superior officers. Our curiosity matched our joy; we could in no way guess what was meant by the appearance of all these weighty epaulettes.

'You really ought to go on deck, Garneray,' said a comrade, 'and then come and explain what's happening up there.'

'But aren't I a prisoner just like you?'

'Not at all. You're the interpreter and as such you've nothing to fear.'

My companions in misfortune put this suggestion so forcibly and urged it so strongly that I eventually agreed and went up on deck. The sentry at the ladder from our deck let me pass without challenge and I soon stood amongst the awesome company who had just arrived. The first thing I noticed was the extreme coldness with which the superior officers acknowledged our gaoler's hurried salutations. They scarcely responded to his compliments save by a mere nod of the head.

'Lieutenant Rose,' said an Admiral, 'cause the signatories of the two petitions addressed to the Board of Transport to be brought before us. Here is the list of their names.'

'But there must be some mistake, my lord,' exclaimed Rose, flustered. 'I transmitted only one petition to the Board of Transport.'

'Both of them are here, sir. You may look over them.'

As he spoke the Admiral handed our turnkey two rolls of paper. As soon as I set eyes on them I recognised firstly the petition against the contractors which we had prepared at Rose's instigation and next the memorandum setting out Rose's cruelties and illegal conduct. The reader will recall we had hidden the latter in the loaf of bread that had been sent as a specimen of the provisions.

The immense dismay, the suppressed fury and despair, felt by the wretched Rose when he saw the trap into which he had fallen can scarcely be described. If he had had the power to hang us all at that moment, I do not doubt that in his rage he would have done it.

'Well, sir,' continued the Admiral, who acted as the president in this enquiry, 'what have you to say?'

'I reply, my lord,' exclaimed Rose, not knowing which way to turn, 'that not even with my ill opinion of the French would I have thought them capable of such foul treachery, such vile ingratitude.'

'Cause the signatories to these petitions to be brought before us. You shall explain yourself after we have heard them.'

I rushed to deliver this good news to the gun-deck and the orlop where it produced transports of joy. Heaven itself had taken pity on our sufferings and we were to be delivered from the detested Rose's hateful tyranny. This good fortune seemed so great that we could not believe it.

Half an hour later the commission of enquiry was settled in the great cabin and summoned the signatories of the two petitions before them. I must do them the credit of saying that their questions were put with the greatest impartiality.

We had to do no more than tell the truth to dispose of our enemy and our part was easily played. There came a moment when Captain Rose was so overwhelmed by the unanimity and accuracy of the testimony against his infamous conduct that he felt a fit of apoplexy coming on and begged leave to withdraw and obtain some fresh air.

The enquiry continued till the end of the day. When night fell and the commission left the *Crown* to go ashore we were certain of our victory and considered Rose's dismissal as inevitable.

Three days later his successor arrived. Poor Rose, what a sad leaving he had! Never in all the world was there a barracking like the one with which we saluted his departing launch as it passed before our ports. It was our last revenge on him and we gave ourselves up to it ecstatically. It seemed that life took on a totally fresh aspect and that we were reborn once our gaoler was gone.[89]

Captain Rose leaves the Crown; *stern view of a hulk.*

CHAPTER XVI

The Vengeance *hulk • A shrewd picture dealer •*
A lucky chance • The incurables • Hate and cruelty •
A stalwart doctor • A young man in love • Altercations •
A suicide

URING THE FIRST WEEKS after Rose's removal I managed to establish myself fairly comfortably and settle down to my painting again. I was working on a large picture in the many leisure hours that remained after my duties when our new Captain announced that his colleague in the *Vengeance* hulk, whose interpreter had just died, had asked that I might be lent to him for a few days. Since our Captain understood French sufficiently well to be without my services for a while he parted with me in this manner.

There could be no response to that order, except to obey. I therefore took my leave of my comrades on board the *Crown*, whom I was never to see again, and embarked for the *Vengeance*.[90] My imprisonment was to come to an end in this hulk, only it was to last a further five years.

I shall not trouble the reader by trying to depict how this new prison appeared to me when I arrived. These floating tombs resembled one another more or less and this one was exactly like the *Crown*.

In my capacity as interpreter I was accommodated in a tiny cabin situated on the upper deck and had much less to complain about than the other prisoners. I quickly arranged with our clerk to let me have, or rather to rent, a narrow cabin he occupied on the larboard side of the after-deck and there I set up my studio. I was utterly absorbed in my work, mixed very little with the prisoners and my time went by, if not happily, at least rapidly.

One day I had a visit from a stout little man who came unceremoniously into my modest studio and without saying a word began examining my productions with perfect assurance.

'To say that these seascapes are painted by a Frenchman, they're not half bad,' he said at last. 'If you'll be reasonable, we can perhaps arrange something between us. I'm a picture dealer from Portsea.'

Since I was very short of money it seemed to me that the heavens had opened and I rapidly replied that I was the easiest man in the world when it came to business.

'Young man,' said the dealer, treating me with a disdainful familiarity like the rest

The picture dealer.

of the English who took advantage of our position, 'you should not talk like that. Had I been a Jew and not the honest man I am, that admission might have cost you dear. Fortunately your lucky star has protected you. I am Abraham Curtis.'

The Englishman pronounced this name so emphatically that I supposed it must have been very well-respected and I did not dare to confess that this was the first time I had ever heard it.[91]

After a short discussion it was agreed that he would take all my pictures, provided they were of a particular size and well-finished, for a pound or twenty-five francs apiece. I was so far from expecting such a price that I was in a transport of happiness. That very day I received six pounds for all the pictures in my studio which Abraham Curtis took away with him.

From that moment my life changed into one of intense work. I left my easel only to take my meals and painted ceaselessly, winter and summer. In this way I managed to produce three and sometimes four pictures a month. Faithful to his word, my dealer paid me with such regularity that I could not have been more grateful to him. I enshrined him in my heart as the fairest and most generous man in the whole world.

One morning towards the middle of autumn, when I had been about six months in the *Vengeance*, the Captain ordered me to announce to the prisoners that a visit would take place that same day from the surgeon charged by the Board of Transport with examining the sick men who were to be sent back to their families as incurables that year. As ever the announcement of the surgeon's visit had a profound effect on the prisoners. Sad to say, each one considered himself a candidate and each one entertained hopes.

Few prisoners were healthy. The dreadful diet we endured, the foul stench from the latrines and above all the sudden changes of air we underwent when moving from the gun-deck or the orlop into the open air multiplied the cases of hæmoptysis or suppuration of the lungs to a fearsome extent. These changes were equal to the difference between a Turkish bath heated as hot as possible and a temperature of ten degrees above freezing. Immediately after hæmoptysis, the principal disease, came marasmus and consumption.[92]

The English loved to make a parade of their humanity, though it was a quality they always lacked. Since nothing is easier to calculate than the remaining time that a pulmonary patient has to live, they sent back those who only had a few weeks left to die amongst their families They boasted of having freed twelve thousand prisoners since the beginning of the war. Seen from a correct point of view the twelve thousand men set free were the victims of as many murders.[93]

The surgeon to whom this important visit was entrusted was called Weir[94] and he deserves a full description. He was a ridiculous coxcomb, about fifty-five years old, exceedingly slight in build, powdered, affected, constantly sniggering and afflicted with the most disagreeable face it is possible to imagine. He had an exaggerated self-esteem and complacently believed himself to be the most eminent practitioner in England. He was remarkably insolent, professed a lofty disdain for the French and did not even pretend to hide the hate they inspired in him. Plays on words and bad puns poured from him, each word he uttered was a quibble and each quibble was an insult. I pass on to his visit.

The first two sick men who presented themselves to this cruel biased judge presented a curious and moving contrast. The first was a handsome old man, sixty-five or sixty-eight years old. He was a true seaman, with skin tanned by the heat of the tropics and hands gnarled by daily contact with hemp and tar. He had lost his right leg and leant upon a good-looking young man of about twenty-five or thirty whose wasted features and body weakened by marasmus proclaimed his approaching end only too plainly. The old man and the young one were father and son, both seamen and both taken prisoner on the same day. They were serious candidates and I had no doubt that Dr Weir would do justice to their claim.

'Ahah!' exclaimed the doctor gleefully, tapping the old man's wooden leg with his cane, 'it seems, my friend, that you put your foot in an Englishman's door. An unwise thing to do. See where it got you. Lord, it was a good job; you got just what you deserved.'

The old man had been rotting in the hulks for six years. He took no notice of the misplaced humour and proceeded to explain his case.

'Sir,' he said humbly, 'I beg you to send me back to France. I feel that I have but a short time to live and I wish to die there, where my father died. After all, what harm can I now do to the English, a poor broken-down wretch like me? What's the use of keeping me on board the hulks? What good does the English government get out of it? Why should it spend money to feed me?'

'You old cripple,' exclaimed the surgeon, 'I really can't see why government should bother with you. How old are you?'

'Sixty-six years of age, your honour.'

'Do you sleep well? How's your strength?'

'I can no longer sleep and every moment I feel so dizzy and weak that I can scarce stand up.'

'That's bad. Let me take your pulse... Dreadful! Show me your tongue... Abominable! I'd hate to be in your shoes, old fellow. Tell me, would you like to see your country again, to go back to France?'

'More than anything in the world, my dear doctor,' cried the poor old man, 'I weep like a child at the very idea.'

'Now then, take comfort and be of good cheer.'

'Oh, my good sir, will you put my name down this time?' cried the poor one-legged man, overwhelmed by the depth of his feelings.

It seemed to me that the surgeon, contrary to his usual practice, felt some pity, since he patted the back of the old seaman's tanned hand and said with an air of kindness that I had thought foreign to his nature, 'I repeat, comfort and good cheer. And this young man, who is he?'

'My son, doctor.'

'Ah! Your son. So doubtless it was you who brought him up as a sailor? He comes from good stock. And what does the young man want?'

'Like myself, doctor, he wishes to go back to France to die.'

'Let me examine him a little... Yes, he is in a truly pitiable state. Poor young man!'

'So, doctor,' continued the old seaman in a tremulous voice, 'will you send him back as well?'

'Never fear. You will have heard that I am malicious, even cruel. These are slanders.'

'You, malicious!' exclaimed the one-legged man, 'just now I think you're as good as God himself.'

The surgeon then shook the seaman heartily by the hand as if to thank him for that compliment and continued tenderly, 'You do well to have confidence in me. One would have to be a monster to drag you away from your son's attentions. I will not separate you. You have my word.'

At this announcement of their freedom, father and son fell into each other's arms.

'Farewell, my friends,' said the surgeon, sniggering, 'I will see you next year.'

'What? Next year!' repeated the old seaman, opening wide his eyes and staring wildly.

'Well, yes, I repeat, next year. Did I not promise that you and your son wouldn't be separated? Now, since I'm honest and keep my word I shall leave you both here together.'

The wretched seaman uttered a heart-rending cry and fell down senseless. The surgeon laughed and continued his rounds. Since the smallest offences committed by French prisoners were so severely punished on board the hulks and so little was needed to constitute an offence in the eyes of our gaolers, not one amongst us dared raise his voice in protest against Dr Weir's despicable cruelty.

I am happy to state that in an honourable but rare exception to the usual rule it was an Englishman who expressed the general indignation. This Englishman, named Fuller, was the usual surgeon assigned to our hulk.

'Sir,' he said, addressing his colleague firmly, 'your duty, if I am not mistaken, consists solely in assessing the prisoners' state of health and not in tormenting them. Now, sir, since you are a surgeon like myself, you must be aware that the cruel violence to the feelings of this poor old seaman and his son caused by your barbarous conduct is surely bound to aggravate their cases most damnably. It is already critical enough. As a man and a doctor I most strongly protest against your unjustifiable conduct.'

At Fuller's words, Dr Weir pursed his lips with a disdainful and malicious expression and then continued in a low ingratiating voice which affected me as if I had heard a serpent hissing.

'Sir,' he answered his colleague, 'your uncivil observations are provoked merely because the Board of Transport lacks confidence in your talents and abilities and has thought fit to send me to inspect your patients. Your vanity speaks, not your outraged conscience. Pray remember that at the general inspection, which I perform today, you are no more than an assistant allocated to furnish me with such details as I may require concerning the state of health of the patients whom you have treated with more or less success for the past year. Your duties, sir, are at present no more than secondary and your position is a subordinate one. Do not forget it.'

Dr Fuller answered sharply, 'Dr Weir, I despise you too much to admit that insolence from you could ever affect my honour and so I do not receive your words as an insult. I merely regard them as a fresh act of cowardice. As to my subordinate position, in which you rejoice, I am ready to give in my resignation at once if you have the courage to step ashore with me.'

At this obvious challenge Weir remained silent for a moment and then turned towards his colleague, smiling amiably.

'Come, my dear Fuller,' he said in his habitual ingratiating tone, 'let us put these childish disputes aside and continue our rounds. We are both too irritable and might do something unfortunate. Here, take my hand.'

Dr Fuller had had lengthy service in the Royal Navy. He had given repeated proofs on many occasions of self-denial and courage and was endowed with remarkable uprightness and fixity of principles. He did not deign to take the hand offered by his colleague and contented himself by saying moodily, 'Very well; let us get on with our visit.'

'Irascible fellow!' exclaimed Dr Weir with a laugh in Dr Fuller's direction. The latter seemed not to notice this latest insult.

The medical inspection had lasted a little more than three hours and two-thirds of the prisoners had already been seen when the two surgeons stopped in front of a sailor who appeared to be suffering greatly.

'Now here's a man,' said Weir, 'who must have dosed himself with some noxious drug to get himself sent home. These French are revoltingly sly and unscrupulous. Come, my friend, stop closing your eyes like that and making out you're dying. Those old tricks may take in students but I warn you, I know my work. I see them every day and I don't fall for them.'

The prisoner to whom I translated this sentence seemed to be suffering agonies. His body was pushed up against the gunwales, he rubbed his forehead with one hand and with the other behind his back he pressed his kidneys. For a while he was incapable of replying.

'Comrade,' he murmured at last, 'tell the Englishman he's a fool and that I've taken no drugs to make myself ill. I'm suffering unbearable pain. All I want is to be well. Tell him to leave me alone.'

It may be imagined that I made significant alterations to this speech.

'Very well,' exclaimed Weir, 'the rogue wants to persist with his performance. Let us go on...'

'Allow me, sir,' said Dr Fuller incisively, 'but on the contrary, this man appears seriously ill to me. In what latitudes were you taken prisoner, my friend?' he asked the sailor.

'Near Florida, coming from Havana.'

'You are simple, my dear colleague,' said Weir. 'According to you, what disease is this rascal suffering from?'

Dr Fuller was about to speak and then, suddenly changing his mind, he put his mouth to Weir's ear and whispered for a few moments in a low voice. I shall never forget the expression of terror that passed across the latter's face as he recoiled abruptly from the sailor with an exclamation of fear and disgust. By contrast his colleague approached the sick man without a moment's pause, started examining him attentively and took his pulse.

'Come, come, Fuller,' exclaimed Weir, 'it's growing dark and we really must get through our rounds today. Order them to take this man to the hospital. But let's be quick, be quick!'

There was such dread in Dr Weir's tone that the most outlandish superstitions passed through my mind. The inspection continued. The last prisoner before whom the surgeons stopped was little more than a child. He was at the most seventeen or eighteen years old, had the most attractive face and might have passed for a girl dressed up as a sailor. Seeing the medical committee appear next to him the young man wiped away the tears that filled his eyes and assumed a respectful demeanour.

'This young little viper's fangs are scarcely grown, so he can't have bitten too many Englishmen yet,' said the jocular Weir. 'How long have you been on board the *Vengeance*, you young jackanapes?'

'Two months and four days.'

'Where were you taken and how?'

'In the Channel after a fight.'

'On a man of war, I suppose?'

'Near enough; on a privateer, the *Éclair*.'[95]

'Ahah! A young privateer. You wanted to rob the English and the English caught you. A good job, and you deserve to be a prisoner. You see where the love of money takes you.'

'Oh! Money,' repeated the child with a sigh, 'money would be nothing to me if old Mignar would give me Angélique without a dowry. But old Mignar loves money…'

This exclamation made me smile and I did not think fit to translate it to the surgeons.

'Well, Fuller,' said the surgeon-inspector to his colleague, 'that ends our task. I have my notes and we can go. Let's go! The foul, close atmosphere on this deck could make us ill. Are you coming?'

The two surgeons were going off, Fuller calmly, Weir in great haste, when the young privateer ran after them and seized the latter by the arm.

'Well! What about me? You haven't examined me, you idlers,' said he, 'I'm ill, very ill. I'm suffering fearfully. Aren't you going to send me back to France?'

'Insolence! You dare to take hold of my arm!' exclaimed Dr Weir, raising his cane to strike the lad.

'Ah! *Sacré mille nom de noms!* Down with your cane or I'll hit you,' cried the little prisoner, with eyes gleaming and fists clenched, bravely squaring up to the surgeon who rapidly retreated.

'Ask the lad where it hurts,' said Dr Fuller to me, laughing.

'Where does it hurt?'

'Where? All over!'

'How's your appetite, my lad?'

'How should I know? For a start, we get nothing to eat.'

'Do you sleep well at night?'

'I must do, because I dream about her, but I wake up suddenly a hundred times.'

'Do you cry often?'

'It's shameful for a man to admit it, but I do nothing else. My eyes stream like fountains. However I can say, hand on heart, it's not for lack of courage. What can I do? It just overcomes me.'

'Sadly, my poor child, it pains me to have to tell you that your case is hopeless,' said Dr Fuller gently. 'You're in love and rightly or wrongly, love is not considered a serious enough distemper to warrant sending a prisoner home.'

'Now then!' exclaimed the young man in astonishment; 'who told you I was in love? Well, it's true! After all there's nothing dishonourable in that. Yes, I shipped on board the *Éclair* just to get money so that I could marry Angélique. And as to being ill, I really am.'

Dr Fuller had no answer to this and was moving off to join his colleague who had already left, when the young privateer also held him back.

'So,' he said in a pleading voice, 'won't you send me back to France?'

'My poor lad, I repeat that I cannot.'

'Is that your last word? Well, if you're an honest man you'll soon regret that refusal. That's all I have to say.'

The little lad pronounced these words decisively, rammed his tarred leather hat down over his head and walked towards one of the darkest corners of the deck.

When we rejoined Dr Weir he was being detained by a crowd of prisoners who were unwilling to let him go before they had brought to his attention the illnesses which they claimed would justify their being sent back to France. The surgeon seemed to take an unusual pleasure in all these pains and petitions and gave rein to his mischievousness. Every sigh provoked a smile, each complaint inspired a pun, but despite the pleasure he derived from inflicting these mental tortures, he appeared in a hurry to quit the after-deck. A barely concealed anxiety was visible on his face.

'Come along, Fuller, let's go,' he said, heading at last towards the ladder over the side.

In the sudden movement he made to break through the surrounding circle of prisoners a paper slipped from his hand, which I swiftly picked up. At the top of the sheet was written in large letters, 'Names of the Prisoners to be sent back to France.'

As you can imagine I refrained from returning this precious document of which Fuller possessed a duplicate. I hid it beneath my coat at once so that I could communicate its contents to those whom it concerned and spare them the anxious delay of a fortnight or even a month which always accompanied the annual revision of the list.

As I mentioned, Dr Weir had pushed the prisoners aside and hurried towards the entry port. Once he was at the foot of the ladder he looked up and turned towards us. When he was certain that we could no longer impede his escape he said with an air of unctuous friendliness, 'After all, my friends, be easy. There are many amongst you who won't be on board the *Vengeance* for much longer.'

'What? Do you mean peace is coming, doctor?' called out one prisoner.

'Not exactly, my excellent friends, my dear French friends, at least not what you mean by peace. The peace of the grave. I kept the good news until I made my farewells to you. Yellow fever has just broken out on board the *Vengeance*.'

This stunning declaration struck us with terror and the surgeon, grasping the side rope of the ladder, made it with a peculiar delight. He then leapt nimbly into his launch and was rowed away.

It is difficult nowadays to explain the dread induced in us by the naming of this terrible and mysterious scourge which the French call yellow fever and the Spanish the *vomito*. Twenty wretches would die every evening as a consequence of various cruel diseases. Our numbers were ceaselessly depleted by an enormous mortality. We never enjoyed an hour of rest or a moment's pleasure. Every night a boat loaded with the bodies of our friends moved silently away from our hulk; we were so hardened by suffering that they went unregretted, unremembered and unaccompanied by a single prayer.[96] Why then did yellow fever terrify us to such an extent? I do not know; I simply state that such was the case.

I must give all credit to Dr Fuller who, when he learnt of his superior's treacherous indiscretion, denounced his vile conduct with sincere indignation.

'My friends,' he said, 'you need not despair. I have resided for a long time in the colonies where the *vomito* flourishes and I can assure you that this malady is in no way contagious. If promptly and intelligently treated it can be completely cured. However, those whose spirits are low and give way to despair or fear run a much greater risk than those who face it with resolution. Take heart, I will answer for curing those of you who may be infected.'

We thanked Dr Fuller warmly for those comforting words. He was about to go away when piercing cries of 'Help! Help!' came from down below, causing him to climb back up the first steps of the ladder which he had already descended. At the same moment a prisoner covered with blood, his face distorted with fright and his clothes in disarray, hurled himself into our midst.

'One of our mates has just stabbed himself,' he said. 'Come and help him. I don't think he's dead yet.'

Dr Fuller, accompanied by the crowd, hurried after the sailor who led them to a place on the gun-deck so dark that it would have been difficult to recognise anyone a yard away. We could vaguely see the suicide's body, stretched out on the deck like a black bundle.

'Carry this poor man up into the daylight,' said Fuller.

We hastily obeyed the surgeon. The shock I felt can be imagined when I saw that the unhappy fellow was the poor little privateer, Mademoiselle Angélique's lover. I recalled his last words and reproached myself bitterly for not having attached more importance to them. He had tried to kill himself with a sharpened file. When lifted up he was drenched in blood and as pale as a corpse, but still breathing.

After getting him to take a cordial brought by his assistant, a French surgeon named Dancret, Dr Fuller examined the wound minutely.

'If the blade had not run against a rib,' he said, 'he would have died on the spot. I will answer for him. He will not die.'

Hardened as we were, this assurance delighted us, since it was impossible after seeing the lad's youth and delicacy not to be concerned for him. In a while he regained consciousness. 'Don't talk, and move as little as you can,' said the surgeon. 'You're in no danger and if you follow my orders you'll be cured in a fortnight.'

'So much the worse, doctor,' the wounded lad replied feebly, 'after all, what does it matter? Once I'm cured I'll do it again.' There was such decisiveness in the way the poor little patient announced this resolution that I promised myself that when he was on the way to recovery I would watch over him to prevent him from putting it into action.

At that moment I was far from imagining that this adventure, so tragically begun, would end in the oddest and most comical manner, giving rise to one of the most curious and extraordinary of all the episodes associated with the history of the hulks.

CHAPTER XVII

The infamous Dr Weir • A medical dissertation •
An epidemic • Expulsion of Dr Fuller

ONCE DR FULLER HAD LEFT I swiftly informed my companions in misfortune of the precious document I possessed, that is to say the list containing forty names of prisoners selected to be sent home. It would be impossible to describe the transports of joy, verging on madness, felt by those who were chosen or to express their unearthly outcries of happiness. The immense despair that these wretches must have felt can be imagined when a fortnight later the roll of the sick men who were to be freed was called and it was found that not a single one of them was on the authentic list.

The paper that Dr Weir had seemed to drop by accident was nothing but a practical joke on his part to vex the French dogs, as he would have put it. He admitted this to us later, whilst at the same time making sport of our credulity. How can such conduct be judged? How can one adequately stigmatise a nation which treated our brave sailors and soldiers in this way, when their only crime was to be losers amidst the uncertainties of war? Turks never treated Christian slaves in this fashion and no one would have dared to behave so to convicts.

Doctors maintain that yellow fever is not a contagious disease and I must take their word for it. However, despite this opinion, it is still true that this terrible scourge soon spread through our hulk with extreme violence and most of our prisoners fell ill.

Dr Fuller handsomely kept the promise he had given us. His solicitude on our behalf was constantly crowned with success. The treatment he used was not only appropriate to the nature of the disease but also to the constitution and habits of sick men weakened by the terrible regime on board the hulks. He saved almost every one of them from death and when I reflect carefully I cannot recall that even a single man died. Peruvian bark taken in strong doses and suitable tonics gave a complete victory to science.

It scarcely needs to be added that the prisoners' spirits, which had sunk for a while, soon revived when they saw that the scourge they had dreaded so much at first caused so little mortality. We even composed a comic song entitled *Monsieur le Vomito*. Sad to say, this happy state of affairs could not last. A fortnight after the *Vengeance* had been boarded by the yellow fever the execrable Weir arrived on the hulk one morning. His arrival was a mortal blow to us.

I can still see the interview between the two doctors. 'Mr Fuller, your servant, sir,' said Weir, smiling at our good doctor with an air of hypocritical affability. 'In case the intelligence has not reached you officially, I regret to inform you that the Board of Transport has seen fit to send me to supersede you in attending the Frenchmen suffering from yellow fever. Doubtless you have done your best and you may well believe that I took your part and spoke up for you. But I am powerless against the truth. Facts are facts; the Transport Board is highly dissatisfied with you in this matter and utterly disapproves of the way you have treated your patients. I don't maintain that they are correct... I...'

'Spare me your hypocrisy,' exclaimed Dr Fuller, shrugging his shoulders contemptuously. 'You coveted my place, you schemed for it and you got it. I see nothing unnatural in that. Each man looks after his own interests and provided you continue the course of treatment I've followed so far, I shall say nothing.'

'If you will permit me, my dear friend, you have on that point touched lightly on a most serious matter. I do not assert that you are lacking in talent. Far from it. On the contrary, I am full of confidence in your abilities and no one in the world esteems your knowledge more than I. But you are well aware that science has many different systems. Now, I confess that in no way do I share your view of yellow fever. Do not be surprised therefore, if my treatment differs entirely from yours.'

'What! Are you going to leave off the strong doses of bark and the tonics which have worked perfectly well for me?'

'Yes, my dear and worthy colleague. What would you have me do? I have a heavy responsibility and must act according to my conscience.'

'May I enquire to what treatment you propose submitting your patients?' asked Fuller, flushing.

'Certainly, my dear colleague. Much bleeding, blistering on the stomach and a low diet. Such is my system.'

'Dr Weir,' exclaimed Fuller in ringing tones, 'your system is that of a madman or a murderer. If you put it into effect I tell you now that not a single one of your patients will recover. You'll kill every one of them.'

'Bah! A few Frenchmen more or less...'

'Ah! Now I see it all,' replied Dr Fuller with growing fury, 'the Transport Board's disapproval of my conduct and their preference for you. I repeat that your task, sir, if I am not mistaken, is that of a murderer. No, this shall not happen! I shall speak, I shall write...'

'First of all, sir,' interrupted Weir, changing his tone of hypocritical amiability to one of command, 'you will leave the *Vengeance* without further delay. You have been long enough in the Navy to know that rank is no trifling matter. I am your superior. You can start by obeying me.'

'I shall go, sir, but you cannot prevent me from speaking or writing. The press will help me to expose your vile and monstrous conduct.'

'You will have no evidence to allege against me, since no one can prove that my system is worse than yours. You will be condemned as a slanderer and that will bring about your dishonour and the ruin of your family,' interrupted Dr Weir again. 'Go, sir, I shall not detain you.'

'The scoundrel is right,' murmured the poor noble surgeon, his anger extinguished by deep sadness, 'I am powerless, powerless…'

Half an hour after this scene which, in my usual way, I have described with perfect truth, the good and upright Fuller left the *Vengeance*, never to return, and Weir assumed his post. Although there was a French surgeon on board each hulk as a deputy to the English surgeon the latter's authority was much greater than that of the former, whose function was practically reduced to that of an assistant. Soon a fearful mortality appeared amongst our sick and without exception all those treated by Weir died.

If the reader wishes to know my own private opinion, I have no trouble in declaring on my soul and conscience that the Transport Board and Dr Weir had tacitly agreed to carry out these murders. If I am mistaken in this opinion, God is my witness that my error is that of an honest man, unmoved by anger, who says plainly what he thinks.

In five weeks we lost about thirty comrades. Then the epidemic suddenly ceased. In the meantime the Captain commanding the *Vengeance* was retired on account of his age and replaced by a very young lieutenant named Edwards.[97]

Chapter XVIII

The excellent Captain Edwards • Justice and humanity •
Preparations for a play • The pretended actresses • Attempted
bribery • A scandalous elopement

OUR NEW CAPTAIN, promoted to lieutenant at the age of twenty-two as a result of a visit to his ship by the Duke of York, had married the daughter of a rich East India Company shareholder and through this influential alliance found himself the Captain of a hulk at just twenty-four years old.

I am only too happy to testify to fine qualities on the part of the English when the opportunity arises and I hasten to say that Captain Edwards's arrival was a great piece of good fortune for us. Although no one was more scrupulous than he in the performance of his duties, he was a man of intelligence and warmth who understood admirably that his almost unlimited power allowed great latitude for doing good. His constant concern was to interpret the spirit of the regulations in our favour and to mitigate our lot as far as his instructions permitted.

The influence of an honest commander is remarkable. Although it cost the English government not a single farthing a year extra, our hulk soon took on a completely different appearance and our conditions, both materially and morally, were bettered to such an extraordinary extent that they became tolerable and almost pleasant.

Since we were treated with consideration and humanity we tried to respond to these benefits (justice and humanity being benefits to us) with gratitude and good conduct. Without any coercion we freely helped the English seamen to do various tasks that we had never previously accepted and lived in complete harmony with our enemies. No one thought any more of escaping, being restrained by the fear of harming our excellent young Captain's prospects, and so the English had scarcely any trouble in guarding the hulk. Violence never had any influence on us, but we were subdued by consideration and justice.

I have said that the appearance of our hulk changed, as if by magic, with the arrival of our new Captain and the reader will understand this when I say that we were soon giving balls and concerts and had a theatre. One of the oddest aspects of French character lies in its incredible gaiety and fertility of imagination, capable of discovering sources of mirth and amusement at the most difficult times when foreigners would lapse into despair and yield to their sufferings. After a truthful narrative (though pale enough when compared to reality) of our horrible life on board the hulks it must be pleasing to the reader to know that by our own efforts and without any outside help we possessed a theatre! And by a theatre I do not mean a puppet show, but a proper theatre where actors and actresses, elegantly turned out, performed in front of scenery to the accompaniment of an orchestra. When I think of the pleasure these plays gave me I consider that they were in no way inferior in dialogue or performance to those of some Parisian theatres.

Those actors, so well-dressed in costumes that cost no more than a few sous, that splendid scenery improvised with paint on a few old pieces of canvas or sometimes on planks, those dramas which made us laugh or weep so much, were all the products of French imagination which makes use of anything and from nothing can create everything.

A pretty large space which had once served as a chapel lay at the end of the orlop. The floor there was lowered by several feet and the ceiling was almost twice the normal height. There we set up our stage. I remember the first performance we gave as if it were yesterday and the reader will soon see why a most strange occurrence associated with it should have impressed itself so deeply on my mind.

A fortnight before the date set for this great occasion no one on board the *Vengeance* thought of anything but the play. Every rag and scrap of cloth was scrutinised and a use was found for each one. A midshipman and a purser, both talented, were commissioned to compose the two masterpieces that were to be performed. The one wrote a farce in two acts entitled *The Adventures of a Sentimental Lady* and the other a five-act melodrama called *The Corsair's Sweetheart*.

These two efforts gained a great and immediate success when submitted to the actors who were to play them and to an *ad hoc* reading committee. Both were unanimously judged worthy of gracing the stage.

It was decided that the expenditure on costumes, lighting and scenery should first be deducted from the gross receipts and if anything were left over, as we hoped, the actors would be rewarded for their work. The protagonists and the main players were to receive a franc, the secondary roles ten sous and the supernumeraries four sous. The orchestra, which consisted of a violin and a flute, offered its services for nothing and was voted an honourable mention.

As for myself, a deputation representing all my comrades waited on me desiring me to create the scenery required for the performance after first agreeing what was needed with the authors. I received the deputation with becoming modesty and having thanked them heartily for the esteem in which my comrades held my talent, I promised to make every effort to justify their confidence. I even carried my graciousness to the extent of refusing the twenty-five sous offered for the five scenes that were expected of me. My disinterestedness and magnanimity were acclaimed as heroic and, like the orchestra, I was unanimously voted an honourable mention.

So that there should be no later dissensions our final concern was to settle the authors' rights. The midshipman and the purser were both in fairly reduced circumstances and it would have been unreasonable to expect the one to abandon his straw-work or the other his slipper-making without offering some compensation for their lost time. Two proposals were made. The first was to pay them thirty sous in cash for the farce and four francs for the drama and the second to let them take their chance and have whatever remained after the settlement of all expenses and disbursements.

On or off the hulks authors are much the same and having complete confidence in the merits of their own works, they preferred the second proposal to the first. In any event it was stipulated that after the first act of the drama any dissatisfied spectators might leave and have their money back. The self-confident authors raised no objections on this score.

The female costumes remained to be made. We were in considerable difficulty since we lacked not only dressmakers (though our tailors offered to do better than mere dressmakers) but also raw materials to work on. In desperation we decided to appeal to the ladies of Portsmouth, Gosport and Portsea with our kind Captain as intermediary. With this in mind we caused a gallantly phrased request to be spread abroad in town with which we made a touching appeal to English feelings. This request succeeded far beyond our hopes. Female cast-offs flowed in from every quarter in such abundance that we thought of establishing a company of dancing girls. This scheme was abandoned for the time being, but was taken up a few months later and in its realisation gained such a colossal success that the memory of it must still linger in Portsmouth.

After entering into such minute details the reader will perhaps think that I have forgotten the most important of all; we had no actresses. By no means; I was reserving this delicate subject till last. There is one matter on which I have not spoken before, for a very good reason. It concerns the Frenchwomen who were to be found on board the hulks. They were in fact nearly all so hideous or so coarse in manners and speech that we had to dispense with their help. These women lived with the men whose lot they had sought permission to share, occupying compartments of a sort on the gun-deck and the orlop with walls made from old cloth or grey paper. Such screens were a sufficient defence against any criminal intentions, since the mere sight of these women was enough to put the most desperate man to flight.[98]

It was therefore impossible to think of using these hapless consorts in our performance. Apart from the fact that probably not one of them could read and that most spoke some dialect, we had our national honour to uphold and no desire to misrepresent the grace and beauty of Frenchwomen. We decided therefore to replace these impossible females with the youngest and most attractive boys amongst the prisoners on board.

Amongst these novel actresses the one who received the greatest acclaim was an acquaintance of the reader's, whom I now reintroduce. I refer to the little privateer who at the time of the surgeon's last visit had so impetuously stabbed himself in his love-sick despair. He had been well for more than a month and was helping me in my painting.

Pierre Chéri was the name of the lad whom I had promised myself that I would keep an eye on. Thanks to his kindly open nature he gained my friendship and found in me a person to whom he could prattle all day about Angélique and dreadful old Mignar. Two or three times daily he went over the story of his love affair, a simple intimate drama made up of a glance, a sigh and one squeeze of the hand; with this outlet for his feelings he bore his affliction patiently. He was, however, more determined than ever to escape when an opportunity might present itself. Pierre Chéri had been chosen to play the part of the corsair's sweetheart and since the authors had agreed at his request to call the character Angélique, the young man learnt his part fervently.

The great day of the performance finally arrived. What an occasion it was! To secure places for his wife and a few relations whom he wished to attend this curious spectacle, Captain Edwards sent us a pound, despite our protests and the fact that the prices had been fixed as low as two or four sous.

How can I express the commotion on board the *Vengeance* two hours before the performance? There was an unbelievable uproar. The actors, and above all the actresses, were running about as if bewildered, all seeming to have lost their wits. At last, at about three o'clock in the afternoon, the chaos began to abate and everyone took up his position.

Soon boats loaded with officers from neighbouring hulks, young ladies and tradesmen converged on us from all sides, bringing a numerous and select crowd of spectators and before long all the fashionables of Portsmouth, Gosport and Portsea were swarming over the *Vengeance*'s deck. Never has a play caused such a sensation.

At six o'clock exactly the curtain was opened, rather than raised. The onlookers were avidly curious and a repeated salvo of applause greeted the scenery and the actors' costumes. It is true to say that there are provincial theatres which can scarcely offer a sight as satisfying as that of our stage.

In the first act of *The Adventures of a Sentimental Lady,* the lady's part was taken by a young apprentice from Paris, who played it with remarkable energy and to universal applause.

'Really, my dear Garneray,' remarked the midshipman who wrote the farce, 'I assure you that we do wrong to keep mocking the English. Excellent critics they are and far from lacking in taste.'

'The proof lies in their applause,' I answered with a laugh.

A few scribbled sheets of paper, ten rhyming couplets which more or less scanned and a cheer or two were enough to extinguish in the heart of a young naval officer both the memory of the past and his hatred for the English. Authors are the same wherever they may be.

The second act of the farce was received with no less acclaim than the first. The finale was greeted with long and repeated applause. The English ladies clamoured for the author who, compliant to their desires, made his blushing appearance on stage.

During the interval after the performance of *The Adventures of a Sentimental Lady* the stewards who kept order received a deputation from the *rafalés,* demanding to be admitted to the theatre without payment. The request could not possibly have been granted and was instantly refused. Despite any desire we might have had to let the *rafalés* forget their miseries in a moment of pleasure, we could not admit them because the sight of their costume, so close to that of nature, would have put the entire female part of our audience to flight. The deputation departed muttering, its sensibilities hurt and hopes dashed.

Then began the drama of *The Corsair's Sweetheart*. When my young friend Pierre Chéri came on stage an exclamation of wonder and surprise greeted his appearance. It would have been impossible to find a sweeter, prettier or more alluring actress than this young man. The illusion was so complete that not a single English lady or any spectator paused for an instant to think that this pretty creature could be a boy.

Pierre Chéri, with his soft, feminine voice, played his part so sentimentally and wept so well each time Angélique's name was mentioned that he succeeded in moving his audience deeply. Soon the ladies were unfolding their handkerchiefs and sobs could be heard on every side.

'Well, Garneray,' asked the purser who wrote the melodrama, 'what do you think of my *Sweetheart*? Isn't it a triumph?'

'An even greater triumph, sir,' I replied, 'since not one of those tearful ladies knows a single word of French. Imagine the extent of your success if they could follow the dialogue!'

The first act finished to the sound of flattering murmurs. There is scarcely any need to say that not a single spectator amongst the prisoners thought of asking for his money back, as had been agreed if the play failed to please.

The second act began in profound silence. The corsair preferred glory to love and took leave of his sweetheart. The poor girl, in the person of Pierre Chéri, was doing her utmost to detain him when there came a surprise that none of us expected. A chorus of fifty voices intoning vespers interrupted the play; it was the *rafalés*, enraged at their exclusion, who sought to halt the performance. In this they succeeded only too well, since the actors' voices were inaudible beneath the formidable chanting. For a moment our spectators were taken aback, but they highly approved of our drama and took this abnormally vigorous plain-chant for an entreacte slipped into the play; they applauded enthusiastically.

As can be imagined, this applause only stimulated the *rafalés* to greater boldness and at that moment they began to intone a doleful *De Profundis*. English astonishment gave way to unbridled enthusiasm. What was to be done? We had been defeated and could only capitulate. It was immediately decided that we would allow ten *rafalés* into the theatre, on the condition that their garb would not outrage the modesty of our audience. I was despatched to the *rafalés* in the capacity of an extraordinary ambassador.

After a few preliminaries which had the immediate effect of halting the *De Profundis* so that the play could continue, the *rafalés* accepted the offer I was authorised to make. They agreed to draw lots amongst themselves for the ten who were to attend. Those who were not successful in the ballot were to strip off their clothes for the benefit of their fortunate comrades. This was done and a quarter of an hour later ten scarecrows, fantastically rigged out in unbelievable rags, made a furtive entry into our auditorium, though naturally only at the rear.

The third act was about to start when an English lieutenant, the commander of one of the Danish hulks in the line before Gosport came and sat down beside me.

'My friend,' he said in a low voice, 'someone has just pointed you out to me as the interpreter on board. Is that correct?'

'Correct, Captain. Can I be of service to you?'

'Yes,' replied the Englishman, 'you can indeed! Not a word more for the moment. Don't seem surprised and don't look at me. At the end of this act, come up on deck. I'll be there.'

I was highly intrigued by this air of mystery and waited impatiently for the fall of the curtain and my meeting with the Englishman.

'My dear sir,' said the captain, drawing me aside, 'I must tell you that I am well-off and accustomed to pay handsomely for services done on my behalf. Answer my questions satisfactorily and you shall have a guinea. What d'you think of that offer?'

'At that rate, Captain, I think you really must have need of me!'

'Oho! I see you're a humorous fellow and a shrewd one too. Now, since I'm generous and open-handed as becomes an Englishman and you, like the rest of your countrymen, are grasping, selfish and conscienceless, our business won't detain us long. Listen carefully to me…'

I was horribly galled by these insults and jibes and thought to myself, '*Parbleu*, if this Englishman gives me the chance to do him an ill turn, I won't let it slip.'

The captain continued after a moment's thought, saying, 'Interpreter, bear in mind that for my guinea I'm entitled to complete frankness on your part. Answer my question truthfully, if the word signifies anything to you.'

'Carry on, Captain, I'm at your service.'

'What's the girl called who is acting in the play?'

'Which girl?' I repeated in astonishment and then, when I realised the Englishman's misapprehension about Pierre Chéri, I took on a matter of fact expression.

'She's called Clara, Captain,' I replied.

'I like that name very much. Tell me, this young woman, is she married?'

'Yes, and no, Captain. Whichever you prefer.'

'I'd prefer her to be unattached. But explain yourself clearly. I don't follow.'

'Oh, it's a long story, Captain.'

'Well, tell me the story.'

'But if you were to betray me…,' I continued, feigning confusion.

'You have my word as an English gentleman that you have nothing to fear on that score.'

'I believe you, Captain. I can definitely assure you that the young lady is not married. She is Mademoiselle Clara. She was betrothed to an officer in the Imperial Navy and was about to marry her future husband when he was obliged to go to sea on the orders of minister Decrès.[99] The wedding could not take place. This was about a year ago. Now, six months ago today, the frigate in which this officer served was captured by the English. You can imagine Mademoiselle Clara's despair. She thought she adored her fiancé and did not hesitate in crossing to England to join him on board his hulk…'

'Indeed! That shows a good heart…but go on.'

'Then she wrote out something like a marriage contract. Armed with this document she appeared before Captain Edwards and begged him to let her share her husband's imprisonment. Doubtless you will know, by hearsay at least, of our Captain's extreme generosity. Mademoiselle Clara's petition was favourably received. In this way a young lady from one of the best families of France, highly virtuous, endowed with the benefits of a brilliant education, now finds herself obliged to act in plays on board an English prison hulk.'

'Indeed! Indeed! Indeed!' repeated the English captain in varying tones. 'This is extraordinary. Yes, extraordinary's the word. But can you point out the young lady's supposed husband to me?'

'Impossible, Captain. He recently tried to escape and he's at present in the Black Hole.'

'What! Tried to escape? And what about his fiancée?'

'They now hate one another, Captain. The truth is he tried to escape to get away from her.'

'What are you saying? This grows more and more extraordinary. What! This girl abandons her family, gives up all comforts, sets sail in the face of every danger, all to rejoin her lover? And he responds with black ingratitude to so much goodness, to so many proofs of devotion! Are you sure you're not hiding the truth from me?'

'Captain, I could never do that; I simply describe things as they are. But I must absolve the young man from the stain of ingratitude which you lay on him. It is not he who has ceased to love his fiancée. Quite the reverse; it is she who first declared that she no longer loved him.'

'Ah! Ah! And why doesn't she love him any more?'

'My God, Captain, if I told you the truth you wouldn't believe me. I prefer to keep quiet.'

'Speak on, … I insist.'

'If you order me, that's different and I must obey. Can you believe that Mademoiselle Clara, having been used to seeing her fiancé on shore, dressed in a brilliant uniform, with his hair curled and pomaded, took an aversion to him when she saw him barefoot and in rags on our hulk, with his beard and hair grown wild? It's really scarcely believable.'

'On the contrary, it seems quite explicable and shows Mademoiselle Clara's nicety in these matters. But, one more question. Since this interesting young lady no longer loves her fiancé, why has she not left the *Vengeance*?'

'Because she dare not go back to her family.'

'God bless me! I hadn't thought of that! You're right. Well, interpreter,' continued the captain, lowering his voice, 'if you want, as I'm sure you will, to earn two guineas instead of one, go straight to Mademoiselle Clara. Tell her that a generous English Captain, touched by her beauty and distress, desires to remove her from the frightful position in which she finds herself. Then return to me with her answer. Now, let's go back to the orlop, since I don't wish to miss any of the play. I'll be back here on deck at the next interval.'

Bowing low to the English captain in an attempt to suppress the laughter that was nearly bursting me, I fled away to give vent to my mirth. This opportunity to hoax an enemy was too good to be wasted and I decided to take it as far as it would go. Thanks to my position as chief scene-painter I made my way into the wings, took Pierre Chéri aside and declared to him the passion he had inspired in the English Captain, who proposed that they should fly together. I ended by asking Chéri if he wanted to help with the hoax.

The little privateer listened to me with the greatest attention and when I had finished said earnestly, 'Monsieur Garneray, it's no joking matter. This English booby must really carry me off.'

'What, carry you off?'

'Yes, of course. What! Don't you understand, even a man as crafty as you, that luck never gave a prisoner a better chance of escaping than this…'

'*Ma foi*, Chéri, I must say that until this moment I thought only of hoaxing this Englishman, but you're right…'

'Of course I'm right! Sure as I love Angélique, I'll sling my hook if you'll only help me.'

'*Dame!* Young man, that's a serious matter, making me an accomplice to an escape.'

'What of it? Do you think the Englishman would report you? Always assuming he discovers his mistake, he'll be too mortified to let the whole world know. He'd never hear the end of it. No, he'll keep quiet. Come, sir, please, I beg you, be a good comrade, don't refuse. Devil take it, you can't refuse to help a friend escape! It's not a favour, it's a duty!'

I recognised that the young privateer might gain his freedom through this grotesque mistake, and though I admired his audacity and presence of mind I still hesitated to meddle with the scheme. Suffering had made me selfish and I was afraid of jeopardising the relatively fortunate position which I held on board the *Vengeance*.

'There's my cue,' said Pierre Chéri quickly. 'Monsieur Garneray, you know that when I say a thing I mean it. Well, word of a seaman, word of a lover too, if you won't help me I'll stick a knife in my heart! Angélique or death!'

The little fellow made his entry on stage, leaving me in deep thought. After the outstanding example he had already given of his keenness and determination I had no doubt that he would keep his word. '*Ma foi*,' I thought, 'what's the worst that I could get for helping in this escape? A week in the Black Hole! To draw back and abandon the lad in the face of such a feeble danger would be cowardly. He'll kill himself and the memory of his death will torment me for ever. I'll help him, come what may.'

Having taken my decision, I sought out Chéri once more and told him of it. I shall never forget the insane delight and gratitude he showed. He promised that if he succeeded in escaping and ever saw Angélique again, the first word that he would speak to his beloved would be the name of his deliverer. Further, he promised that he would try to get Angélique to write me a line. With such happiness in store, how could I have hesitated? A line in Mademoiselle Angélique's handwriting! To Pierre Chéri that was worth a million and I am certain he thought he was promising me the richest of all rewards.

'Where's the Englishman?' he asked, and when I had pointed out where he was seated, he continued, 'Now, sir, take note how I'm going to look at him. I'll try and imitate Angélique. Oh, I'm certain to succeed!'

Bent on enchantment, Pierre Chéri overwhelmed the English captain with a profusion of smiles and glances, until by the end of the performance the man had completely lost his wits.

'Interpreter,' asked the captain in the last interval, 'have you done as I asked?'

'Certainly, Captain. I've spoken to her.'

'And what says Mademoiselle Clara?'

'She thanks you for your generosity and accepts your gracious protection.'

'Really! Interpreter, you are a persuasive fellow! Here, take the two guineas I promised. If peace is ever signed between England and France and you'd care to enter service as my valet, just seek me out...'

I was at first inclined to reject the money proffered by the Englishman. However, I thought that such honesty was incompatible with the low and shifty part I supposed to be playing. The amorous captain's suspicions might have been aroused, thus preventing young Chéri's escape. Humbly and respectfully bowing, I took the money. The very next morning I distributed the two guineas to the *rafalés*, thereby gaining an enormous reputation for magnificence and open-handedness amongst those gentlemen.

It was about nine o'clock in the evening when our performance ended. There was a double guard on duty and the light of the torches made the deck as bright as day. I was exceedingly agitated as I waited impatiently for the conclusion of the little three-handed drama we were acting out. I kept the English captain in sight and after a few seconds' hesitation he appeared ready to perform his part. Stepping

The escape of Pierre Chéri.

openly up to Pierre Chéri, he offered him his arm; the young privateer immediately accepted it and both approached the ladder leading down from the hulk to the water.

Being afraid, and with good reason, that one of our comrades might take the captain's gallantry as a joke and speak to Chéri, I walked behind the pair, ready to stop the first man who attempted to accost them. Fortunately the crowd was so dense that nobody took notice of them.

'Thank you and farewell, sir,' murmured Chéri in my ear, as they passed by the first sentry, 'Angélique and I will never forget you.'

Since I could go no further, I stayed where I was, with my heart beating violently, to see the outcome of this episode. Everything ended as satisfactorily as could be. The English captain, with Pierre Chéri still on his arm, stopped close to the sentry, who saw only a young lady with an officer and never thought for a moment that an escape was going on before his eyes. The captain hailed his launch and shortly afterwards disappeared from my sight with his supposed conquest.

CHAPTER XIX

Captain Edwards's confidence • A dignified protest against barbaric orders • A meeting with an old acquaintance • An ingenious means of communication • Transfer of Captain Edwards

I WENT BACK TO MY CABIN pondering on the oddities of chance. 'How strange is fate,' I thought. 'I have spent four years in the hulks, dying by inches, using my intelligence and imagination to devise ways of escaping. The first time I nearly drowned. The second time I mistrusted the chance of freedom and refused it. Later I was betrayed by Duvert, but here is a young man, scarcely more than a child, weaker, less determined, less confident than myself who manages to regain his freedom, without trouble or effort through the most incredible deception that anyone could imagine. It proves one thing to me, that man's fate is fixed and that our will can change none of it. Suffering is my destiny and I must resign myself to it.'

I must add that in these pages concerning my private life I try to depict myself truthfully and I say that Pierre Chéri's good luck did not make me in any way envious. On the contrary I applauded his success and hoped fervently that he would not fail.

I must confess that at this time my position on board the hulks had been so particularly improved and my life had become, if not agreeable, at least easy enough and quite tolerable. Thanks to my position as interpreter I enjoyed greater freedom than was allowed to my comrades, I earned more money than I could spend and my painting was a powerful distraction from my sad thoughts. Short of freedom, I had nothing to envy. Yes, short of freedom! Despite my relative good fortune, I still had much to regret and in real truth I was unhappy.

One day Captain Edwards summoned me. I found him downcast and anxious.

'Monsieur Garneray,' he said, 'escapes from the hulks are increasing. With the object of preventing them the British government has issued a regulation, which I have just received. Pray be good enough to translate it, so that I can inform the prisoners in the *Vengeance* about it.'

I set to work at once, but as soon as I had cast my eyes over the official document I ground my nib violently on the table with a spontaneous and uncontrollable movement. 'Cowards! Villains! Englishmen are nothing but a vile set of butchers!'

'Doubtless you forget in whose company you are at the moment, Monsieur Garneray,' said Captain Edwards in a tone of mild reproof, 'or with an upbringing such as yours you would not speak in that manner.'

At these friendly words I became my normal self again. 'I beg your pardon, Captain, for that outburst,' I said, 'but it was more than justified by the cruel and abominable regulation I have just read.'

'Sir, I agree, and take note that I speak as Mr Edwards, an ordinary English citizen, not as the officer commanding the *Vengeance*. I agree with you, I say, that in putting out this regulation the British government has violated and dishonoured the most sacred and indefeasible rights of justice and humanity. But is it fair to blame an entire nation for one bad action done by no more than a few men? I have no doubt in my opinion that the English people would also despise such a monstrosity.'

'For the sake of England's honour I trust you are not mistaken, Captain. But whether the government's underlings approve of it or are outraged by it, must they not enforce it? Imagine the crimes and irretrievable miseries that must ensue.'

'Sir,' replied Captain Edwards, after reflecting for a moment, 'I think I can assure you that the commander of the *Vengeance* will never be an accomplice to such a monstrous betrayal of humanity.' After a further silence he added forcibly, 'No! I will never obey such an order. I would rather resign my commission a hundred times. As for you, sir, I trust that you will keep this conversation secret. I have spoken to you as an equal, a man of honour, not as a prisoner under my supervision. For the moment, not another word on this painful matter, I beg you. It would be an impropriety on your part. Pray finish your translation as quickly as you can.'

I bowed my head without replying and cursed the injunction to silence which prevented me from expressing all the admiration and gratitude inspired in me by the humane conduct of this noble young man.

This regulation, which had just been promulgated by the Council of the Regency and had so rightly incensed me, stated that the British government had decreed that 'the escape of one prisoner will be punished by hanging two prisoners in his place if the fugitive is not retaken.' The commotion caused by the publication of this regulation on our hulk can be imagined. Shouts of rage were heard everywhere.[100]

Our officers immediately assembled in council and after long deliberation wrote the following letter. I reproduce it without changing a word or a comma, firstly as an historic document and secondly as evidence of the existence of this monstrosity, which might seem to many like an idle invention.

Copy of the Letter addressed to the Council of the Regency in reply to its Order dated 6th March 1810, by virtue of which the escape of any prisoner, etc, etc.

Gentlemen, we can find no words, to express our astonishment on receiving the order which you have done us the honour of addressing to us; we have been obliged to peruse it several times to persuade ourselves that persons belonging to a nation deemed civilised can issue threats of the barbarous nature contained in the said order and, above all, address them to officers. It is a breach of all propriety and feelings of honour for which we were unprepared, notwithstanding the ill-treatment and numberless humiliations which you have hitherto laid upon us.

Gentlemen, you make us responsible for our comrades' escapes. Those appointed to guard the prisoners are no longer responsible; the prisoners themselves are required to be their own guards on pain of being hanged. What an overthrow of all the common principles hitherto known amongst civilised peoples!

Are combatants who are only prisoners because of a violation of the laws of mankind to be thus addressed? This cannot be ignored by the President of the Council.

What nation can furnish an example of the like injustice? The peoples whom you would call barbarians, who take slaves not prisoners, never presume to punish those who remain in their power for the disappearance of those who escape.

For how long has it been thought that we would descend to denouncing one another out of mere attachment to existence? Have you forgotten that you address combatants who have proved on more than one occasion that they did not fear death? If there should be any amongst us who lacked sufficient experience in war not to have faced death as a matter of course in the field, they have had time since they came into your hands to familiarise themselves with an image that you hold before their eyes every day.

Gentlemen, you have a very slight understanding of our nation's character if you did not foresee that such humiliating measures, far from lessening our wish to escape, could only add to our desire to rejoin our brothers in arms and even more so to distance ourselves from a people capable of putting such extreme barbarities into practice.

Gentlemen, we cannot doubt that you wish to reduce us to despair, but together we swear that we will endure whatever fate you have allotted to us with the nobility suitable to the great nation to which we have the honour to belong. Death we prefer to dishonour and at the proper time we will submit to it in such a manner as to leave behind us an example of courage and resolution, as you will leave one of injustice and cruelty.

Signed: Lachapelle, Petiet, de Lespée, &c, &c, &c, all French officers reduced to captivity by the violation of the capitulation of Santo Domingo.

Since chance has turned me into an author let me say in passing that the wording of this letter appears to leave something to be desired. It was followed by innumerable petitions submitted from all the hulks and the atrocious measure ordered by the English government was never put into practice.

At this time I had a curious encounter on board the *Vengeance* which I cannot pass over in silence. With the devious policy that makes them so formidable to their friends and allies the English had just seized the Danish fleet at Copenhagen.[101] The crews of the fleet, kept prisoners in their own vessels and then transported to the hulks, shared our unhappy fate a few cables' length away from us in the Gosport River. One morning a Dane was sent on board the *Vengeance*; he had given information about an escape by some of his comrades who had threatened to kill him.

I was on deck when the Dane arrived and it seemed to me that I had seen him somewhere before. When he saw me the traitor appeared completely abashed for a moment and turned away with such obvious awkwardness that my suspicion became a certainty. I was trying vainly to recollect where, how and in what circumstances I could have met this man, when I suddenly remembered. I went straight up to him and looked directly at him.

'You wretch!' I said, 'do you remember me?'

'No, sir,' he stammered in bad French.

'Liar! Nearly five years ago you commanded a merchant ship which was anchored in Portsmouth harbour…'

'I swear to you, sir, you're mistaken.'

'You're still lying. Be quiet and listen. One night, two French prisoners who had succeeded in swimming away from their hulk took refuge on board your ship. They were dying of weariness, hunger and cold. Ah, now you go pale and quiet! Now you know me. There's no need to continue with the story, no need to add that one of these two prisoners, good, brave Bertaud, threw himself back into the sea so as not to be given up to the English as you threatened. He died there, a victim of your pitiless cruelty. The other one, tied up on your orders, was brought back to his hulk in your boat by your crew. He has been cursing you for the last five years.'

'Yes, sir, I recognise you,' said the trembling Dane, 'but have pity on me, don't speak so loud. You'll ruin me. I have a little money…'

'You dog, do you think you can buy me off? You're a traitor and I'll expose you as one everywhere. Oh, good, brave Bertaud, I'll avenge you!'

The sight of this wretch had recalled the poor Breton's tragic end so vividly to me and I pronounced these last words with such force that several of my comrades hurriedly approached to learn why I was so furious. I had no difficulty in explaining my animosity towards the Dane. As soon as I had finished I knew from the shouts of rage arising on all sides that I had exceeded my intentions. It was no longer a question of putting the man in *quarantaine* as I had wanted; they spoke of nothing less than killing him.

I did not want to be the cause of a murder. I sought out the captain at once and having told him in a few words how everything stood, I begged him to send the Dane to another hulk, adding that I could not answer for his life if he were left for twenty-four hours on board the *Vengeance*. Captain Edwards immediately complied with my request and a boat took the Dane away.

The wretch believed that he had escaped with no more than a fright. How mistaken he was. Before eleven o'clock next morning the whole line of hulks knew that a Dane who had once betrayed two Frenchmen and had lately done the same to his own countrymen had been sent on board one of our hulks by the English. His comrades in misfortune were advised to do him justice.

The reader may be surprised by the ease with which we communicated from hulk to hulk. I hasten to say that the English never suspected for a moment how we managed our communications and never discovered the secret. It was done by a highly original telegraph.

We communicated by means of a table, turned upside down on the highest part of the deck, which a carpenter seemed to be mending. Each leg of the table, according to the diagonal, horizontal or vertical position in which it was placed represented a letter of the alphabet. A mallet left between or leaning against the legs of the table in one way or another also represented another letter. From long use we attained such skill in making these signals that we could compose fairly lengthy sentences in a very short time.

Let me conclude the Dane's story. The wretch was followed everywhere by the abhorrence he so well deserved, and was always received with contempt and distrust. Constantly placed in *quarantaine*, always despised, threatened and beaten, he at last conceived such an aversion to life that he poisoned himself with verdigris and died in atrocious suffering. I must confess that the memory of his death has never weighed on my conscience.

The reader may perhaps reproach me for not having spoken further about young Pierre Chéri. To this I reply, that the memories of my imprisonment are so scrupulously truthful and unlike the scenes in a novel that I am forced when chance does not come to my aid (as it seldom does) to leave most of my stories without a conclusion. I would like to believe that Pierre Chéri managed to escape. At any rate, I can only say that I never received any letters from Mademoiselle Angélique.

I have already said that my time on board the *Vengeance* passed happily enough for a prisoner, but unfortunately this state of affairs could not last for ever. Towards the middle of 1811 our excellent Captain Edwards left our hulk to take command of a corvette.[102] The day of his departure was one of mourning and how often we regretted his going! If ever, in the high position he now occupies, these lines should come to his notice, I trust he will receive once more the renewed expression of my deep respect.

CHAPTER XX

A stroke of good luck • Gambling for a man's life •
I try to prevent a murder • Persecuted by Abraham Curtis

SINCE I DID NOT WISH for reasons of discretion to name the *Crown*'s atrocious Captain, I will also designate the kindly Edwards's successor by a mere initial, Lieutenant T___ being worth not much more than Rose.[103]

He had not been in command of the *Vengeance* for more than a fortnight when all the old abuses that Captain Edwards's firmness and justice had suppressed made their appearance again. The contractors took their revenge with such enthusiasm that a fortnight later my poor comrades resembled living skeletons.

As for myself, thanks to my brushes which were never idle and also to the promptness with which my worthy picture dealer, Abraham Curtis, paid me ready cash, a pound for each of my productions, I was well above necessity.

One afternoon I was finishing a picture which I had to deliver the following day, when someone came to tell me that a visitor wished to speak to me. Almost immediately a man dressed from head to foot in black entered my cabin and after thrice bowing deeply, addressed me as follows:

'Are you, sir, the person named Garneray?' he asked.

'The same, sir. What do you want?'

'I wish to render you a great service.'

'I am most grateful. Whom do I have the honour of addressing?'

'Mr James Smith. My name is probably not unknown to you.'[104]

'Your pardon, sir, it is completely so. But if you are a person of note do not let my ignorance offend you. We live here so far from the world that it is no wonder if I am unaware of what everyone knows.'

'I am not famous, sir, but I enjoy a general regard. I am a picture dealer and I flatter myself that English artists are pleased to do business with me.'

'I don't doubt it, sir. May I ask, to what do I owe the favour of your visit?'

'Your interests and mine. However, before we pursue this conversation, I should like to ask you a question. At what price do you sell your pictures to Abraham Curtis?'

'Ah! So you know that my productions are bought by that good man Curtis?'

'Do you mean the Jew, Abraham Curtis? Will you answer my question?'

'I see no reason not to satisfy your curiosity. Curtis pays me a pound each.'

'A pound! I'd never have thought him so generous. Well, do you know, sir, what price Abraham gets for your pictures? He sells them onwards for twenty-five guineas, sometimes thirty.'

'What are you saying?' I exclaimed in utter astonishment. 'What, my daubs find such a market! You must be mistaken.'

'I'm never mistaken when it comes to business. As for what you call daubs, they may be weak from the point of view of art, but they have truth and likeness to nature, which are rare qualities. That is my view and the public is of my opinion. Your work sells well. For my part I had no idea that you were on board a hulk and I was very far from guessing it. Now, having given these explanations, let's settle to business. Will you supply me with your pictures for five pounds apiece? If your reputation increases, I'll raise my price.'

'*Ma foi*, I don't see how I can refuse such an advantageous proposition!' I exclaimed rapturously.

'In that case I'll begin by carrying away the two finished pictures that I see there. When I leave I shall give you my direction and you will kindly write to me whenever you have a new production ready. Here are ten pounds. Monsieur Garneray, it has been a pleasure to make your acquaintance.'

'Not at all, Mr Smith, it is I who am delighted to find myself doing business with you.'

As soon as the generous Mr Smith had gone I was so overjoyed and proud of my success, which represented independence to me, that I could not continue with my work. I decided to celebrate my unexpected good luck by treating some of my poor comrades and I went straight down to the orlop.

In the last months of his command Captain Edwards had succeeded in doing what no one before him had accomplished, the suppression of the *rafalés*. Thanks to his resolution, fairness and the judicious steps he took, the foremost of which was to forbid games of chance, the *rafalés* had gradually come back into our common life. As soon as Captain Edwards was gone *roulette*, *passe-dix* and *biribi*,[105] which had been put aside for a while, emerged anew and as an inevitable consequence the *rafalés* came with them.

It was to the *rafalés* that I set off to accomplish my generous project.

'*Ma foi*,' I thought, 'if Mr Smith had delayed coming on board the *Vengeance* until tomorrow instead of coming to see me today, the Jew would have carried off my pictures for three pounds. That chance has gained me twelve pounds. I can well afford to devote a quarter of that to treating fifty starving wretches. Their joy will be a pleasure to me.'

The first two *rafalés* that I caught sight of were sitting astride a bench playing *écarté*, with great concentration, surrounded by a numerous gallery of spectators.

'To judge by the silence of the crowd this game seems of particular interest,' I said to a prisoner who was leaning forward with his eyes wide open, apparently absorbed in the spectacle.

'That it is, mate,' he replied, 'It's for the life of Linch the boatswain.'

'What do you mean, for Linch's life? What the devil are you trying to say?'

'The truth. Don't you know Linch?'

'What a question! I know him perfectly well. The most violent and brutal fellow. He'll never die for the love of France.'

'No, but a Frenchman will kill him.'

'Don't talk in riddles, comrade. Explain it all a bit more clearly. Why do you say that these two *rafalés* are playing for Linch's life? What do you mean?'

'I mean just what I say. Petit-Jean and Leroux, these two honourable *rafalés*, being as it seems particularly affected by Linch's brutality, have decided to kill him. Now, I repeat, they're playing twenty points of *écarté* for who'll rid us of the cruel boatswain by stabbing him.'

'Impossible! There's some trick behind it.'

'Not at all: it's a very serious game.'

'No, I can't believe it! Look at Petit-Jean and Leroux. They're winking at one another and they keep bursting out laughing. I tell you they're hoaxing you.'

'I know 'em both and I can assure you that the stakes are serious. Now, comrade, kindly let me follow the game. We'll have time enough for talking later.'

Petit-Jean was then winning. His score was nineteen points and it was his turn to deal; his opponent had only seventeen.

'Now then, Leroux, what happens if I turn up a king?' he exclaimed after dealing, poising the card that was to come next between his fingers.

'And what of it?' replied Leroux calmly, 'I can pay you. I won't cheat.'

'Won't you feel a trifle irritated when they hang you?'

'*Dame,* to tell the truth I'd rather be shot. But after all, you must be philosophic and thankful for what they give you. Instead of bullets a hemp cravat isn't to be sneezed at. Anyway, before they launch you into eternity, as the Goddams say, they give you a bloody good dinner, three courses, as much tea as you like and a pint of beer. Now then, Petit-Jean, play your card. The company's getting restive as you can see.'

'This Leroux's pretty sharp,' exclaimed Petit-Jean with a laugh. 'If I win, as is likely, he'll have no difficulty in paying. I can expect ready money.'

'You're annoying me. Will you deal, yes or no?

'*Salpêtre,* here goes! The queen of hearts! What d'you say to that?'

'To that I say,' replied Leroux calmly, 'that I can match it with the king.'

'Ah! Then that gives you eighteen. Do you want to discard?'

'Hardly, since with the king I've a jack, an ace, a ten and the nine of trumps. The whole lot! Eighteen and two make twenty. I reckon I've won.'

'*Sacristi,* what bad luck,' exclaimed the hapless Petit-Jean, striking the bench so violently with his fist that the cards scattered in all directions.

'You complain, but you got nineteen points. It's a very honourable defeat.'

'And going to the gallows. How would *you* like that?'

'Then you shouldn't gamble. Are you trying to wriggle out of paying?'

'Me! Not at all. I'm honest. You won fairly and I'll pay you, never fear. It's just that…it suits me to be angry. And I'm angry now, that's all!'

'I've nothing to say to that. Each to his own. If you want to make a row about it, then make one! But let me remind you that to avoid any dispute we agreed before we sat down to play that the loser would settle up at once.'

'Yes, yes, I know and I'm ready,' replied Petit-Jean, getting up immediately from the bench. 'Well, would you believe that at this critical moment, when the time to settle has come, I no longer loathe that blackguard Linch quite as much as when we sat down to play a little while ago. I must confess that the brute doesn't care for the French, that he's ill-bred, unfair and violent…'

'Well! Add to all this the fact that he's English and isn't it enough?'

'It certainly is, and more than enough. Only I believe that beneath it all he's not quite the evil devil he seems. At any rate, I'm going.'

After embracing his comrades Petit-Jean set off towards the upper deck, seemingly unconcerned, but I held him back.

'You villain,' I said, 'are you going to do a foul cold-blooded murder? I won't let you, do you hear? I forbid it.'

My words were met with fierce murmurs. Leroux advanced towards me.

'And why won't you allow it?' he asked fiercely. 'By what right do you forbid him to pay me what he owes?'

'Any honest man has the right to prevent a crime.'

'A crime, Monsieur Garneray,' continued Leroux forcefully, 'ah! You call it a crime, do you? Don't you know that Linch takes his only pleasure in our sufferings? He's a hundred times more cruel than the Captain and doesn't give us a minute's peace or rest! Every Frenchman who gets into his grasp receives some abuse or injury! But how would you know that? You're the Englishmen's pet. They treat you more like a friend than a prisoner. You don't live life as we do, you're not one of us.'

I gathered from the hostile whisperings that spread through the crowd after these words that Leroux's tactics against me were skilful and to the point. I was fairly well liked and it would have been easy for him to make me unpopular or even distrusted by exploiting the jealousy inspired by my position. Accordingly, I did not let him go on but interrupted sharply.

'Leroux,' I said, 'not everyone believes your insinuations. I'm a better Frenchman and a better comrade than you, and I'll prove it. How do you live on board the *Vengeance*? As a beggar and a cheat living off others. You boast about France but you represent it so badly. What would they say there if they knew about your shabby ways? Did we grow to be noble and respected like this? As for myself, instead of being a burden on my mates, haven't I been very glad to serve them well on a thousand occasions? I don't bring this up out of vanity, but so that no one shall degrade me by setting me at your level. Come, gentlemen,' I continued turning back to the crowd and raising my voice, 'is there anyone here who's ever had to complain about me? Speak up now.'

'I don't say that you're a bad comrade, Monsieur Garneray,' replied Leroux in a far less arrogant tone than he had used before, 'I simply say that living with the English must have made you friendly with them.'

'Me, friendly with the English!'

'*Dame,* if that's not so, why do you defend Linch so warmly? He's our cruellest enemy. We don't want help from you. All we want is that you shouldn't interfere with our revenge or side with England against France.'

'Do you believe I'd do that? Not at all. What I want is to stop Petit-Jean from going to the gallows.'

The *rafalé* Petit-Jean, who had not taken part in this altercation, broke his silence with, '*Dame!* Listen to me comrade. In all honesty I can't deny that I've lost. If I don't kill this scum Linch I'll be dishonoured for ever. What the devil, just because you're a *rafalé* it don't follow that you've no conscience at all! Thanks for your good intentions. I'm in debt and I intend to pay.'

'Bravo, Petit-Jean!' clamoured the prisoners.

'Embrace me again, my dearest friend,' cried Leroux, falling into the villain's arms, 'you have my highest respect; I expected no less of you. Good luck! And don't forget the dinner they owe you before they march you to the gallows. Three courses, as much tea as you like and a pint of beer. You've a right to it. And if you're well-behaved, they might even add a little tot of gin or brandy when they turn you off. Farewell and good luck!'

Petit-Jean went off and I had to renounce all hope of saving him. Being watched, as I was at that moment, the least false step on my part could have brought me into the gravest trouble.

Scarcely five minutes after Petit-Jean had left us a loud shriek was heard on deck. The wretch had kept his promise and paid his debt only too well. The shriek announced that Linch was dead, stabbed with a knife in his chest. Petit-Jean was immediately arrested and taken ashore. A few months later we learnt that he had been hanged.[106]

The day after the visit of my new picture dealer, the generous Mr Smith, the Jew Abraham Curtis sought me out. I now knew at what rate to value him but wishing for my own amusement to have confirmation, I asked him to allow me an extra five shillings for each picture.

'God bless me!' he replied, looking slyly at me, and raising his eyes to the heavens. 'Are you mad, my friend, to make such a request? This is what comes of wanting to be useful to your sort. They become unfair or demanding. But you don't know, you can't know, that I haven't yet managed to sell a single one of your pictures. To avoid humiliating you, I've always concealed the fact from you. I have them all in the shop, every one of them. Moreover, far from giving you the five shillings you ask, I feel forced to abate the price by the same amount. In future I will pay you no more than fifteen shillings.'

'Then in future I will no longer work for you.'

'What! I beg your pardon! What's that you say?' exclaimed Abraham Curtis, with an apprehension that did not escape me. 'Come now, you have a quick temper. I'm too tender-hearted, but I can never resist the desire to succour the needy. Come now,' he continued in a wheedling, paternal tone, 'work conscientiously, do better, finish your pictures more highly, for your latest work has been weak, and I'll try to continue paying you a pound.'

I replied coldly to the Jew, 'Thank you for the interest you display, but I warn you that if you want to have more pictures from me, I'll not let you have any at less than ten pounds.'

'Ten pounds!' exclaimed Abraham Curtis, turning pale. 'My God! My friend, are you ill? Are you out of your mind?'

'No, my dear Abraham, I'm not in any way mad,' I replied with a smile, 'after all, I don't see why my suggestion should astonish you. It doesn't seem unreasonable if I sell you pictures for ten pounds and *amateurs* pay you fifteen or twenty for them.'

'I sell them for fifteen or twenty!' replied the Jew, looking fixedly at me as if trying to read my thoughts. 'Mr Garneray, I see it all. You've taken advantage of the confidence I foolishly placed in you. You have seen that dealer Smith.'

'You've guessed it at last! Yes, it's true. Mr Smith visited me yesterday and you may like to hear that I was delighted with him and the proposals he made.'

'Frenchman,' exclaimed Abraham the Jew, interrupting me, 'I won't speak to you of gratitude. You would just mock me and rightly so. I shall merely observe that in your position an enemy is not to be underestimated and that if ever I have a chance of doing you harm I shall seize it. You don't trifle with a man like me with impunity.'

'My honest Jew,' said I, taking Abraham by the arm and shoving him to the door of my cabin, 'I don't give a fig for your threats.'

Unfortunately, I was then far from suspecting that the scoundrel would soon take a stunning revenge on me, as the reader will shortly learn.

CHAPTER XXI

The prisoners from Cabrera • The Pegase • The deadly baths • Colonel Lejeune • A terrible epidemic • I become infected • Reappearance of Fignolet • Green Parrot and his conjugal affections

TOWARDS THE END OF 1811 the Spaniards handed over to the English the remainder of the French division that had come into their hands after the deplorable surrender by General Dupont at Baylen. These men had been held for two years in the island of Cabrera and had been dreadfully decimated by disease and hunger.[107]

On their arrival in England these unfortunates were spread around amongst all the hulks and the *Vengeance* received about thirty of them. It would be impossible to depict the sad state of these wretches. The cruelty of the Spaniards had been such that the prospect of being thrown on board the hulks seemed to them an unexpected mercy, and one in which they could scarcely believe.

The prisoners from Cabrera come on board the Vengeance

Buard del.

Ferdinand sc.

9. Louis Garneray. *Engraving by Buard after Ferdinand, from* La France Maritime, *1845.*
Private Collection.

10. *Wreck of the Frigate* **Atalante** *in Table Bay on 6th November 1805.*
National Maritime Museum, Greenwich. (Ref. F0824).

Garneray and the Atalante*'s crew were saved and he was sent on board the* **Belle-Poule.**

11. **'22 Ventose, 3ième position'**; *14th March, 3rd position;*
National Maritime Museum, Greenwich (Ref. F0825).

This probably represents the Belle-Poule *with the* Amazon *on her starboard quarter during the battle between Admiral Linois' squadron and Sir John Warren's fleet off the Cape Verde Islands on 14th March 1806.*

Two examples from a remarkable series of seventy-two wash and ink drawings by Duclos-Legris, a seaman on the Marengo, *one of Admiral Linois' ships; he was captured with Garneray and imprisoned on the* Prothee *hulk at Portsmouth from 1806 until 1814.*

12. 'Le Prothee, prison flotante.' *The Floating Prison*, Prothee. National Maritime Museum, Greenwich. (Ref. F0826).

Duclos-Legris' naïve view of the Prothee, with smoking chimneys and the prisoners' washing in close proximity, expresses the day-to-day discomfort of hulk life more forcibly than Garneray's large scale paintings. The rambade or bulwark preventing the prisoners from gaining access to the poop can be seen.

13. Exterior of an English Hulk. Musée national de la Marine, Paris.

14. Interior of an English Hulk. Musée national de la Marine, Paris.

Two engravings by Legrand after Garneray to illustrate the Histoire du Sergent Flavigny, *1821, to which Garneray contributed notes. The floating platform round the exterior of the hulk is visible, together with sentry boxes on it.*

15. A Traitor's Punishment. Lithograph from Alexandre Lardier's Histoire des pontons et prisons d'Angleterre, *1845.* Private Collection.

This unfortunate prisoner has been tattooed on the forehead with the words, J'AI VENDU MES FRÈRES Le 8 AOÛT 1809, *'I betrayed my brothers on 8th August 1809.'*

*16. Playbill for a theatrical performance on board the **Crown** hulk at Portsmouth on 10th July 1807.* National Maritime Museum, Greenwich. (Ref. F0823).

17. French prisoners of war on the island of Cabrera fighting a duel with razors attached to sticks. Private Collection.

Engraving from The Wars of Europe, *1838. Garneray describes a fatal duel with similar weapons on board the* Prothee *hulk at Portsmouth.*

18. Taking in a topsail and an outer jib.

Engraving by Pardinel after Garneray, from La France Maritime, *1845.* Private Collection.

*19. Garneray and an assistant
drawing the port of Brest.*

A vignette from Vues des
côtes de France dans
l'Océan et dans la
Méditerranée,
*a series which was published
in fifteen parts over nine years
from 1823.*
Musée national de la
Marine, Paris.

*20. Garneray's grave in
Montmartre Cemetery.*
Photograph, Richard Rose.

*The grave was restored recently;
the device with the palette and
brushes, cutlass, anchor and
boarding axe was saved from
the original monument.*

Nevertheless they all arrived, or at least those who were sent to the *Vengeance*, in such a desperate state that it appeared plain to us that not one of them would live. I can still see the lighter that brought them, a distressing sight. The wretches lay in the bottom of the vessel uttering cries of pain and writhing in a feverish delirium. They were thin as skeletons, pale as corpses and scarcely covered by miserable rags, although it was intensely cold. The hardest heart could not have viewed them without pity, but the English treated them with the greatest inhumanity and hated them because of their nationality. To the English these were not suffering human creatures; they were French prisoners of war.

Of the thirty wretches brought to us by the Transport Office scarcely a dozen were well enough to climb on board. The others lay stretched out in the bottom of the lighter, incapable of moving.

'Captain,' said the *Vengeance*'s surgeon, addressing our commander, 'I object to bringing these vagabonds on board the hulk. They have some contagious disease and before a fortnight's out they'll turn the *Vengeance* into a charnel house.'

'What ought we to do, doctor?'

'Send them to the hospital, Captain.'

'Very well, you're right. However, since they're not expected on board the *Pegase*, I'll dispatch a boat to warn the Captain there.'

The *Pegase* was an old vessel of dismal appearance, her sloping tar-blackened sides ruined by the weather and topped by sheds of all sorts and sizes which made her resemble a Chinese junk when seen from afar. She had been a French 64 captured in the war of 1780 and since that time had had no other purpose save the confinement of prisoners of war of all nations or the storage of naval equipment.[108] *Pegase* had eventually been transformed into a hospital and was secured by four enormous chains at the head of eleven other hulks in the main channel of the Portchester River.

During the entire time that the boat was absent on its errand to warn our commander's colleague in the *Pegase* that further inmates would be coming, that is to say for nearly an hour, our unfortunate countrymen made continual heartrending groans of pain as they lay exposed to the bitter cold in their lighter. We vainly begged the Captain to bring the wretches on board but he would by no means consent.

'It's not worth troubling my crew for the few minutes that these people will have to wait,' he replied. 'Anyway, when you have a fever you don't feel the ill-effects of cold.'

At last we saw the boat returning. We hoped that our comrades' cruel ordeal would come to an end, but it was not to be. The commander of the *Pegase* desired his colleague on board the *Vengeance* to give orders that the Frenchmen in question should take a bath before they were sent. His hospital was so crowded that there was no room to carry out this essential operation to prevent infection.

'My colleague is right,' said our commander. 'Well, take these people to the wash-house and have them bathed.'

This barbarous order was immediately executed. Our poor comrades were hauled unconscious on board and carried to the wash-house, a sort of hut erected in the bows of the *Vengeance*. They were stripped completely naked and plunged several times into tubs of icy water. It would have done as much good to shoot them. After this fatal operation they were again put in the lighter which set off at last for the hospital ship.

In my capacity as interpreter I was obliged to write down and register in the entry ledger the surname, Christian names, age and rank or profession of the newcomers. This formality was neither very difficult nor complicated, but needed to be done with the greatest care, because it was most important. This was the register that was consulted in all questions relating to exchanges and the distribution of money remitted from France. The alteration of a single letter in a name might sometimes deprive a prisoner of his liberty for the length of the war. I had just finished my work of registering my new companions in captivity when I saw a truly singular character enter my cabin.

Imagine a tall handsome man of about thirty-six or thirty-eight years old, with a fine open countenance, and a proud assured bearing, advancing towards me with

Colonel Lejeune in Garneray's cabin.'

a haughty patronising air. He was dressed in a proper harlequin's jacket, though the squares of the cloth were blue instead of red. He addressed me brusquely.

'See here, Englishman's clerk,' he said, 'trim your pen and get on with your job. Hurry now, I'm not a patient man, I warn you.'

'I don't know who you are and it doesn't matter to me,' I answered the harlequin, with an anger that the reader will readily understand, 'but from your manners it's easy to guess that you were very ill-bred.'

'You dare to speak to me like that, you miserable traitor!' exclaimed the handsome man, apparently about to spring at me. 'Have a care, or I'll make you regret your insolence.'

The anger that was brewing within me boiled up and over at this. I advanced menacingly and told him in the lowest terms[109] what I thought of him. I expected that this exchange would lead to blows, but the harlequin seemed charmed by my attitude and at once became calm.

'Ah, comrade,' said he, 'you must be all right if you dare to speak to me like that. I thought that all interpreters were spies. You aren't a spy, are you?'

However unfair the question, the harlequin asked it so ingenuously that I could not be offended.

'I only took the post of interpreter,' I replied, 'because it allows me to serve my companions in misfortune. Enquire about me from the first person you meet and you'll be told who I am and what I'm like.'

'Well, my apologies! Shake hands!' said the harlequin, holding out his hand, 'I like you. If I stay on your damned hulk, I fancy we'll get along together. I like angry fellows. They're generally sincere.'

There was so much good breeding, sincerity and goodwill in the harlequin's voice and expression that I shook him warmly by the hand and made my peace with him.

'Will you answer a few questions, comrade Harlequin?' I said with a laugh.

'Naturally, and no more insults.'

'*Dame*, you started it. Your name?'

'An enemy to the English – Lejeune.'[110]

'Where were you taken and by whom?'

'*Mille tonnerres*, by brigands, at Badajoz in Spain.'

'Very well.' *Lejeune; taken by the Spanish*, I wrote.

'Not at all, I don't want you to write that,' he exclaimed, flaring up again, 'why do you alter my answers? *Brigands* I said and you write Spaniards. I know it's the same thing, but I stick to my version. Brigands I answered, so write brigands.'

'But I can't do that, comrade!'

'Bah! And why not? I'm prepared to concede that interpreters aren't spies, but your behaviour shows them to be foul toadies at least.'

My calmness deserted me at this fresh insult. '*Ah! Tonnerre!*' I exclaimed, 'if interpreters are toadies I'll show you, if you're worth my while, that at least they don't shrink from the point of a sword.'

'A duel! And why not? Who bothers about rank on board a hulk? It'll do to pass a morning. Your name?'

'Garneray, mate in the Imperial Navy.'

'Are you related to the celebrated painter, Isabey's rival?'

'Do you mean the instructor of Queen Hortense,[111] that excellent woman, that devoted patron of the arts and artists?'

'Exactly. Do you know him?'

'He's my brother.'

'You're Auguste Garneray's brother? But I know your brother well, and your father too. Old Garneray gave me my first drawing lessons. Your mother was the daughter of the Marquis de Courgy who was murdered by the revolutionaries. Your brother Hippolyte is very promising and will be a distinguished painter. And I was thinking of cutting your throat!' exclaimed this strange character, shaking my hand again before I could prevent him. Then without allowing me any time to recover from my surprise, he continued, 'and speaking of painting, what do I see on your clothes? Stains of oil and colour. Are you a painter too?'

'Not exactly, but I'm trying to become one.'

'So you're able to paint on board the hulks?'

'There's your answer,' said I, indicating a seascape I had just finished.

'Ah! That's one of yours? Let me see.'

The harlequin immediately approached my picture, gave it a prolonged and silent inspection and then turned back to me.

'Monsieur Garneray,' he said with exquisite politeness, and in the tone of a man of cultivation, 'pray accept my sincere compliments. You are a worthy bearer of your family's name. Really, this picture is fine, very fine. It has some imperfections here and there, revealing a certain lack of mastery and skill, but I can say again that on the whole it is excellent.'

I was as much surprised by the stranger's compliments and politeness as I had been at first by his violence and rudeness. I could not make him out.

'Are you a painter, sir?' I asked, to renew the conversation.

'Yes, from time to time. When I have leisure from my other concerns, I use it in daubing battle-scenes.'

'Ah, you're a military man,' I continued, pointing to the open register in front of me. 'May I put down that reply, without abusing your confidence?'

'*Parbleu!*' said the harlequin with a laugh, 'you remind me that I haven't yet answered your questions. I was so angry when I found myself on board a hulk that I forgot for a moment what I was saying or doing.'

This delicate and indirect manner was, if not an excuse, at least an explanation of his behaviour towards me and confirmed my opinion that this tall handsome harlequin was not a simple soldier but a man of quality.

'Pray take up your pen again and I'm at your service,' he continued, with a nod in my direction.

I stood at my desk and continued my questions.

'Your profession, please?' I asked.

'Colonel of engineers, part of the French army in Spain,' he replied with a smile. 'Yes, I imagine that my rank appears a trifle out of step with the grotesque garb I'm wearing, but having been made a prisoner, plundered by the Spanish guerrillas and brought directly to England in a merchant transport, I was only too glad to get this mountebank's coat. After all, if it's my fate to rot on board the hulks, as looks only too likely, then my new uniform seems about on the right level.'

'Colonel, you can be reassured,' I replied, 'that you won't remain long in the *Vengeance*. When your rank is known, which it shall be today since I will seek out the Captain at once, you'll be taken ashore immediately. The hulks aren't intended for superior officers.'

'What, do you think they'll set me free on parole?'

'Yes, in a parole town. Only I'm sorry to tell you that the fate of Frenchmen in parole towns is scarcely better than on board the hulks, thanks to the suspicions and distrust of the English.'

A few days later Colonel Lejeune was sent to Odiham.[112] 'Au revoir, my dear Garneray,' he said as he went into the launch, 'remember, anything that I'm allowed to do for you ashore will not be forgotten.'

I smiled ruefully at that promise. I had so often been the victim of ingratitude and forgetfulness on the part of my former fellow-captives that I no longer had any faith in promises. After all, I reasoned, I had done no service to Colonel Lejeune, so why should he trouble himself with me? Because we both indulged in painting? A foolish idea. I badly misjudged the excellent Colonel. On the contrary, he was the only man who looked after my interests.

Since chance has brought up Colonel Lejeune's name I take this opportunity of saying that in my opinion his battle scenes, highly regarded as they are even today by connoisseurs, are the most remarkable productions of their type in France. In a few slight aspects they may have minor faults but no other battle painter has achieved the same reality. The widow of Lejeune, who died as a general a few years ago, exhibited his paintings with great success and they gave me the keenest pleasure.

To return to my narrative. The contagious disease affecting the prisoners from the isle of Cabrera who were put on board our hulk spread amongst us with terrifying rapidity. The *vomito* from which we had suffered was as nothing to the new epidemic. Soon the *Vengeance* bore a sad and mournful appearance. Those of my companions in misfortune who were in low spirits were child-like in their despair and expected only a hideous death.

As for myself, a comfortable life without material privations had left me with more strength, and my work had occupied my attention, thus keeping at bay the fatal influence that weighed on my fellows. I took little notice of the scourge and felt very well.

However, one day I felt myself taken with a mild shivering and a fairly severe headache. I was in hopes that this indisposition would have no consequences when it suddenly seemed as though the hulk was spinning rapidly in every direction and I fell down unconscious.

When I came to myself I was in a boat with other sick prisoners on my way to the hospital. It would be difficult to describe the hideous impression made on me by this discovery. Though my mind was hovering between reason and delirium I had enough intelligence left to understand my situation but insufficient strength to endure it. The thought that tormented me most, which I can recall with pain to this day, was that of the deadly freezing bath which all patients were made to undergo on the pretext of cleanliness when they arrived on board the *Pegase*.

Soon however the delirium overcame me and I ceased to struggle against my illness. I was beaten. When I recovered consciousness I was in the wash-house of the *Pegase*. The sight of great tubs full of icy water drew a shriek of horror from me and for a moment restored all my wits.

'I don't want to be bathed!' I cried loudly. 'Let no one lay a hand on me! I'll resist!'

Needless to say the Englishmen and the French orderlies gave not the slightest heed to my cries and protests. They were busy with my companions in misfortune whom they plunged over and over again into the great tubs of freezing water. From the haste with which they performed their task they seemed determined to get it over as rapidly as possible.

With horror I saw my turn come round. A French seaman who helped the English in their task came up to strip me of my clothes and had already laid hands on them when he suddenly exclaimed in joy and surprise, 'What! Is it you, Monsieur Garneray? Ah! How good to see you!'

'Don't let them bathe me!' I cried, clinging to the one idea in my head.

'Never fear, the English won't touch you. I won't let them,' replied the orderly, lifting me in his arms and carrying me out of the wash-house. I cannot tell what length of time passed before I regained consciousness for a few moments and found myself lying in a cot.

'Well, Monsieur Garneray, are you feeling better?' asked a Frenchman, seated by the head of the cot, who seemed to be watching over me. I recognised the seaman who had saved me from the icy bath and thanked him with a nod. 'I had you put near the door,' continued the seaman, 'so I shouldn't lose sight of you. That way the English won't be able to take you to the dead-house whilst you're still alive.'

This dismal sentence had a deep effect on me and though I should have liked an explanation from my unknown friend, I was so feeble and exhausted that I could not ask. I soon fell into a troubled sleep and passed a dreadful night, oppressed by fearful dreams in which I had a fixed idea that the English had declared me dead and might bury me alive.

I shall not weary the reader by describing all the stages of my illness but will resume my narrative from the day when my convalescence began. That this happened at all was due to providence, because the treatment we were forced to undergo in the *Pegase* was utterly unsuited to our illness and almost always resulted in death.

'Well, Monsieur Garneray, that was a rough passage, but it seems from what the surgeon says that you're out of danger,' said a French seaman assigned to help the English orderlies, whom I found seated by my cot when I opened my eyes again. He continued, 'No matter, so long as you've got your strength, but I'm sure you'd have been done for if I hadn't saved you from the cold bath.'

'What!' I exclaimed, 'was it you, my friend, who carried me from the wash-house to my cot?'

'Yes, of course it was me! *Dame,* it was the least I could do for an old acquaintance.'

'What do you mean, an old acquaintance? Have we met before today?' I asked the seaman, looking at him more attentively than before.

'Don't you remember me?' he exclaimed. 'So that's it. I said to myself, the lieutenant doesn't seem at all pleased to see me. That offended me. But then, looking back on it, it's nine years since we were together. Well, from seventeen to five-and-twenty a man changes quite a bit. Now do you know me?'

'Not at all, my friend; however much I look at you, I don't recollect you at all.'

'What! Have you forgotten the *Doris,* Captain Liard, the niggers and their mutiny and our friends Combaleau, Périn, Ducasse and me, Fignolet, midshipman Fignolet?'[113]

'Fignolet!' I exclaimed, looking in astonishment at the strapping, athletic seaman before me. 'Are you Fignolet?'

'Yes, lieutenant, it's me and more. Ah! *Dame,* I admit I've grown and filled out nicely. I always had a good appetite.'

'Really, Fignolet, seeing you in the *Pegase* is like a dream. I can't believe my eyes. I recall you very well now.'

'My God, lieutenant, there's nothing strange about my being here. I was nabbed two years ago by an English frigate and put on a hulk. Then, being trustworthy, I was sent as an orderly on board the *Pegase*. Yes, I know you'll say that we aren't well liked, *croque-morts* they call us, but what could I do? There I was, dying of hunger and I was promised triple rations if I agreed to work in the hospital. So I had to accept.'

'And you did right, Fignolet. Without you, I'd be dead.'

'Oh, you're not out of danger yet, lieutenant. Don't count your chickens.'

'I assure you, Fignolet, I feel very well, despite being extremely weak.'

'As to how you feel, so far so good. What troubles me is that you won't be able to stand the strict diet they'll put you on. However, if you'll swear to be careful and not get caught, I might be able to help you.'

'I'll swear whatever you like, Fignolet.'

'Very well. Now, I'll give you part of my rations every day. In that way you'll be able to get up in a fortnight.'

And that very evening, good kindly Fignolet brought me a little cup of broth which induced in me a night of deep repose. During the ensuing two or three days my convalescence progressed rapidly and I began to observe what was going on about me. First of all my attention was naturally attracted by my neighbours. To my left lay a poor soldier horribly affected by the fever and on my right a dying sailor. These companions were not such as to give me any cheerful ideas. On the day after my conversation with Fignolet my right-hand neighbour perished from the severity of the disease and the unsuitability of the treatment administered to him. The English orderlies swiftly carried his corpse to the dead-house up on deck.

An hour had scarcely passed since this death when I saw the arrival of one of my acquaintances from the *Vengeance* to occupy the vacant cot. This was a prisoner named, or rather nicknamed, Green Parrot. I never knew the reason for this nickname because Green Parrot was a big devil with a face burnt brown, unassuming manners and no resemblance at all to the bird whose name he had been given. Green Parrot was, however, a very original fellow of great strength of character. He had been thrown half-naked and penniless on board the *Vengeance* and by busying himself in all sorts of ways and doing drudgery for the other prisoners, had soon amassed a small capital. This had enabled him to set up as a *ratatouille* seller. Green Parrot's culinary superiority over his rivals was soon unquestioned throughout the hulk and the sale of his victuals expanded to the point that he was forced to employ an assistant.

Ratatouille no longer satisfied Green Parrot's ambitions. He set up a sort of restaurant, and a roulette table which were also highly successful. Soon he was a millionaire, that is to say he made scandalous profits, nearly a hundred francs a month.[114]

With such wealth the celebrated Green Parrot could have led a sybaritic life, held court and had his sycophants, dined well, employed at least two servants and eclipsed the rest of the prisoners with his luxuriousness. On the contrary, he did nothing of the sort. He dressed himself nearly as badly as a *rafalé*, scarcely ate and never shrank from any menial task. When it came to material things Green Parrot was the most miserable of all the prisoners in the *Vengeance* but in his own view he enjoyed the greatest blessings. He was deeply in love with his wife and it made him the happiest of men to send her all the money he earned.

'How my wife will enjoy herself this Sunday,' he said occasionally, 'I can see her in a lovely muslin gown making her entry at Vauxhall with all the women glancing jealously at her and all the young men paying her court. She's the queen of the ball! I'll try and send her more next month so that she can go to Ranelagh.' Now, the woman on whom Green Parrot doted was known to various prisoners, who informed us that she was at least fifty-five years old and hideously ugly.

It was the celebrated Green Parrot who came to occupy the empty cot on my right. Even whilst being put to bed he was raging in the grip of an intense delirium. Two men were obliged to watch over him and his cries prevented me from sleeping for nearly the whole night. My astonishment can be imagined when I woke up fairly late the next morning and the first man I saw was Green Parrot, standing upright with a little bundle under his arm, preparing to go. I thought I was dreaming.

'Good morning, Garneray,' he said calmly, 'I'm glad to know you're out of danger. I'm going back on board the *Vengeance*. If you've any messages for your friends, I'm at your service.' These words, spoken in a matter of fact way, merely increased my amazement.

'But, Green Parrot,' I answered, 'I saw you in utter delirium last night. How can you even be thinking of leaving the hospital? You won't go a yard before you fall over.'

'True, mate, I was pretty bad last night,' he replied.

'And you've managed to get better in a few hours?'

'Yes, by God. I said to myself, Green Parrot, my friend, if you let yourself lie about in idleness here you'll get seriously ill and even if you don't die, it'll be six weeks before you're out of bed. What'll your lovely wife think when the end of the month comes without the cash you normally send her so promptly? She'll reckon you don't love her any more, that you're courting some English lass, or you've eloped. So, comrade, when I thought that, I said to myself, Green Parrot, if you're a man you won't be ill, you'll get straight back to work. You've wasted enough time as it is, a whole half-day. So, get better now and quick! And I felt better. Get up! And I got up. Off you go! And so I do. Farewell!'

Green Parrot gave me a little nod, walked steadily to the door and disappeared from my sight. I would not have believed it if I had not seen it and this gave me much to ponder on. Perhaps will-power could overcome illness. I decided to follow Green Parrot's example, but sadly I was so weak that my strength failed me and despite all my efforts I could not get up.

CHAPTER XXII

The thieving orderlies • Fignolet excels himself •
Dr Dancret • Monsieur de Bonnefoux from the Belle-Poule
• Captain T___'s conduct • Abraham the Jew again

THAT SAME EVENING I was writhing and tossing sleeplessly on my cot when my eyes fell on the patient in the cot to my left and I noticed something gleaming brightly. On looking more closely I soon made out that the gleam came from the sparkling of a diamond set in a ring worn on his right hand which rested on the bed. This patient, a soldier of the army in Spain, had along with many of his comrades brought back jewels as the spoils of war.

I had conquered my restlessness and succeeded at last in sleeping, when I was half awakened by the sound of a conversation almost next to my ear. The words I heard seemed so remarkable that they soon engaged all my attention. At any rate, I kept my ears open and my eyes shut whilst feigning sleep. The conversation I shall relate was between two English orderlies.

'See here, Snow, I can't pull the ring off. It won't come. This French dog's let his hand hang out of bed. The blood's run down into his fingers and swollen 'em up. What'll we do?'

'My God! Devil take the brute! Leave the ring. We'll get it when he's dead.'

'If it's still there, which ain't likely. A pretty job if we lose it.'

'Indeed, a pretty job. The dog's at a low ebb. Likely he won't last the night.'

'No, he won't. And in the few hours he's got left we'll lose our best chance. It's enough to break your heart. Now then, Snow. I've a notion. I reckon the man's dead.'

'Are you mad? Can't you hear him breathing?'

'No, you're mistaken, that's the cove next door. I tell you, Snow, he's dead. In that case, ain't it our duty to get him to the dead-house straightaway?'

'You're a sly one! Now I see your game. Aye, of course, we'll get him up to the dead-house. Lend us a hand.'

Without a moment's delay the two orderlies dragged the bed-clothes off, laid hold of the unhappy soldier and carried him away on their shoulders. What I felt can easily be imagined. Above all I feared, and rightly so, that if I resisted this abominable action by the English orderlies the villains would stop at nothing to silence me since I knew their secret. Without uttering a word I let them go. Only when they were out of the door did I sit up, shouting for Fignolet at the top of my voice. He ran in at once. Time was short and I told him in a few words of the crime that had been committed. What I said caused no great surprise or outrage to the former midshipman.

'Never fear, lieutenant,' said he, 'I'll attend to it.'

'Have a care, Fignolet, these English orderlies…'

'Oh! Don't worry, they know my fists are hard.'

For five minutes whilst Fignolet was away I remained in terrible anguish. Then I saw him returning, carrying my neighbour in his arms.

'Well?' I asked.

'Well, he's still alive, lieutenant,' he replied. 'As for the orderlies, I banged their heads together. That's all.'

'If you like, we'll complain about it tomorrow morning, Fignolet.'

'Complain, lieutenant! What good would that do us? First of all they'd pretend not to believe us. Next, even if we had proof, which we haven't, they still wouldn't prosecute them. Every day some patient is carried off to the dead-house so they can rob him more easily. It isn't allowed, but it's tolerated. Goodnight, lieutenant. Sleep well!'

And Fignolet returned yawning to his bed, with an indifference that amply proclaimed how used he was to such daily horrors. The soldier whom the orderlies had pretended was dead recovered, as I later learnt. Alas, how many wretches fell victim to the hateful greed of the English orderlies and died unavenged?

Thanks to Fignolet, who generously shared his rations with me, I convalesced rapidly and was soon able to get up and go on deck. The ceaseless examples of cruelty that I had before my eyes revolted me and made my stay on board the *Pegase* intolerable, so I hailed with joy the day when I could at last return to the *Vengeance*. It would be difficult to convey to the reader the barbarity with which the French were treated on board this hospital ship. The memory of it still arouses my anger. There are cruelties that the pen should not describe and since I do not wish to cause public revulsion, I shall describe only one of a thousand similar events I witnessed.

One day, during the English surgeon's visit, Fignolet spoke to him and asked him to order wine for a young midshipman who was dreadfully weakened by sickness.

'You fool, are you mad that you make such a request?' replied the Englishman. 'Strengthen an enemy! You're out of your mind.'

For my part I sincerely believe that not a single one of us would have escaped if we had been treated by the English surgeons alone. Fortunately for us the French assistant surgeons in the *Pegase* supported us and succeeded in mitigating our misfortunes. Amongst them I must mention with gratitude Monsieur Dancret, who now lives at Nogent-le-Rotrou.

The time for my return to the *Vengeance* came at last. My encounter with

Fignolet had been very fortunate for me and I embraced him warmly before going down under escort into the waiting boat. A quarter of an hour later I nearly wept for joy when I found myself once more in my little cabin amongst my attempts at painting. My first task was to visit the Captain who received me with extreme coldness. I judged that whilst I had been ill some scheme had been hatched to displace me as interpreter and I resolved to be wary.

Amongst the new guests who had graced our hulk whilst I was away, was an old seaman called Dupart or Dubard (I cannot recall his name exactly) who had been made a prisoner at the same time as myself on the *Belle-Poule*. He gave me sad news of our old companions and officers. Very few had been released, many were dead and the rest were suffering in English prisons. He also told me that Monsieur de Bonnefoux, the young Ensign who had conducted himself so brilliantly in the action before the *Belle-Poule* was taken, in which he had acted as sailing-master,[115] had already tried to escape twice. The English kept a careful eye on him and he was then quite ill on board the hulks at Chatham. 'I doubt if our Ensign will let himself be discouraged by his lack of success,' said Dupart, 'he's in a fever to escape. I very much fear that he'll get himself shot one of these days.'

Happily Dupart's prophecy was never fulfilled. Monsieur de Bonnefoux, who gained such a distinguished reputation in the navy, later retired from the service with the rank of Captain. He told me recently that he intended to publish an account of his captivity in England and I sincerely hope he will do so.

I took up painting again with a sort of enthusiasm that bordered on frenzy and in strict accord with our arrangement the generous Smith paid me exactly the agreed price of five pounds for each picture. Far from lacking money, I was able to save a considerable sum. Leaving aside thoughts of freedom, which came to me ceaselessly, only one thing troubled me. This was the Captain's coldness, which became increasingly marked and sometimes degenerated into real boorishness. To tell the truth, I had little liking or respect for this worthy successor to Rose and I was earning large enough sums not to have any need of the daily twelve sous which were my allowance as interpreter. However, I feared that the loss of my employment, which would also put a stop to my use of the cabin I had on deck, would make it impossible for me to continue painting.

I was therefore equally circumspect and submissive in my dealings with our commander, but all in vain. His aversion to me increased by the day and I did not know why. A day came when my patience was exhausted and I could no longer endure his insults and incivilities. I offered him my resignation as interpreter.

'You perform your duties with intelligence and accuracy and you are useful to me,' he replied, 'I refuse your resignation.'

'With your permission, Captain, you have no right to do so.'

'A legal right, no, but I still have the power to do it. The proof of this is that if you persist in your resolve I'll make you so wretched and miserable that you'll soon plead to be taken back. You didn't come on board the hulks yesterday. You know what a Captain can do with the almost discretionary power he holds. Believe me, continue to act and nothing shall happen to you.'

'Captain, that is all I wish, but I must confess that your conduct towards me is become so odd that...'

'Enough, sir. I please myself, that is all. Is there anyone who is irreproachable? Of course not. Do you not find that even you are guilty of some unfair dealings? Go back to your duties and leave me be.'

I could only submit to this reply and so I did. I hoped that this start towards an explanation might render my relations with the Captain less disagreeable and that since he recognised my abilities and the correctness with which I did my duties he would in the end treat me more properly. Unfortunately, I was deceiving myself. Far from being appeased, his ill temper increased and sometimes came close to violence.

One day whilst I was contemplating some extreme and decisive resolution a launch approached the *Vengeance* and soon one of my old acquaintances, the Jew Abraham Curtis, appeared on deck.

'May I see my cousin the Captain?' he asked the officer of the watch, looking shiftily at me and placing emphasis on the word *cousin*.

'No, sir,' replied the officer, 'he has just gone ashore.'

I saw it all; a Captain in the Royal Navy had taken it upon himself to avenge the wrongs done to a tradesman's interests. What French officer would ever have dishonoured his uniform in such a fashion? Abraham Curtis was preparing to return to the boat that had brought him, or rather pretending to do so, when he seemed to notice me for the first time.

'Upon my word, Mr Garneray, are you still here?' said he, with a well-feigned astonishment, which did not deceive me. 'Well, are you happy with your lot? Does Mr Smith still buy your pictures for five pounds apiece? Is my cousin, the Captain of the *Vengeance*, treating you well?'

'Mr Smith always pays me scrupulously,' I answered. 'As for your cousin, he's the damnedest villain that I either know or can conceive of! Such downright language takes you aback, I see. Miserable Jew that you are, you don't know the lengths to which a Frenchman will go to avenge his insulted honour. I don't boast. I don't threaten. I merely warn you. I'm even-tempered and mild. I abhor violence. But I'll never forget that I have the honour of belonging to the French navy and I'll always make the English respect that. I live a dreadful life and I've nothing to fear from a firing squad or the hangman's noose.'

'The scoundrel!' exclaimed Curtis, turning pale, 'he might do something desperate!'

'And the responsibility would lie with those who made me desperate!'

'Come now, let's be calm, I beg you, Mr Garneray,' continued Abraham Curtis, in a wheedling tone. 'You're a good man, let's talk without getting heated.'

'I haven't yet tried to throw you overboard, so you can see I'm completely calm.'

At that reply the Jew swiftly recoiled. When he saw me smiling contemptuously at him he approached once more, saying with an air of good nature tinged with cynicism, 'You despise me too much to cut my life short. Let's talk and not be angry.'

'Go on, lie away if it amuses you.'

'Lie? Me? You're mistaken. I want to play fair with you, openly and with my cards on the table, because my game is too good to lose. You say that the Captain of the *Vengeance* treats you very inhumanely and you put this down to the fact that he and I are related. Well, you're not mistaken. You've guessed right. It was I who stirred up my cousin the Captain against you. I alone am behind the discomforts that you now suffer. Am I right or wrong to do so? It doesn't matter. What's important is that I'm able to make myself very disagreeable to you and I can influence your future for good or ill, just as I please. Having got that out of the way, let's take a cold look at what you can do, from the sole point of your own self-interest. Should you continue your relations with Mr Smith or renew the ones we had before, which you so rudely broke off? That's the question.'

'*Ma foi!* I admire your impudence,' I exclaimed, interrupting the Jew.

'And you are right to admire it, my dear sir,' he continued, 'because it shows a superior mind. Let us proceed. You are young, you are talented. Sooner or later the war will end and you will be called upon to play some part in society and to make your mark in the world. I look on this as a certainty. Do you think it would be clever to sacrifice that future for shabby considerations of present need and petty importance? I think not. If you persist in working for Mr Smith, because of some infatuation that I cannot understand, what will become of you? Troubles will crowd in upon you till you come to some disastrous end, as you yourself recognise. It would be a pretty ending if you were shot or hanged just to be able to put aside a few more pounds. Now, supposing you listen to reason and renew our old relations by supplying me with pictures at a pound apiece, then everything will alter. My cousin owes me money and is in no position to refuse me anything. He will become charming towards you and leave you to work in peace. He will help your work by exempting you from a thousand little duties. He finds these indispensable at present, but then they will seem unnecessary. Perhaps I'm mistaken, but it appears to me that you can hesitate no longer after this fair and frank explanation.'

I set down this conversation as one of a hundred thousand examples of how the French were exploited by the English. It made me reflect seriously. The Jew was right and common sense told me to submit.

'Abraham,' I replied, 'you are an abominable rogue, but after all, what of it? You hold all the cards and I've lost the game.'

'I like to hear you speak so plainly and with such good common sense,' he said coldly. 'What do you expect? I'm not rich and I mustn't neglect anything that helps me to a poor living. So, we understand one another and are agreed. From today onwards you will resume handing over your pictures at a pound apiece.'

'From today, no, because I've already promised the one I'm just finishing.'

'And when will it be done?'

'In four days at the latest.'

'Very well, I'm perfectly willing to give you this last concession. It shows that I'm not so hard in business matters as you pretend to believe. Goodbye, I shall return next week. Try to hurry because I have several delayed orders for your pictures.'

'So you admit that you're selling my pictures?'

'Selling them? They go very well. Smith's good opinion and his business sense have swollen your reputation. Nowadays I don't let your productions out of my shop any more for less than twenty pounds each.'

The cynical Abraham then proffered his hand. I ignored it, which made him smile. He made his way towards the ladder. I held him back. 'Now we're in agreement, Abraham,' said I, 'try to speak to your cousin as soon as you possibly can.'

'I'll see him in half an hour,' he replied, 'he's at my house...'

Chapter XXIII

*Mr Smith • Colonel Lejeune honours me with his friendship
• On parole • An Englishman's crime goes unpunished • An
attempt to suborn me • I am pursued • My escape*

AFTER THE JEW HAD LEFT I wrote hastily to Mr Smith, telling him that he must come and see me as soon as possible. Thanks to five shillings which I gave a sailor to deliver the letter to his address at once, Mr Smith received it a few hours later. The next morning he came on board early to see me.

'I can't blame you for having accepted that rogue's terms,' he said, 'because you really couldn't have done otherwise. We now have to find some way of evading him.'

'Apart from reducing the Captain of the *Vengeance* to beggary, I don't see how that can be done.'

'I have an idea and here it is. But first of all, a question. Do you know anyone ashore who can work on your behalf? A Member of Parliament, for example, or a French general?'

'*Ma foi*, no! But wait! Yes, I know Colonel Lejeune!'

'Well, perhaps the Colonel has some influence in English society. Yes, that's it. Write to him without delay so that he can request your discharge to the parole town where he's living.'

'But perhaps the Colonel won't remember my name.'

'What does it matter? You lose nothing by writing.'

'As you please. Now, always supposing that this plan succeeds, which seems unlikely, what then?'

'A good question. Once ashore you'll have no more to fear from the Captain of the *Vengeance* and you can work for me.'

'*Ma foi*, that's so simple that I hadn't thought of it.'

Half an hour after this conversation Mr Smith left with my letter to Colonel Lejeune, assuring me on his part that he would set all his friends to work for my deliverance. A week went by with no change in my position and I had almost stopped thinking about my ambitious scheme when one day a letter arrived from Colonel Lejeune. He told me that he had already made overtures on my behalf and had done so several times without informing me, so as not to raise vain hopes on my part. None of these had succeeded, but this time he had better expectations.

'I have good news for you,' said Smith, who took advantage of the Captain's absence ashore to come and see me during that day. 'As I promised, I set all my acquaintances to work on your behalf and now I'm more in hopes than ever.'

And a fortnight later I was indeed summoned by the Captain who told me that the Board of Transport had directed that I should be sent to the parole town of Bishop's Waltham. Any idea that the reader may conceive of my joy at this news falls far below reality. My ecstasy was beyond description. I was to be allowed to breathe fresh air in the fields, to rest under shady trees and live like everybody else. I could not believe such good fortune. Now, if I had known then what parole really meant, my joy would not have been so intense. I had often heard officers who had come from parole towns talking about them but I had never paid much attention, for the good reason that my inferior rank kept me firmly fixed on board the hulks and it was of little importance to me to know exactly about parole. Yet, after all, I must confess that parole offered a very tolerable life compared to the hulks.

When I arrived under escort in the little village where I was directed to live, the same place in which Colonel Lejeune was living,[116] I saw with some disillusion that more than twelve hundred Frenchmen of all ranks had only a few miserable and decayed houses in which to dwell. These were rented out at such an exorbitant rate that a year's rent was fully equal to the value of the house itself.

After having thanked Colonel Lejeune, who received me with the greatest affability, I managed to obtain for ten shillings a week, not a room, but the right to put my bed in a sort of hovel where five officers slept already. It was of no consequence to me. I was ashore!

The day after my arrival, being anxious to make the most of my freedom, I was up and dressed by five in the morning and ready to go abroad.

'Where are you going like that?' asked one of my room-mates.

'To take the air and roam about the fields,' I replied.

'Take care, or you'll be arrested.'

'Arrested! But why?'

'Because we're not allowed to set foot outdoors before six in the morning.'

'But that's impossible. There must surely be equal treatment of prisoners on both sides. English prisoners on parole in France can go out of their lodgings when they like or even stay out all night as long as they don't go outside the prescribed limits.'

'True. English prisoners in France can go about within a radius of six miles and if they like to increase that area they can do it informally by a simple request to the commander of the place or the head of the *gendarmerie*. In France they can go to all private and public assemblies, plays, concerts and balls. But Frenchmen are treated differently in England. We aren't allowed out before six in the morning and we have to be back before sunset. We're suffered to go a mile out of town, but even in this narrow area we have to stay on the highway. We can't go into the fields or byways.

'For the better observance of these severe regulations the Board of Transport allows any inhabitant who finds a Frenchman infringing them to attack him, as if he were a wild beast, and to take him prisoner or knock him down. This makeshift constable gets a reward of one pound. These rules have given rise to innumerable ambushes. I don't exceed the truth when I say that at least two thousand Frenchmen have been killed or wounded since they were put into strict execution.[117] As for the recreations we're allowed by the English government, they are no more than painting and reading.

'In various parole towns French prisoners wished to indulge their artistic tastes, to give concerts and set up little theatres, but the Board of Transport swiftly ordered these places of assembly to be closed. The excuse was that these meetings, to which the local inhabitants were admitted, would promote intimacy between the two nations and corrupt English principles. That's the way we're treated on parole, my dear comrade. Now you can see that your removal from the hulks wasn't such a cause for rejoicing as you thought.'

This information, given by my neighbour in the next bed, a young naval lieutenant, was far from an exaggeration and covered only a small part of the annoyances and sufferings we had to endure from the English.

During the day I arranged with an old woman who owned a tumbledown house that nearly touched the one where I lodged, to rent a room under the eaves. This I made into my studio. My establishment ashore might have been wretched but it was still so splendid and comfortable compared to my little cabin on board the *Vengeance* that I was entirely satisfied.

During the first four months of my stay ashore, until the spring of 1812, I worked constantly and eagerly at painting and the time passed rapidly for me. I bore my hardships patiently and did my best to put constantly recurring thoughts of France out of my mind. Then a fatal event occurred which completely altered my position.

One morning when the weather was extremely beautiful (a rare event in England) Monsieur S___, the Captain of a corvette, Monsieur V____, a Major in the dragoons, and myself decided to go and dine at a farmhouse on the highway about a mile from the town. It was about ten o'clock when we set off and since the sun was beaming down strongly on us, we resolved to cut across a field along one of those footpaths that are so common in England. This would have halved the distance that we still had to cover.

Whilst leaping a wide ditch I fell so awkwardly on a stone that I thought I had broken my ankle. Happily it was nothing, a mere sprain and a very little one at that. I was therefore about three or four hundred paces behind my companions when it seemed to me that I heard shouts of distress. Unhappily, I was not mistaken. Here is what had happened. A labourer cutting a hedge had noticed my two companions and had hurled himself brutally at them with his bill-hook in his hand. Major V___ had been severely wounded in one arm and having no means of defence had begun calling for help.

Captain S___ spoke a little English and swiftly threw himself between the hapless Major and his assailant, to try and make the latter see reason. This intervention cost him very dearly. The labourer rushed upon S___, brandishing his bloody bill-hook, and without stopping for the slightest explanation struck two terrible blows to his head which laid him on the ground, apparently dying.

As I came round a bush which had concealed this hideous scene from my eyes until that moment, I saw the dreadful position in which my two companions found themselves. I cannot express the despair and fury aroused in me by this lamentable sight. At that moment I believe I would have given ten years of my life to have had some weapon and been able to avenge my companions.

At the howl of rage I uttered the assailant noticed me and ran towards me, menacing me with his bill-hook. I thought I was lost, but just then I noticed a knotty cudgel, thrust into the ground and supporting the corner of a hedge. It was the work of a moment to seize this and rush swinging it towards the English peasant. I was in such a state of fury that I no longer felt my sprained ankle, whilst the heavy cudgel in my hand weighed no more than a straw.

The rustic was both a brute and a coward. Seeing not only that I did not flee from him but that on the contrary I was running towards him, he took to his heels. His agility said little for his courage and he had soon put so much distance between us that I had to abandon any hope of avenging my unfortunate companions.

I was in a very delicate position. Had I left S___ and V___ they might have been exposed to fresh violence from the monster who had struck them down. On the other hand, it would have been impossible to stay and guard them whilst waiting for some passer-by who might go and alert our friends in the town, since both victims were losing blood at such a rate that there was not a moment to spare to fetch help and staunch their bleeding.

I was agitated, undecided and had no idea what to do. Then I saw a number of country people running towards me armed with pitchforks and guns. At their head was the assailant who had attacked my friends and I had no doubt that they were coming to finish off his bloody work. I believe to this day that this was their intention, but at the sight of the two victims stretched out in a pool of blood they took pity on them and gave up their murderous design.

I explained the terrible scene that had just taken place in a few words. To give them due credit, they added their own reproaches to the curses I heaped on the cruel assailant. He was trembling like a coward and kept behind his companions, never taking his gaze off the cudgel with which I was armed.

The Englishmen improvised a stretcher with their pitchforks, placed the apparently lifeless bodies of S____ and V___ upon this litter and set off towards the town carrying their melancholy burden. The assailant followed the sad procession at a distance for a few moments, then shrugged his shoulders with an expression of disdain and went quietly back to his interrupted task of cutting the hedge.

Our arrival in the town created less of an impression than I had expected. The French prisoners were so used to such catastrophes that they took little notice of them. However, on this occasion the attack had been perpetrated on undeserving victims with such excessive cruelty, whilst the excuse for it was so futile and implausible, that great indignation was aroused amongst those on parole when the circumstances were known. The higher-ranking officers assembled immediately and on the spot composed a vigorous protest in French, addressed to the English government.

It only remained to translate the document. Colonel Lejeune had recommended me as very competent to perform this task and it was entrusted to me with a request to finish it as soon as possible. I set to work and completed it in an hour.

I was about to take it to the assembled officers when a large man, whom I took at first from his appearance to be a tradesman, suddenly came into my room. As the reader can well imagine I was very ill-disposed towards the English at that moment and I raised my eye-brows at this rude and unmannerly way of introducing himself. The stranger began to speak hastily.

'Sir,' said he, 'I believe your colleagues have asked you to translate a petition which they intend to send to the English government and publish in the press. Believe me, this business could get you into a great deal of danger and you would do well not to meddle with it.'

'Who are you, sir, coming here to spy on me and give me advice?' I exclaimed. 'Are you some informer from the Board of Transport?'

'If that were so,' replied the stranger coldly, accompanying his words with a false, crafty smile, 'then you would be wrong to express yourself as you do.'

'You're mistaken, you spy! I break no rule by translating this petition and I don't see what penalty I face or what risk I run by saying that an informer is a low, foul, contemptible creature that no honest man would ever keep under his roof.'

I accompanied this with a menacing gesture and pointed towards the door. The stranger remained unmoved, saying coldly, 'Tell me, yes or no; do you intend to translate that petition?'

'I tell you again, I have no notion who you are or what right you have to question me. However, it hardly matters to me. Yes, I will translate that petition.'

The stranger turned on his heel and departed as he had come, without a bow or a civil word. I hurriedly took what I had done to the waiting officers.

I had just left the meeting when Mary, a pretty little English girl of about twelve years old whose portrait I had painted, passed close to me and pulled me gently by the sleeve. She put her finger swiftly to her lips to indicate silence and with a little nod made it very clear that I was to follow her. This mysterious conduct made me uneasy but I began walking after my pretty little guide and after two or three minutes saw her go into a miserable cottage that stood on its own at the edge of the village. A moment later I entered the hovel and in the first room found Mary's grandmother, an elderly woman.

'My dear sir,' said she urgently, 'every moment is precious, so I'll be quick. From overhearing two constables I've just learnt by chance that you are to be arrested. Now, since you've always been very good to us and did Mary's picture for nothing, I thought it my duty to warn you, so I sent my little girl to fetch you here. You must think about what to do.'

'Many thanks for that warning, my good woman,' said I, 'and believe me I'll not forget your kindness. As to what to do, I can only think of one course, which is to flee. Thank you again and farewell!'

I put a guinea into the little girl's hand and then hurried back to my painting-room. After taking my gold and bank notes from a hiding place where I had concealed them from English greed and treachery, I crammed them into a leather belt which I had obtained on board the hulks and never took off. Then, after burning a few letters and certain papers, I locked up the room and went swiftly away to a naval lieutenant who I knew owned an excellent pair of English pocket pistols.

I was fortunate enough to find him in and having briefly explained my position I begged him to sell me his pair of pistols at whatever price he wanted to fix. '*Ma foi!* I'll readily let you have them,' he replied. 'They're of no use to me and I could be horribly compromised by owning them. They've been causing me sleepless nights. I'm very glad of a chance to be rid of them, because at this moment I've no money at all. My pistols cost me six pounds, if that price is agreeable to you.'

'Agreed, with a thousand thanks. Here are the six pounds.'

I put the loaded pistols into my pockets and without waiting to hear another word from the lieutenant I shook him by the hand and set off on the road into the countryside. About a mile from the village I hid in a ditch sheltered by a hedge and decided to wait there for nightfall, believing that no one would look for me so close to the town. As it proved, this precaution was by no means ill-conceived since I saw several constables hurrying onwards who never thought that they were leaving me far behind.

Although I was very well concealed by the hedge that overspread the ditch in which I crouched it was nevertheless with some pleasure that I saw the day giving way to night. Towards nine or ten o'clock that night I thought I heard the sound of a vehicle moving rapidly. I emerged from my hiding place and set off walking down the middle of the highway at a normal pace, like a peaceful traveller.

Ten minutes later the vehicle came up with me and I saw it was a stage coach. I hailed the driver who drew up at once. There was one vacant place inside, which I took and was thankful that I did not have to ride outside on what we in France call the *banquette* or *l'impériale,* for that was full of travellers and there I might have run the risk of recognition.

I would be lying if I said I was not nervous when I found myself in my seat and the guard had closed the door on me. I was very agitated. Little by little I began to recover when I saw that my three fellow-travellers (English stage coaches at that date only carried four inside passengers) took no notice of me. Beside me sat a man who seemed asleep, whilst two women occupied the opposite seat.

At the first stop to which we came my neighbour roused himself and contrary to the normal English habit, spoke to me. This put me in a great difficulty. Not to reply would have been an obvious discourtesy, but if I answered my accent might have betrayed my nationality. I knew not what to do or how to proceed, but one of the women, whose soft melodious voice went straight to my heart, spoke up and answered my interlocutor on my behalf.

In less than five minutes I understood that I was with a father and mother and their daughter. The father was a protestant clergyman, the mother a complete cipher and the young lady a poor child, quick-witted and full of grace, who was being taken to her situation as governess in a peer's household. I was afraid of being quizzed again and feigned a deep sleep.

My alarm can be imagined when I heard the clergyman say to his daughter, 'Remember, I must ask at the next stop if the escaped prisoner they're after has been retaken. I'd gladly give a crown if he were.'

'Pray don't talk so, dear father,' answered the girl, 'why desire harm to a fellow-creature?'

'The French are not our fellow-creatures, Flora,' exclaimed the clergyman disdainfully, 'they are fanatics who slavishly bow down to Rome and acknowledge the Pope's monstrous authority. For our part, we are men of discretion who hearken only to the voice of reason. Yes indeed, I repeat, I most earnestly wish that that escaped Frenchman, that parole-breaker, will be taken.'

'You curmudgeon,' said I to myself, 'how I'd like to get you on some neutral ground without your daughter to hide behind. I'd soon show you what I thought of you.'

Flora did not see fit to reply to her father and soon resounding snores from the highly uncharitable minister and his wife proved that they were heavily and deeply asleep. How foolish one is when young! At the risk of giving myself away I was wondering whether or not to thank the young pretty Flora for her concern on behalf of an escaped French prisoner, when all of a sudden the vehicle came to a halt.

I put my head out of the window at once and with unspeakable anguish perceived that the coach was surrounded by five or six constables, carrying lanterns.

'*Je suis perdu!*' I exclaimed in French.

'Perhaps, sir,' said Flora earnestly, 'but lean on my father's shoulder and pretend to be asleep.'

I scarcely had time to obey the charming young woman's direction before the interior of the vehicle was flooded by a bright light.

'What's the matter?' asked the clergyman's daughter with astonishing calm. 'Have a care, gentlemen, or you'll wake my parents.'

'Who is that young man, ma'am?' said the constable, and he may have pointed at me.

'My brother, whom my father has brought out of the Navy so he can enter into orders.'

'Very well, ma'am, pray excuse us for having disturbed you, but we're looking for a Frenchman who's broke his parole and we're obliged to search all the coaches.'

'No apology is needed for performing your duty,' observed the young lady sententiously, as she pulled up the glass.

'I'm saved,' said I to myself, 'as long as they don't question the coachman. But if he should talk...' And then my uncertainty was cut short as the coach moved off again. For the moment I was saved.

'Ah! Mademoiselle,' I said to Flora, 'God will reward you for that good deed!' I took her hand and raised it respectfully to my lips. I am not ashamed to say that I let fall a tear of gratitude. She withdrew her hand gently with no appearance of having understood me. She was right. What good would it have done to answer a man whom she had never seen before and would never see again? It no longer matters but, Flora, if by chance these lines should come before your gaze, be assured of my heartfelt gratitude for your noble conduct.

For fear of raising any suspicion I had still not dared to enquire in what direction the coach was travelling and it was only at the third stage that I learnt from a few words exchanged between the guard and a servant at the inn that the vehicle was not going towards Portsmouth. I therefore decided to continue my journey no further but to stop where I then found myself, both to take some sorely needed food and to prevent myself going away from Portsmouth, where I hoped to find refuge. I paid my fare to the guard and asked for a room in the inn. Before retiring I was careful to feign a toothache which prevented my speaking without a handkerchief held to my mouth.

I requested the chambermaid not to disturb me until the next day, an hour before the Portsmouth coach was due. Then I carefully closed the door of my room, put my pistols close by and threw myself fully clothed on the bed. At nearly five o'clock the next morning I heard a gentle knock at my door when a maidservant came to warn me that the Portsmouth coach would soon arrive. I developed my sham toothache into an inflammation and took my breakfast with a black scarf around my head and cheeks, completely disguising my face.

I had just drunk my last glass of port and eaten my final mouthful when the coach arrived. My lucky star caused the inside to be completely empty. Chance seemed to favour me; no other traveller came to join me during the rest of the day and I arrived in Portsmouth about nine o'clock in the evening, without having run the slightest risk.

CHAPTER XXIV

Curtis again • I treat him roughly • My arrival at Mr
Smith's • I take lodgings with him • His enquiries •
The smugglers • A fatal change of servants

FOR TWO DAYS the heat had been intense, although it was then only towards the end of May. When I descended from the coach a heavy shower began to fall, driving all passengers from the streets. This was a very happy circumstance for me since it would allow me to reach Mr Smith's house, where I hoped to find refuge, without attracting anyone's attention or raising the slightest suspicion. Unfortunately, obstacles are not overcome in real life with the same ease as in novels. It may seem a childish detail at first sight but although I knew the picture dealer's address, I knew nothing of the town of Portsmouth where I had been only once before, under escort for Duvert's trial.

I had to ask the way. But to whom could I speak? I did not dare go into a shop. I pondered as I paced rapidly onwards, in hopes that luck would help me and lead me to the street where Mr Smith lived. Then, a few yards in front of me, I saw a man sheltering under the porch of a house, waiting for the storm to pass over. I went straight up to him.

'Sir,' I said, 'would you be kind enough to direct me...' and then I stopped, my sentence cut short by a gasp of horror and surprise. The man from whom I had asked directions was the Jew, Abraham Curtis!

'Ahah!' he said, with a chuckle, 'it appears that you've become an inhabitant of Portsmouth, my dear Garneray. I can't tell you what pleasure it gives me to meet you. I'd like to think that we could start business again. Come along with me, I'll be your guide.'

I understood that I would be lost if I weakened and that the Jew undoubtedly intended to lead me into a trap and give me up to the authorities. A happy inspiration came to me and I pretended to act my part boldly.

'Upon my word, my dear Curtis,' I replied, 'I'm as pleased as you are with this meeting. I'm in a very delicate position and since I know you're an ingenious, clever sort of man, I'm tempted to believe that providence sent you to get me out of this scrape.'

'You need never doubt my partiality for you,' replied the Jew mockingly, 'I've given you proof enough in the past for you to believe that.'

'You have. But may I be very frank with you?'

'Speak on, my dear friend, I'm listening.'

'Firstly, I must confess that my presence in Portsmouth at this moment is just a trifle irregular. I've run from the town where I was on parole.'

'I thought as much! And what else?'

'What else? By God, that seems enough to me! What else! Well, I've no idea what to do. I rely on you to give me some friendly advice.'

'I'll give you better than good advice.'

'Ah! Really! My good friend, I expected no less from you. What will you do?'

'Take you to a place where you'll be in no more danger of arrest.'

'You overwhelm me. Some police office, I expect.'

'He! He!' replied the Jew, with a laugh, 'I can see you're a clever young man. You know how to take a joke and submit to circumstances. Yes, my friend, I intend taking you to the watch-house nearby.'

'Will you allow me to say one word?'

'By all means, ten, twenty, as many as you like. It's still raining. We've time to spare.'

'Well, my dear friend,' said I, 'here it is. If you shout, if you try to raise the alarm, I'll blow out your brains like a mad dog,' and I took him by the throat and clapped the muzzle of my pistol to his temples. Curtis expected this so little and it was done so swiftly that he scarcely needed the warning. He opened his eyes wide in fear, his jaw dropped and he stood there, speechless and terrified.

'Now then,' I said, 'I'm absolutely determined never to go back to the hulks. I'll die rather than do that. I swear on my honour that if you don't do as I say, if you offer the least resistance, I'll blow out your brains, even before witnesses. Now that I've warned you, I'll take your arm and you'll guide me out of town. Above all, if you value your life, don't lead me astray.'

'I'll do as you say,' said the Jew in a trembling voice. 'Never fear, I won't give you away.' I took Abraham by the arm and gripping him hard, with my hand in the side pocket of my coat where I kept my pistols, we set off.

In less than an hour, after having passed all the watchmen, we were out of town and in open country. I gagged my guide with my handkerchief and tied his hands with my neckerchief.

'We're going to stay here without moving for an hour,' I said, 'only remember this and mark it well. If ever you inform on me and I'm recaptured, I swear that sooner or later once peace comes, even if I have to hunt you down in England, I'll have my revenge on you.'

After uttering these words I left the Jew and walked away at a normal pace. But as soon as I was out of his sight I bounded forward and sped with all my strength towards the town, arriving there twenty minutes later. It might then have been nearly eleven o'clock.

I could hesitate no more. I could not loiter any longer in the public street for fear of being taken up as a vagrant. Every shop was shut and, summoning up all my courage, I went into a public house and spoke to a lad who was half-asleep with his head on the counter, asking him to direct me to the street in which Mr Smith lived.

'First on your left, quarter of a minute's walk,' said the lad, without even looking at me.

A few seconds later I was discreetly knocking and ringing at the picture dealer's door. After scrutinising me closely, bearing in mind the lateness of the hour, an elderly servant eventually admitted me to the parlour where Mr Smith was finishing his pipe and a glass of grog. The good man was so far from expecting me that for a while he did not recognise me and I had to introduce myself.

'You here!' he exclaimed at last, 'but have you lost your wits?'

'By no means, but I nearly lost my freedom.'

I related all my adventures, which he heard without interrupting.

'I'm sorry that it has all happened in this way,' he said, when I had finished, 'because your life on parole was quite tolerable. But since they'd want to send you back to the hulks ... Upon my word, what's done is done. We must now think of some means of extricating you from your difficulties. In the meantime my house is at your disposal and you shall stay here as long as you please.'

Mr Smith then summoned the old servant who had opened the door to me. 'Sarah,' he said, 'I know you have no love for the French. Nevertheless, you're an honest woman and trustworthy, as you've proved by twenty years good and loyal service. I can count on you. This gentleman is an escaped French prisoner. Make ready the upstairs room for him and try not to jeopardise the young man's freedom by a misplaced word. You know you're inclined to gossip, which is your greatest fault.'

Old Sarah shrugged her shoulders in an ill-tempered way and answered her master brusquely. 'Aye, I hate the French,' she said. 'You know my poor son was killed by them on a voyage in the Indian Ocean. True, I could have wished above all that this young man had not sought refuge here. But since he's trusted himself to you and is under your roof, I must bow to it. Hospitality is sacred.'

'Well said, Sarah, spoken like a proper Scotchwoman,' replied Smith, 'I've no fear of your gossiping now.'

Next day, having completely recovered from the previous day's turmoil, thanks to a long night's sleep, I began coolly to consider my position. I concluded that I must try every means of getting to France. I had just finished a substantial breakfast which Sarah brought to my room when Mr Smith came to see me.

'You must pardon me for not inviting you down to the parlour,' he said, 'but I'm afraid that Abraham Curtis may have spoken to the authorities. I wouldn't be surprised if the house were watched. I think it would be wiser if you kept to your room, until further notice.'

'My dear sir, I really don't know how to thank you.'

'Thanks are not needed. I do no more than my duty. Now, let's speak seriously. What are your plans?'

'I have but one aim; to find some way of reaching France.'

'Upon my word, that's the only reasonable decision, but it goes clean against my interests. What do you need to do it? Money?'

'Thank you, but no. Because of you I have enough. My belt's full of gold. What I need is to know a few honest smugglers who would lighten the weight of that belt, or to speak plainly, would take a large bribe to risk a passage across the Channel with me on board.'

'Good. I'll make discreet enquiries amongst my many acquaintances as to where and how one can come across such smugglers.'

'Since I don't know how to express my gratitude, I'll keep quiet and let you proceed. For the time being, could you get me some painting materials? That would help me to pass the time.'

'A good idea! Goodbye, I'll send an easel up to you with canvases and colours. Above all, keep well hidden. I meet Curtis fairly often close to my house and I fear he may have arranged for it to be watched.'

'I understand. I'll take an escape from the hulks as the subject for my first picture. That'll make me happy.'

I had been working on a sketch for more than two hours when Mr Smith appeared in my room again with an air of triumph.

'Hurrah! Victory!' he exclaimed light-heartedly. 'A great stroke of luck, good news…'

'Tell me, my dear Mr Smith,' said I excitedly.

'Here it is, briefly told. One of the gilders I employ has a cousin who is a sailor and does nothing but smuggling and helping prisoners escape. What's odd about it all is that my workman mentioned it for no reason and without my asking. Luck like that is a good omen! I didn't want to question him straight away and trust myself to him, since he has a fairly bad reputation, but tomorrow I'll broach the subject again and find out where his cousin the smuggler lives.'

The thought that I might soon see my homeland and be reunited with my family excited me to the extent that I could not sleep all night.

Next day, though I waited impatiently for Mr Smith to come, yet the day wore on without his appearance and it was nearly three o'clock before I heard the stair creak beneath his heavy tread. My heart leapt at the sound of my host's boots, as if I had been a youth anxiously waiting for the swish of a silk gown.

'Well?' I exclaimed, before he had had time to shut the door.

'Well,' he replied, 'one day's different from another. Good news yesterday, but today I bring bad.'

'Did you see the smuggler? Did he refuse?'

'I would be very wary of seeing him. At any rate, he certainly hasn't refused.'

'Explain, I beg you, tell me…'

'That won't take long. I was on my way to see my gilder when I met a friend of mine, the captain of a merchant vessel, whom I hadn't seen for a long time. You can imagine that I soon brought the conversation round to smugglers. The captain hates the French, and so as not to raise his suspicions I set about deploring the greed of smugglers and how they conspire with the French with the result that so many prisoners escape from the hulks. *"Don't trouble too much on that score,"* says the captain, with a laugh, *"the number that escape and see their native shore again is far from being as great as you might believe. Smugglers save England from more enemies than they help."* At this I feigned great surprise and my friend told me the painful story that I must repeat to you.

'Smugglers are the worst villains in the world and not to be trusted in any respect. They risk death when they are taken at sea with escaped prisoners bound for France and the penalty is always exacted. When they are closely pursued they throw overboard the evidence that might convict them, by which I mean the Frenchmen who have trusted their good faith. These are the more honest smugglers. Others have fewer scruples. Once they lay their hands on the large sum of money fixed for the passage they murder the poor creatures they'd agreed to take to France.'

'But this is unspeakable!' I exclaimed.

'Oh, that's not all,' continued Mr Smith, 'a third class of smugglers exists, not such a bloody band of villains, but no less villainous. Smugglers who are spies linked to the Board of Transport.'

'Both spies and smugglers!'

'Exactly. This sort, being in league with the Board, don't murder prisoners or harm them. They're happy to relieve them of a large payment down, then they plunder their goods, take them prisoner and hand them over to the Board which pays them a reward of five pounds a head. These smugglers are pretty numerous, since they run no risks and make a good living. A Frenchman wanting to escape has the least worst fate if he gets into their hands.'

I was downcast for a while, but soon took heart.

'My dear sir,' I said to Smith, 'I confess that if the details you have given me are right they're enough to discourage anyone. Nevertheless, I'll pursue my scheme as much as ever.'

'You'll pursue it? Are you mad?'

'Only,' I continued, 'I'll alter my plan so as not to follow it without some chance of success.'

'What will you do? I can't guess what you intend.'

'It's a very simple idea. I shall take two or three companions with me.'

'Which will make three victims.'

'Not if we are three men ready for anything, well-armed and with our eyes open. Now, if we're strong and careful, it may be possible to use a smuggler's boat.'

'Aye, you may be right. That way, I agree you may succeed. One thing troubles me, though. How will you get a couple of companions without leaving your room? Portsmouth town is scarcely bursting with escaped prisoners.'

'Alas, I acknowledge the difficulty. But I have various friends on parole. I'll write to them about it.'

'Very well, it's bound to be difficult, though not impossible. No matter,' added Mr Smith determinedly, 'don't lose heart yet. Whilst you work on your pictures and your letters I'll set about finding some men for you, be they smugglers or companions in the escape. That'll probably take some time. No matter, I've always succeeded so far when I wanted a thing determinedly and wasn't deterred by trouble and weariness. This time I want to succeed and, mark you, so I shall.'

I remained hidden in Smith's house for nearly a year, until the month of April 1813, and nothing happened to break the monotony of my unvarying existence. I had excellent food and a comfortable room; I lacked nothing to make life agreeable, yet I was nearly as miserable as I had been in the hulks and perhaps more so.

I heard the noises in the street, I cautiously lifted the corner of my curtain, saw the free and busy world passing and repassing up and down the road and found my voluntary seclusion unendurable. During the whole of that year I scarcely dared to go out other than for two or three drives in a carriage. Only working at a desperate rate brought me some relief and whilst daylight lasted I never left my easel.

Mr Smith always behaved excellently towards me, but suffering makes one unreasonable and I had begun to suspect that because my slavery was profitable to him he was not trying to shorten it but was seeking in some underhand way to prolong it as much as possible. Sarah, the old Scotchwoman, who had in the beginning frankly avowed her detestation of the French to me, softened her heart to my captive state and became my greatest friend. She was really a most excellent woman, full of kindness and concern for me.

At the beginning of the spring of 1813 I was so low that I began to neglect my painting. Soon a complete lack of appetite and an inability to sleep brought on an illness which forced me to take to my bed for several days.

'My dear friend, don't be downcast,' said Mr Smith every evening before he retired, 'remember my concern for you and that I won't neglect any plan that might help you get back to France.'

'You know the plan,' I replied, 'I only need to find travelling companions.'

'An easy thing to do in a large town like Portsmouth, to unearth French prisoners hiding there after escaping from the hulks, always assuming there are any. I'm not a Bow Street runner, you know!'

'Still, you boasted that you always succeed in whatever enterprise you undertake. I've been waiting for a whole year.'

'Upon my word,' he replied one day, 'I think I've had a good idea. I'll ask my gilder to bring me together with his cousin the smuggler.'

'What good will that do, since those villains aren't to be trusted?'

'What you say proves that it's hardly surprising that I didn't think of this idea before, since you yourself don't yet understand it. Be patient and listen, I'll be brief. My opinion of smugglers' ways hasn't changed and I think it would be utter folly to trust them, but that doesn't stop us making use of these villains, as you so rightly call them. They alone could tell me, firstly, if there are any escaped Frenchmen in Portsmouth and next, where they are.'

'Ah! My dear Mr Smith,' I exclaimed, shaking my host's hands in gratitude, 'what an excellent idea! Yes, get intelligence from the smugglers.'

'And so as not to arouse their suspicions,' continued Mr Smith, 'I'll tell them that I know a Frenchman who's not rich enough to hire a boat on his own and wants to meet some of his countrymen who wish to get to France.'

'Perfect! It couldn't be better.'

A week later Mr Smith came and announced in a manner combining sadness and triumph that he had succeeded in obtaining from some smugglers the address of three recently escaped Frenchmen who were preparing to cross the Channel. My joy at this news can be imagined.

I could contain my impatience no longer. Despite the danger that the step entailed I decided to lose no time in seeking out my intended companions. When night came I took a carriage and went to them. They had been warned beforehand of my arrival and received me like a friend. Without any delay we began talking of the serious business we had in hand. They informed me that they had the greatest confidence in the smugglers to whom our enterprise had been entrusted and that the only thing keeping them in Portsmouth was lack of money. They expected to receive funds from France in a few days and as soon as they had them they would set sail.

'If that's the only obstacle preventing your escape,' I said to them, 'I can easily remove it. I have far more money than is needed to satisfy the smugglers' demands. But that's not the difficulty for me. The uneasy part of our scheme, for me at least, is the distinct lack of good faith on the part of smugglers. You judge them too favourably. Here's what I know of them.'

I then disclosed to my new friends the information that the merchant captain had given to Smith and which he had carefully passed on to me.

'After all, gentlemen,' I continued, 'what does it matter if these men are cheats and murderers, as long as we're forewarned and on our guard? If we each have a good pair of pistols I'll answer for our success.'

'Will you get the weapons for us?' asked one of the Frenchmen.

'Nothing easier; I'll do it.'

'Well then, what prevents us fixing a day for our enterprise?'

'The sooner the better for me. Warn me a few hours in advance and I'll be ready.'

I then left my address with my associates and took my leave. These fellow-countrymen thrown in my way by a lucky chance, or so it seemed, were called Lemonier, Lebosec and Vidal. All three were privateers. They had been taken by the English towards the end of a profitable cruise and having sent their prize in to port, each of them found himself possessed of a fairly large capital in Bordeaux. I could advance money to them without particular risk for our common escape; I was in such haste to regain my freedom that I would have done so even if I were never to see the money again.

The next morning I received a note from my associates informing me that the smugglers were busy with an urgent venture and would not be able to help us for a fortnight. This delay dejected me greatly and seemed a bad omen. At this juncture Sarah fell dangerously ill and Mr Smith was obliged to employ another servant to replace her for the time being. This little incident made us uneasy and above all it was awkward, because my host was himself obliged to bring up my meals since he did not know the new woman sufficiently well to risk confiding in her.

It can easily be imagined that hiding the presence of a stranger from a servant in a house as modest as Smith's was a complete impossibility. The new servant, whose name was Ducket, had not been more than three days in the picture dealer's house before she had guessed that he was harbouring and escaped Frenchman from the hulks.

Mr Smith made the best of the matter by confiding to Ducket what she already knew, whilst trying to make this appear like a valuable mark of his trust. Although Ducket always showed herself obliging towards me I took an inordinate dislike to her. Why, I could not have said. Mysterious presentiments exist without any explicable reason. Much as one tries in vain to dismiss them and is annoyed at oneself for listening to them, they should never be neglected.

'Is it true, sir,' said Ducket one day as she was cleaning my room, 'that government pays a reward of five pounds to anyone who gives an escaped Frenchman up to the Board of Transport?'

I was perturbed and astonished by the question. I answered, 'Yes, Ducket, it's true. You need only denounce me and you'll get the money.' After a short silence, I continued with a smile, 'Are you thinking of giving me up to the authorities?'

'Oh! Sir!' she exclaimed with a blush. 'What an opinion you must have of me!'

After finishing her work Ducket left me, making her most gracious curtsey as she went. I began to ponder.

'Why shouldn't that woman betray me?' I said to myself. 'She's English, she has no concern for any Frenchman and she may be as treacherous and venal as most of these creatures who work as charwomen. However, if she were thinking of betraying me, she would never have ventured to put that question to me. Bah! Why not? I think she's treacherous but she could equally well be dim-witted. She might have been afraid of making a mistake and knowing that no one could inform her better than myself, was foolish enough to ask me.'

'Then, after all, it might not have been so artless on her part. That frankness might have taken me in, if it weren't for the inexplicable aversion I feel for the woman and the fact that she frequently gossips with the butcher over the way, who is a friend of Curtis. Some slyness is so brazen that one needs to be suspicious beyond measure to detect it. Yes, definitely, the more I think of it, I've stayed here too long. I should have forsaken the house on the day Ducket came and taken refuge at the inn where my new friends Mercadier, Lebosec and Vidal are lodging. As soon as Mr Smith returns I'll put this plan into effect.'

As I was leaning on the window sill, reflecting in this manner, my eyes strayed past the curtains into the street and I suddenly saw Ducket leave the house. 'She's going to betray me!' I thought. I dashed downstairs, opened the street door and began boldly following the servant. To this day I still wonder how I could have been so foolish, after having continued for nearly a year without going abroad. I was so taken with the idea, a certainty in my mind, that Ducket was betraying me, that it was no surprise to catch sight of her at the corner of the street talking to a man whom I instantly recognised as Abraham Curtis. I knew all I needed to know; the butcher had blabbed. I hurriedly retraced my steps and as I reached the door I found myself face to face with Mr Smith, who was coming home from the opposite direction. The sight of me drew from him an exclamation of surprise, almost fright.

'Are you mad, my friend?' he said when we were indoors.

'I admit I've been extremely foolish,' I replied, 'but fortunately luck has been with me and has saved me from the hulks.'

'From the hulks! What's happened?'

'Your maid Ducket wanted to earn the five pounds reward offered to anyone who hands over a Frenchman.' Then in a few words I related to Mr Smith what I have told the reader.

'Oh! The slut!' exclaimed my excellent host, colouring with rage, 'I'd like to kill her.'

'That punishment would be a trifle hard,' I replied with a smile, 'but with your permission I'll give the wretch the fright she well deserves.'

'Do whatever you like,' exclaimed Mr Smith, in a passion, 'the foul slut! Don't spare her.'

My excellent host was still speaking when Ducket returned. Her manner was as calm as if she had not committed a vile betrayal, but her shortness of breath proved that if she did not much mind her guilt she was anxious not to be suspected.

I knew that she had run all the way back from her meeting with Abraham Curtis.

'Ducket,' I said politely, 'would you kindly come up to my room for a minute. I need your help to put up a picture.'

'Certainly, sir,' she replied, following me with a crafty expression. As soon as we were in my room, and Mr Smith had followed us, I closed the door, took out my pistol and turned towards Ducket. She went deadly pale.

'My dear girl,' I said, 'it's entirely natural that you should want to earn five pounds, which I was however going to give you when I left the house. Only you shouldn't be surprised that for my part I want to keep my freedom. If you need to pray, be quick about it. You've less than five minutes to live.'

'Yes, yes, blow out her brains!' exclaimed Mr Smith, whose rage was so high that he took this shamming for reality, 'blow out her brains! She fully deserves it!'

To this day I cannot recall the scene without amusement. Ducket, believing her hour had come, fell at my feet and begged for mercy.

'No! No mercy!' said my host. 'Shoot her! Shoot her!'

I raised my pistol and the wretch, thinking this was the end, uttered a hollow moan and fainted away.

'Quick, fetch water and smelling salts,' I exclaimed.

'Not to bring that slut round,' said Smith, 'let her die, and serve her right.'

'That's not at all what I want. I don't want to take the poor girl's life. She has information which may be valuable to me. Help me, Mr Smith, if you please.'

'Yes, we must know what we're about. Yes, you're right; bring her round.'

My attentions succeeded and five minutes later Ducket revived.

'When are the authorities coming?' I demanded.

'Tonight, sir, at ten o'clock,' she replied, trembling.

'You're not trying to deceive me?'

'Why should I lie when I'm going to die?' replied the wretch, even more convinced that I was serious in my performance.

'Good,' I said. 'You've told the truth and saved your life. For the time being you'll stay in this room. Don't go near the window to shout for help or it'll be the worse for you.'

'Well,' I said to Mr Smith, 'what shall we do now? To my mind, my only course is to go and join my companions at the inn.'

'Upon my word, it worries me to see you going out in broad daylight, but I agree. You can't stay here any longer. I'll go and get a carriage. Keep an eye on that slut Ducket till I return.'

*Garneray threatens
to kill Ducket.*

CHAPTER XXV

*An interesting meeting • An unwise drinking bout • Jeffries
the smuggler • A bargain • An ambush • A murder • We
sight France • Back to the hulk*

HALF AN HOUR LATER I arrived without any incident at the inn
where Mercadier, Lebosec and Vidal were lodging and told them of my
misadventure.

'You came just in time,' they said, 'we were about to write and let you know that
the smugglers are ready.'

'Well, then,' I said, 'let's leave tomorrow.'

About six o'clock the next evening Mercadier, Lebosec, Vidal and myself were
coming to the end of a lavish meal in the company of the four smugglers who were
our confederates. I can only say that the example I had before my eyes did nothing
to dispel the prejudices that Mr Smith had raised in me against the Honourable
Corporation of Smugglers. Their faces proclaimed their natures. From a couple of
miles off they would have made you think of the gallows. A closer inspection
showed that our smugglers combined their tell-tale features with the most typical
demeanour and picturesquely cynical speech imaginable.

Our meal, which had been going on since ten in the morning, had put these
honest rovers into a very good humour and caused them to shed some of their
habitual caution. They dropped hints, winked and nodded at one another and I
caught them exchanging mysterious leers. They were plainly delighted with the
stroke of luck that had delivered us into their hands and had already planned what
to do with us. The leader of these villains was called Jeffries and it was he who gave
his men the word to go.

'Now lads,' he said, 'we must set to work. We'll drink a health to these gentlemen
with one more glass of brandy, and then we'll be off.' As he spoke, he filled up one
of those pewter vessels containing half a pint which are used for beer in English
public houses, and continued, 'Gentlemen, I drink to the success of our
undertaking! I'm sure you'll join me in that.'

As he said this, he indicated an enormous earthenware vessel that the pot-boy
had brought in. It was full of gin. My friends Mercadier, Lebosec and Vidal were
already heated from over-much drinking and hailed the toast enthusiastically. With
the intention of showing themselves as valiant as the English smugglers each of
them poured himself half a pint of gin.

'Gentlemen,' I said sharply, 'in heaven's name, be reasonable and leave that gin alone! Don't forget that we need all our wits about us.'

'Bah!' said Mercadier, seeing Jeffries looking wryly at him, and raising his glass to his lips, 'drink and privateering go together!'

'I'm as much of a privateer as you are, Mercadier,' I replied, 'and Surcouf who was my commander reckoned I was one of the most reliable men in his crew. Don't treat me as a novice. I've seen drinking bouts in the Indies and I know what drinking is. Well, I tell you again, after seven hours at the table, that gin will finish you.'

'Ah! So you sailed under the great Surcouf,' exclaimed Mercadier, interrupting me. 'Well, my dear sir, you won't take it ill that I drink to the illustrious Breton's health. To the glory of the French navy!' As he spoke and before I could stop him, he briskly raised his glass to his lips and drained it at one draught.

'A health to Surcouf!' repeated Vidal and Lebosec, following Mercadier.

'And you, sir, won't you drink?' asked Jeffries in a peculiar tone.

'Thank you, no,' said I, pretending to stagger, 'I can take no more.'

'You're not used to liquor, as it seems?'

'True. I feel very poorly.'

My answer seemed to please the smuggler and I thought I saw a conspiratorial glance between him and his companions.

'Farewell for now, gentlemen,' he said, 'we'll make ready for putting to sea. For your part, you must leave here at nightfall so that you'll be at the spot fixed for our meeting by ten or eleven.'

'Agreed!' replied Mercadier.

'You haven't forgotten the landmarks I told you of and the road to follow?'

'I remember them exactly,' I replied. 'Never fear, we're word-perfect.'

Once the smugglers had gone I railed at my companions for their sottishness and told them what I had noticed and how I was convinced that the smugglers were plotting against us. My tone of conviction appeared to make a deep impression on them and they assured me that from that moment onwards they would act with the greatest caution.

'And anyway, my dear friend,' said Mercadier, 'what have we to fear, armed as we are with a pair of pistols and a cutlass each?'

'*Pardieu!* If it comes to it I hope you won't be incapable of using them because you're drunk.'

'Be easy on that point. You, Vidal, and you, Lebosec, you're both capable aren't you?'

'That we are!' stammered Vidal and Lebosec in slurred tones that gave the lie to their words.

The rendezvous fixed by the smugglers was at a little inlet about three leagues from Portsmouth. An hour later I said to my companions, 'Come, it's dark now, let's be off.'

After paying our score to the inn-keeper who, let it be said, charged extortionately for his dubious hospitality, we carefully examined the priming of our pistols and set out.

I had hoped that the fresh air and the march would settle my companions' exuberance. It was not so at all. The further we went their intoxication, though scarcely apparent at first, became disturbing. We were scarcely out of the town before Mercadier began bawling the *Marseillaise* at the top of his voice.

'Shut your mouth, you fool,' I said furiously, ' do you want to give us away to the English?'

'The English!' repeated Mercadier, 'what do I care for 'em. Let 'em come, I'll show 'em. I've got my pistols, haven't I? Cowards, they won't come…'

Vidal and Lebosec were scarcely better. They were talking of heading for London, seizing the Tower and, once in control of it, of bombarding the capital of Great Britain into unconditional surrender. My discomfort can be imagined. At one point I was tempted to retrace my steps and go back to Mr Smith's. I would certainly have done so had I not been afraid of Ducket.

The landmarks that the smugglers gave us were so precise that I had not a moment's hesitation about the road we had to follow. At eleven o'clock we arrived at the place fixed for our rendezvous. The little open boat in which we were to cross the Channel was hidden in an inlet at the foot of a cliff.

'Now then, gentlemen,' said Jeffries, 'the night's dark, the sea's fine and the wind's set fair. Let's waste no time, but get aboard.' Then he noticed that my companions, heavy with drink, were having difficulty getting into the boat and continued with, 'Ahah! It seems that gin's not your usual tipple. Still, no matter, a few hours sleep and fresh sea air will set you to rights. Stretch yourselves out in the bottom of the boat.'

Five minutes later the bows of our boat were cutting through the swell, pushed onwards by a fresh south-west breeze. I cannot describe the terrible uneasiness that gripped me. I expected to be attacked at any moment. My pistols were at full-cock and I kept my hands on them whilst trying to catch some word or tone which would let me take the offensive first. But the smugglers spoke so low, if they spoke at all, that no sound came to me save the waves slapping in our wake.

An hour passed in this way and my apprehensions were beginning to abate when I seemed to hear a muffled whispering coming from forward. A little later I heard a smuggler climbing carefully over the thwarts of the boat, for we were then under sail, and apparently coming our way.

'Who's there?' I cried, raising my pistols.

'Damn me, don't be afeared! You can be sure it's not the preventives,' answered a voice, which I recognised as that of Jeffries.

'I'm not afraid,' I replied, 'but don't come any further, if you please. You might hurt my friends by treading on them.'

Jeffries gave no answer, save an oath and went back to his place. An animated conversation shortly broke out between him and his companions but in such low voices that I could not make out a single word.

'*Ma foi*,' I thought, 'I'm foolish to be worried about such a little thing. After all, what have I to fear? An attack? But I have my pistols and my cutlass. Yes, but there are four of these villains and I have only two shots. *Pardieu*, I've an idea. I'll take the pistols from that sot Lebosec, who's snoring next to me. In that way I'll at least be able to face them all.'

Another hour passed without incident. The moon, which had until then been hidden by clouds, began to gleam through from time to time when the wind swept the horizon clear.

'See here, my friend,' said Jeffries, the leader of the gang, during one of these clear intervals, 'you know we don't need you for the meantime. If you're tired, make yourself easy and sleep.'

'No, thank you,' I replied drily, 'I prefer to stay awake.'

'All right! Then, let's talk. It'll help to pass the time.'

'Thanks for suggesting it. I'd rather just think.'

'You might, but I'd rather talk. I've a bit of business to settle with you and you'd best listen.'

'Business? Tell me about it.'

'I will, in very few words. But one question first. Do you know what punishment we smugglers risk if we're caught carrying escaped prisoners to France?'

'Perfectly. They hang you.'[118]

'That's right. I'm glad to see you're well up in English law. Aye, I'm glad, because that's a help in what I've got to say.'

'Now then,' I exclaimed, beginning to grow impatient, 'leave off chattering and come straight to the point. If I'm not mistaken, you do have a point and something in mind.'

'Right! Why go round the bush when we, that's me and my mates, I mean, are on the right track. Here it is in a couple of words. We asked you for ten pound each, forty pound the lot, to carry the four of you to France. Now, you'll agree that's not dear. Others in the trade ask twice as much.'

'You should have asked more. As for that, it doesn't matter. Yes, I agree, you were very fair in what you asked. So?'

'Well, we were so easy with the price of your passage because we reckoned on reaching France without running the least danger, thanks to our skill and cunning.'

'Well, so much the better, and I hope that'll be the case.'

'Only being careful and having done it before ain't enough. Them as are in with us must help us and back us. Can we count on you?'

'My dear Jeffries, this is all idle talk. I don't know why you ask such a question. It's perfectly clear that we have the same interests. In anything to do with all our safety you can count fully on our help.'

'Very good! Very good! Bear with me, I'm coming to the point. Now I think, and my mates are of the same mind, that it'd be wise for you all to change your clothes so that any English vessels we run across when daylight comes won't see that you're French.'

'I must say that I don't see the use of it. We can hide ourselves at first, but if any ship comes close enough to see the cut of our clothes, we'll be taken anyway. However, if you insist on our disguising ourselves, I see no reason not to humour you.'

'Spoken like a good honest lad,' said Jeffries. 'I'll take your word for it.'

'But what clothes shall we put on instead of our own?'

'I thought you'd ask that and here's my answer. All our clothes are in the chest in the boat, where we keep our things. Choose any you like.' Then he added, 'Only, after we've been so obliging to you, you'll be far too gentlemanly to use our clothes without paying us a little trifle.'

'Ah! Very good, I begin to see what you're after. And how much might that trifle be?'

'The right price. What d'you expect? Four pair o' shoes, ten pound; hats, six pound; jackets, forty pound; trousers, twenty pound; neckerchiefs, five pound. Eighty one pound in all but, because we're partial to you, we'll say eighty. How's that suit you? What d'you think?'

'You're a generous man, Jeffries, with an endless store of wit. Ships cruising about to spy on the cut of our clothes; your tailor's bill for disguising us; with your jovial humour you'll never be bored. Thanks for diverting me just now.'

'Listen here, Master Frenchman,' exclaimed Jeffries menacingly, 'I warn you, I don't care for being made a game of!'

'What! You mean to tell me you were speaking seriously? No, you're still joking…'

'I'm serious, you French dog,' shouted the smuggler violently, 'and if you don't deliver the eighty-one pound I'm asking for, we'll sling you overboard.'

I maintained my coolness and answered the villain, 'You're very much mistaken, my dear Jeffries.'

'We'll see about that. Come on, lads!' said the smuggler, making a lunge towards me.

In the moonlight I could see the blade of a knife gleaming in his hand. I stood up to my full height and pointed my pistols at the villains.

'Another step and you're dead!' said I. At the sight of my pistols the smugglers stopped hastily and Jeffries let out a yell of rage.

'You didn't expect this, did you, you precious lot of butchers? I know how to deal with your sort. I knew too much about your tricks to come on board without taking precautions. There's four of you and I've got a bullet for each. You managed to fuddle my friends with your gin, but I'm well able to keep you at bay till they wake.'

'Those dogs you call friends won't be awake for a long while yet,' said Jeffries, regaining his calmness and audacity, 'because I mixed a draught with their gin. You wait. You'll see.'

At this confession I was strongly tempted to shoot the rogue, but I reflected that on a rolling boat in the darkness it was highly likely that I might miss and then all four might hurl themselves on me at once and succeed in disarming me. I judged that it would be wiser to stand guard over my companions and wait for daybreak. Jeffries seemed to guess my thought and spoke again mockingly.

'You poor fellow,' said he, 'you're bound to fall asleep as well. When that happens, I swear we'll heave you overboard. You can have a word with the fishes at the bottom of the sea.'

Without taking my eyes for a second off the smugglers in the bows, I began to kick my companions who were stretched out in the bottom of the boat. All I could elicit was a few incoherent words. With my enemies in front of me I thought I was safe from any surprise, not thinking that my back was turned to the smuggler at the tiller. I was to pay dearly for this carelessness.

Day could not be long in coming. That idea kept my spirits up and made me look on my position with a certain resignation. Then I saw that Jeffries and his companions were moving from their positions in the bows.

'Jeffries,' I called out, 'have a care what you're about! Remember I'm watching you and I'm ready for anything.'

'You're position's too strong for me to think of attacking you,' answered the smuggler, 'we'd do well to come to some agreement. Perhaps I was hard with you and my demands were a bit steep. Now then, see here, let's make a fresh bargain on both sides and end our differences.'

'Since I'm not afraid of you in any way, I'd rather part with a little money than come to blows. I agree that the ten pounds each we're paying isn't enough. Shall we settle for fifteen pounds?'

'Spoke like a proper gentleman,' replied the smuggler. 'Accepted with all my heart and on my honour I swear that from now onwards there'll be no more demands. Please to consider me your true friend.'

'Very well, Jeffries, I'm delighted that I no longer have to blow your brains out.

Now we've made peace, kindly tell me what drug you mixed with the gin my friends drank and how I can bring them round.'

'It's a certain quality of a particular type of Cayenne pepper. As for bringing 'em round, I know naught better than to pour cold water over 'em.'

'That's true, I should have thought of it earlier. I'll try it.'

I filled my tarred hat several times with seawater and poured it over my companions' faces. Soon they began to emerge from their lethargic sleep. Seeing that Jeffries' advice was producing good results I was leaning out of the boat again with my hat in my hand to fill it, when I received such violent blows, almost simultaneously on my head and shoulder, that I fell into the bottom of the boat with a cry of pain. At nearly the same moment something heavy seemed to be crushing my chest and I saw the glitter of a knife blade passing before my eyes like a flash of lightning.

Luckily I had kept a pistol in my left hand and I instinctively pulled the trigger. There was a burst of flame and the smuggler who had struck me from behind, the man at the tiller whom I had forgotten, fell upon me without a cry. He was dead, his skull shattered by the ball from my pistol. 'Help, Mercadier, Vidal, my friends! Murder!' I shouted, before losing consciousness.

When I came to myself again it was daylight. A melancholy sight met my eyes. In the bottom of the boat, soaked in blood, lay two bodies. One was that of Jeffries and the other of the smuggler I had shot. My companion Lebosec lay by my side, deathly pale, seemingly about to breathe his last. He had taken a blow from a cutlass which had laid open part of his shoulder and chest.

'Well, Garneray,' said Mercadier, who was holding my head between his knees, 'how do you feel?' It was a while before I could reply, for I was so stunned that I could take little notice of what was going on about me or what was said. At last I gradually recovered my senses.

'I was badly mauled,' I said, 'but I don't think I'm seriously wounded.'

'Oh! Nothing but a scratch! A thump with a cudgel, blood everywhere, but you don't die of that! Really, we are to blame,' added Mercadier shaking my hand, 'if it hadn't been for you it'd have been the end for us. Thank you, sir! Now you and I are friends for life.'

'What happened? What about the smugglers?'

'Don't talk, it'll only tire you. Your shot and your shouts stirred us up pretty sharply and there was a dreadful scuffle all round. We didn't even have time to use our pistols because the smugglers chucked themselves at us like wild beasts, but we managed to beat the villains off with our cutlasses. Jeffries got killed. Who did it, I can't say. It was so dark and we were so confused that we may well have won more by luck than courage. As for the other two smugglers, I'm afraid they seem to have gone overboard. In the end, apart from your wound and poor Lebosec's, all's well.

The wind keeps favourable, we've a fine boat, we made plenty of way last night and we've nothing to fear, barring any ships cruising. *Vive la France et la liberté!'*

I was exhausted by walking three leagues the previous night and by my loss of blood and so, after talking for a short while with my companions, I fell into a deep sleep.

'Sir,' said a voice in my ear at the same time as my arm was roughly shaken, 'wake up!'

'What is it?' I asked, opening my eyes and sitting up on one of the thwarts. The question was futile. I knew the answer when I saw a corvette, scarcely half a mile off, coming straight towards our boat.

'Oh! My God!' I exclaimed, 'the English! We're lost!'

'We don't know it's the English,' replied Mercadier. 'I woke you up to ask your opinion. Take a close look at that corvette…'

'I'm afraid I can see it only too well. But what's that in front of us?'

'That's the coast of France. There's the Montagne du Roule overlooking Cherbourg!' replied Mercadier in a dull broken voice.

'France! That land is France!' I exclaimed in ecstasy. 'Oh, my God! Protect us!' And I burst out sobbing. That hazy line, scarcely visible on the misty horizon, representing the land of my birth, raised emotions in me such as I had never before

We sight Cherbourg after defeating the smugglers.

felt in my entire life, a life so full of accidents and catastrophes.

'Well,' said Mercadier, 'and what do you think of the corvette?'

I dragged my eyes away from the coast of France and fixed them on the vessel.

'Alas! She's English!' I shouted in despair.

Quarter of an hour later we were once more prisoners of war. It was an odd chance, but the corvette, the *Victory,* which was instrumental in throwing me back into the hulks, was the same vessel which had saved me from pirates in the Indian Ocean fifteen years before.[119] Two days later, at nightfall, I was put back on board the *Vengeance.*[120]

Chapter XXVI

The Black Hole • The Jew again • A drunkard's folly •
In and out of the Black Hole • Peace • I am freed •
My farewell to Mr Smith • I return to my family

SOME SORT OF ENQUIRY was swiftly opened, as much into our escape as into our fight with the smugglers. But it soon became clear to the English that we had done no more than resist force with force and that the only crime of which we could be accused was that of not wanting to let ourselves be murdered. Once started, the enquiry was almost immediately abandoned.

As for myself, I had scarcely set foot on board the *Vengeance* before I was taken to the Black Hole where I stayed for a full fortnight. Nobody troubled about my wound in that time and I suffered horribly. I emerged as thin as a skeleton and in a deplorable state of health.

How I regretted not having stayed peaceably ashore and how I repented attempting my last escape! My lot was truly no longer bearable. I was deprived of the small cabin I once occupied on deck and the little space I had been allowed on the upper deck because of my duties as interpreter. I found myself mixed in with the prisoners without any means of taking up painting or mathematics again.

I had forgotten to say that before embarking with the smugglers I had left all the money I possessed, amounting to a substantial sum, with Mr Smith. Unfortunately, the wretched commander of the *Vengeance* was so severe that great difficulties attended our communications with the shore and Mr Smith found it impossible to send me any help. I was therefore reduced to the ordinary rations, that is to say I was dying of hunger.

This state of affairs had continued for a month when one morning I received a visit from the loathsome Abraham Curtis. I cannot express the horror I experienced at the sight of him. I felt as though I was in the presence of some hideous reptile and I had immense difficulty in restraining my anger.

'Garneray,' he said, 'let me reassure you that I've not come here to insult you in your misery. I'm far too indifferent to you for that...'

'Then why did you want to inform on me, you wretch,' I said. 'You're the cause of my arrest. Without your vile, vengeful character and the fear it raised in me, without your spies, I would never have thought of embarking for France and I'd still be in the house of that good man, Mr Smith.'

'I didn't want to have you arrested for revenge,' he said, 'since I have neither hate nor spite towards you. To me you're no more than a matter of business. Nothing else. I only sought to keep you in England so as not to lose a source of profit. Now, listen carefully to me. I don't like repeating myself.'

'Speak on. I'm ready to hear everything.'

'Oh, I won't pick and choose my words. You are miserable, without a farthing in your pocket, dying of hunger and a prey to your Captain's tyranny, so you won't refuse what I want from you.'

'Pictures, I suppose, my worthy Abraham?'

'As ever. Tomorrow I'll send you whatever you need to start work again, an easel, brushes, canvas and colours. And I'll ask my cousin to let you have your cabin again.'

'I'd be a fool to stand on my dignity with a knave like you,' I exclaimed. 'I accept your proposal. If I have my cabin and if I can communicate with the shore and get the things of which I'm deprived, it's a bargain.'

'From tomorrow you shall enjoy as much freedom as is compatible with being a prisoner. On that point, since you wouldn't be able to work without my help and because freedom can't be too dearly bought, I'll reduce the price I used to pay for your pictures.'

'It hardly matters. Do what you like.'

'By God, and I will! I'll buy your pictures at six shillings each.'

I was then so overwhelmed with misery that I accepted his offer unhesitatingly. Next day I resumed possession of my cabin.

At the end of 1813 and in the beginning of 1814 the English redoubled their ill-treatment and poured insults ceaselessly upon us. Every day brought intelligence of some fresh reverse for French arms and our defeats made our tormentors immeasurably insolent.

Although my condition, materially speaking, was much less dire than that of my hapless companions, I was no less the butt of our gaolers' endless insults. Every moment I heard the Emperor and our armies spoken of with utter contempt; the French were poltroons, who turned tail and fled at the sight of an enemy; they were good for nothing but massacring children and violating women; shot and shell were wasted on them when a few blows with a stick would do, etc., etc. It was enough to make one mad with rage.

One day in April I went up on deck early, as was my habit, to start work. The boatswain of the *Vengeance*, who had a grudge against me because I had refused to paint his portrait, approached me and hailed me mockingly.

'You lad, did you serve in the Imperial Navy?' said he, staggering as he did so, and with a voice that showed he was drunk.

'Yes, I've often had the pleasure of seeing the British flag strike to the *Tricouleur*,' I replied coldly.

'Well, if you served in the Imperial Navy, you'll know how the French salute the English. So, salute me!'

'I don't follow you, sir.'

'Down on your knees, you rascal, and abase yourself like a Frenchy to a British tar! Quick, on your knees and salute!' With a lewd, coarse action the drunkard turned his backside towards me.

'Salute, you scoundrel,' shouted a sailor who was as drunk as his superior, taking me by the collar and trying to force me to my knees. I ought to have treated such an insult with contempt, but my patience was exhausted. I struck the sailor who had dared to seize me so violently with my fist that he fell down three paces away, his face all bloody.

'Kill the Frenchy,' cried several Englishmen, instantly surrounding me. Fortunately a handspike was near at hand. I seized it in a fury, let loose a cry like some wild beast, and hurled myself at the English soldiers and sailors in an explosion of all the anger that had so long festered inside me.

There followed a furious and frightening brawl. I felt no pain and my sole idea was to do as much damage as I could to these cowards who stooped to such despicable abuse of those in their power. If the Captain had not come on the scene

Garneray breaks his easel and brushes.

I do not know how it would have ended. Perhaps with my death.

At the sight of their Captain the Englishmen scattered and left me, covered in blood and bruises. The Captain swiftly consigned me to the Black Hole. In all my life I cannot remember having felt as disheartened as I was at that moment.

'*Ma foi*', I said to myself, 'it seems I wasn't born to be happy. The sooner I'm done with either prison or life itself the better for me. Once I'm out of the Black Hole I swear that not a day shall pass without my trying to escape. In that way I'll either see France again or have my skull cracked. One way or another my fate will soon be settled.'

Every morning in the damp narrow pit that the English called the Black Hole, though it would have been more logical to call it a well, the gaoler brought me a stale heavy lump of bread, which was deemed enough to support me till the following day.

On the fifth day of my confinement he came earlier than usual.

'You can come out,' he said most politely. 'You're free.'

I rose with difficulty and set off for the upper deck as quickly as my strength allowed to breathe the fresh air. When I reached the gun-deck I was astonished to see my companions acting like madmen, dancing, embracing, weeping and whooping incoherently. For a moment I thought I was in a dream.

'What's happening?' I asked a comrade, an artillery sergeant who, like myself, had been nearly ten years in the hulks. He made no reply, but threw his arms round my neck and hugged me to himself, whilst two streams of tears trickled from his eyes and soaked my cheeks. I was more and more astounded and repeated my question.

'Peace has just been signed and we're free!' he replied in a choking voice. I am not ashamed to confess that I broke down and wept at these words. My joy was so overwhelming that my breath was taken away. Running like a madman, I hurled myself up to my cabin on deck where I began breaking my brushes and smashing my easel to pieces.

A week later I was in the excellent Mr Smith's house. My happiness was so complete that I no longer felt either hate or anger towards the English. I was to see France again and to dwell on the past was useless. Even the name of Abraham Curtis did not once cross my mind.

On 16th April I embarked for France. I shall not try to express the depth of my feelings when I came ashore at Cherbourg. Some joys are so immense as to be almost unbearable and cannot be described. I wrote to tell my family of the day and time of my arrival.[121]

On the 20th I saw Paris again after an absence of twenty years. By an odd coincidence, an accident on the road caused the route of the coach to be changed and I went in at the very same *barrière* by which I had come out. In the Allée des Veuves I saw a man who appeared to be expecting someone. It was my father. He had altered much, but in my heart I knew it was he. At last, on the same spot where twenty years before he had kissed me farewell, my father clasped me in his arms.

*Garneray reunited
with his father.*

Epilogue, 1814-1858

GARNERAY WAS RELEASED during the emptying of the hulks and prisons that began very shortly after Napoleon's abdication in April 1814. The prisoners who were subsequently brought to Britain during the Hundred Days and after the battle of Waterloo were imprisoned or paroled ashore and the hulks were never used again for prisoners of war. *Prothee, Crown, Vengeance, Pegase*, the vessels known to Garneray, were all broken up by 1816 and most of the floating prisons that had once been such a formidable feature of ports from Chatham to Plymouth soon ceased to exist. Shore prisons were sold off or their leases allowed to lapse, castles and buildings adapted to receive prisoners of war reverted to emptiness and decay, whilst Dartmoor Prison, the one great reminder in the twenty-first century of the Napoleonic period and its captives, remained void for a generation until reopened as a convict prison in 1850.

During the sixty years after Waterloo practically nothing of any historical value was written in English about prisoners of war and by the time interest in the subject revived only the elderly could recall that as children they had seen or known of French prisoners in Britain, usually in some parole town whose historian would record a few accessible facts on the subject. Remembrance of the men on parole and their families faded, whilst the memory of the prisoner of war hulks dwindled into almost total oblivion. If prison ships meant anything to the English popular imagination in the second half of the nineteenth century the idea was undoubtedly derived from the convict hulks that overshadow Dickens's *Great Expectations,* all the more terrible because never described and only once glimpsed by the narrator.

When he emerged from the hulks in 1814 Garneray was thirty-one years old. He later claimed that he had intended to return to sea after his release and had taken up painting as a temporary expedient when the examinations that would have qualified him as a captain *au long cours* were postponed because of the events of 1815. '… This temporary measure still continues; such is fate,' he wrote ironically many years afterwards. However, the temptations of a seafaring life were perhaps not great when compared with the opportunity to join his two brothers and his sister, all artists, and his father, still active as a painter, and make use of their contacts in society and the world of the arts.

It might have been expected that after the success of his first two books Garneray would have written an account of his long artistic career from the restoration of the French monarchy to the reign of Napoleon III, but the promisingly titled *Scènes Maritimes faisant suite aux Pontons* is largely a collection of rather tedious adventure tales, in the manner of his *Voyages, aventures et combats,* and contains very little of genuine autobiographical interest. This is unfortunate, for though the facts of Garneray's life over the forty years following his release can be assembled from details of commissions, correspondence, exhibitions, travels, money matters and changes of address, a first-hand account of his career and the circles in which he moved, especially the political ones, would have been valuable.

Like most of his fellow-citizens, Garneray appeared to accommodate himself pragmatically to the restored regime. He asserted in *Scènes Maritimes* that a painting dating from 1815, *The Landing of the French Émigrés at Quiberon,* was acquired by *Monsieur,* the future Charles X, and led to commissions from Louis XVIII and members of the nobility, but this extremely early success and even the existence of the painting seem doubtful. Nevertheless in 1817 he won, in competition against distinguished rivals, the post of marine painter to the Duc d'Angoulême, who became the Dauphin on the accession of Charles X in 1824.

By the 1820s Garneray was already in the first rank of marine artists, rare specialists at that period in France. In 1820 he married Anne-Julie-Joséphine Cavaroz. The marriage proved to be childless and Madame Garneray seems to have devoted herself to promoting the career of the husband whom she referred to somewhat impersonally as 'Garneray' in surviving letters.

That career was a remarkable one in terms of the quantity and quality of the work produced, in respect of Garneray's versatility in different media, including engraving and aquatint, his scientific curiosity[122] and his determination to depict entire categories of maritime topography and activities systematically. His aquatints included a series of *Vues des côtes de France dans l'Océan et dans la Méditerranée* published over nine years from 1823. In oils he painted naval battles, historical genre scenes with naval or colonial themes, views of the ports of France and, over a lengthy period, a succession of canvases on which he displayed specific types of fishery 'with a truly documentary care'.[123]

The fisheries series contains some of the finest examples of Garneray's handling of atmospheric effects, such as *Dieppe boats fishing for herring.* Much was based on personal observation but Garneray did not shrink from depicting activities with which he was not familiar, such as the southern whale fishery, and managed to do so with considerable success. His celebrity, spread by engravings of his work, reached the United States where his pictures of the pursuit of the sperm and right whales were seen by Herman Melville.

'Who Garnery [sic] the painter is, or was, I know not', wrote Melville in 1851. 'But my life for it he was either practically conversant with his subject or else marvellously tutored by some experienced whaleman. The French are the lads for painting action.'[124]

Although Garneray claimed in *Mes Pontons* that he abhorred violence, he was in some respects a turbulent man; after an expedition to Navarino in 1828 to make sketches for his painting of the previous year's battle he quarrelled with Captain Reynouard who commanded the vessel that brought him back to France. On 12th August Garneray shot and mortally wounded Reynouard in a duel at Toulon.[125]

In 1832 Garneray became the curator of the musée de Rouen, but his proposal in 1836 to rearrange and classify the gallery's collections, which included the possibility of disposing of some works of minor importance, created a storm which led to his departure in 1837. The following year Garneray began an association with the Sèvres porcelain factory during which he supplied and painted designs for plaques and dinner services, the most elaborate of the latter consisting of eighty-five pieces decorated with fishing scenes surrounded by marine emblems in gold and platinum on a blue ground.[126] In 1848, shortly after the abdication of Louis-Philippe, the factory terminated Garneray's employment.

A hundred and fifty years after the artist's death dismissals such as Garneray suffered in 1837 and 1848, together with other checks to his career, may look like the ordinary vicissitudes of a long and active life. Laurent Manœuvre has, however, pointed out that despite Garneray's talents and energy he received no public appointments after 1817 and although official commissions were awarded to him he did not share equally with his contemporaries in such patronage. His requests to accompany naval expeditions as an artist in a semi-official capacity were invariably turned down, the government rejected his manuscripts after long delays and even membership of the *Légion d'honneur* was not conferred on him until late in life. The reason was political; Garneray was not only a Bonapartist sympathiser but an active Bonapartist agent.[127]

As early as 1838 Garneray had rented a room under a false name in the St Lazaire district of Paris which became a centre for intrigue and correspondence between Louis-Napoleon and his adherents. The most notable of these was Persigny, the future Emperor's devoted schemer and Minister of the Interior from 1852 to 1854, a period that coincides with Garneray's late and brief official favour.[128] The extent and importance of Garneray's clandestine activities are unclear but early in 1852, shortly after the coup d'état by which the Prince-President Louis-Napoleon assumed effective, absolute power, Garneray was decorated with the long-delayed order of the *Légion d'honneur*. Later in the year he was commissioned to organise a mock naval battle on the Seine to celebrate the national festival on 15th August.

On 12th December 1852, within ten days of the decree that transformed the Prince-President into the Emperor of the French, Garneray was received in audience by Napoleon III, thanked for his services and 'promised a place'.[129]

The Emperor's promise does not appear to have been substantially fulfilled, apart from the payment of a small pension. Garneray continued painting and exhibiting until the year of his death, though with increasing difficulty as the effects of a 'tremblement sénile' became more pronounced from the early 1850s onwards. Requests he made to the Director-General of the *Musées impériaux* for the acquisition of his pictures by the state were politely declined and the artist complained that the works he exhibited were either skied or hung obscurely.

In December 1856 Garneray wrote to the Emperor, reminding him of his earlier promise, and in response received a commission in March 1857. Garneray was to be paid 3,000 francs to depict the episode in which Napoleon I on his return from Elba on the brig *Inconstant* passed a royalist vessel unrecognised. It was a subject that Garneray had previously painted in 1831 and a comparison of the earlier picture with the later version emphasises the decline in his powers.

At the age of seventy-four on 11th September 1857 Garneray died of apoplexy in his small apartment on the second floor at 24 Rue des Martyrs and was buried in Montmartre Cemetery. His artistic career had brought him no riches and his widow was left in distressed circumstances. To the enduring mysteries of the artist's life one dreadful enigma concerning Madame Garneray must be added. On the night of 13th January 1858 she was clubbed to death by an intruder who attempted to destroy her corpse by setting fire to the bedclothes. Nothing was stolen from the apartment and even the medals awarded to Garneray for his art were left untouched. The murderer was never caught.[130]

APPENDICES

APPENDIX A

PRISONER OF WAR HULKS AT PORTSMOUTH

Ship's Name	Rate & Guns	Origin & Year Launched	Dates as Hulk	Broken Up or Sold
Arve Princen (formerly *Heir Apparent Frederick*)	3rd, 74	Danish, 1788, taken 1807	1807–15?	1817 S
Assistance	See *Royal Oak*			
Crown	3rd, 64	British, 1782	Powder Hulk 1802–06 Prison hulk 1806–16	1816 BU
Guildford (formerly *Fame*)	3rd, 74	British, 1759	1799–1814	1814 S
Kron Princessen	3rd, 74	Danish, 1791, taken 1807	1807–14	1814 S
Marengo	3rd, 80	French, 1795, captured 1806	1806–13	1816 S
Niger (Hospital or Convalescent Ship)	5th, 32	British, 1759	1804?–13	1814 S
Pegase (Hospital Ship)	3rd, 74	French, 1781, captured 1782	Prison hulk 1794–1801 Hospital Ship 1801–15	1815 S
Princess Sophia Frederica	3rd, 74	Danish, 1775, taken 1807	1807–15?	1815 S
Prothee	3rd, 74	French, 1772, captured 1780	1795–1815	1815 BU
Royal Oak/ Assistance	3rd, 74	British, 1769 (renamed *Assistance* 1805)	1796–1815	1815 BU
San Antonio	3rd, 74	Spanish, 1785, captured 1801	1801–14 Powder Hulk 1814	1827 S
San Damaso	3rd, 74	Spanish, 1775, captured 1797	1800?–14	1814 S
Suffolk,	See *Sultan*			
Sultan/Suffolk	3rd, 74	British, 1775 (renamed *Suffolk* 1805)	1797–1816	1816 BU
Vengeance	3rd, 74	British, 1774	1808–16	1816 BU
Veteran	3rd, 64	British, 1787	1809–16	1816 BU
Vigilant	3rd, 64	British, 1774	1795–1816	1816 BU
Waldemar	3rd, 80	Danish, 1798, taken 1807	1812–16	1816 BU

This table may not be exhaustive since other vessels (not necessarily hulks) may have been used temporarily to house prisoners of war.[131] However all the principal hulks used from 1797 onwards are named above, the dates of their use being taken from David Lyon's *The Sailing Navy List,* with adjustments where later research gives differing periods. The dates of origin of the Danish vessels are the dates of building stated in *Papers presented to the House of Commons relating to the Expedition to Copenhagen, 1808.*

Not all vessels were occupied simultaneously and at times prisoners were moved *en masse* when major repairs were required or space had to be made for a fresh batch of men. For example, the prisoners on board the *Guildford* were shifted to the *Marengo* in February 1812 to enable the *Guildford* to be surveyed and the *Marengo* herself was taken out of service in 1813. At the end of 1811 the *Veteran* was cleared to receive approximately 400 of the 'miserables' (one of the names of the *rafalés*) from Forton Prison and Portchester Castle and it appears that this ship was, at that time at least, set aside for escapers and refractory prisoners.[132]

The *Niger* hospital ship may also have been known as the *Negro*, but occasional references to the *Negro* Prison Ship suggest that a vessel other than the *Niger* might have been used at some time as a separate hulk for black prisoners.

Garneray mentions that there were nine hulks moored in a line when he went on board the *Prothee* in May 1806. A drawing by his fellow-prisoner Duclos-Legris confirms this arrangement and indeed bears some resemblance to the compositions of Garneray's own paintings of the hulks. Later, when Garneray describes his stay on board the *Pegase* hospital ship he states that she was moored at the head of a line of eleven ships. All seventeen hulks on the table above can be identified from details given by the anonymous author of *Les Souvenirs d'un Prisonnier de Guerre*, who arrived at Portsmouth in May 1809. The Danish *Arve Princen* appears in his account (p. 15) under the name of *La Demie Princesse*, which suggests that *she* was locally called the *Half Prince*, much to the author's confusion. According to Garneray the Danish ships, surrendered to the British at Copenhagen in 1807, were moored in a line in front of Gosport.

In 1810 all the prison ships were directed to be paid off from the Royal Navy, with the exception of the *Assistance*, and put under the direct control of the Board of Transport. Each was to be commanded by a lieutenant earning 8s 6d a day and these officers were to be lent to the Board by the Admiralty. The lieutenants then serving in the hulks were allowed to keep their commands.[133]

APPENDIX B

FRENCH OFFICERS ON BOARD THE HULKS AND ON PAROLE

GARNERAY SAYS in Chapter I, 'It is needless to add that when the newcomer was an officer the English either denied his rank or took no account of it and treated him as if he were an ordinary seaman. Complete equality in suffering was the rule in these appalling prisons.' This is a considerable distortion of the truth when applied to the prison hulks as a whole. As a general rule, most officers of the army and navy were entitled to parole and remained just a short time on board till parole arrangements could be made. Privateer officers were subject to stricter rules and were not admitted to parole if the vessel in which they were taken was of less than eighty tons and mounted less than 14 carriage guns of at least four-pounder calibre.[134]

In certain hulks at least the officers were given separate quarters, termed the *demi-prison*. According to Lardier (*Histoire des Pontons*, p. 29) the *demi-prison* of the *Guildford* hulk at Portsmouth was at the after part of the upper deck. It appears from the anonymous *Les Souvenirs d'un Prisonnier de Guerre* (p. 14) that on board the *San Antonio* the hulk's French clerk or interpreter and the French assistant surgeon lived in the *demi-prison* with the officers not entitled to parole.

The officers found on any normal hulk would therefore have been those who were waiting to be paroled, those who refused to give their paroles, parole-breakers and other offenders, privateer officers not entitled to parole and occasional poor individuals without enough money to travel to their allocated parole towns. Certain hulks, particularly amongst those at Chatham, were appropriated to escapers, trouble-makers and parole breakers; officers there who had forfeited their rights to parole because of misconduct certainly suffered equally with the other ranks.

The rules relating to comings and goings by officers in parole towns are summarised with reasonable accuracy by the naval officer at Bishop's Waltham in Chapter XXIII but his statement that the regulations permitted 'any inhabitant who finds a Frenchman infringing them to attack him...' and that 'at least two thousand Frenchmen have been killed or wounded since they were put into strict execution...' is nonsense. There was a reward offered for the apprehension of prisoners who infringed the rules by straying beyond the permitted boundaries or who stayed out after the evening curfew and though many instances of assaults, disturbances and quarrels relating to such infringements can be found, serious incidents were rare. I have not encountered a single example of a prisoner who was murdered in these circumstances in a parole town. Every negative story concerning misconduct towards parole prisoners can be matched with accounts of hospitality and respect from individuals and local inhabitants generally.

APPENDIX C

GARNERAY'S SOURCES

THE ORIGINAL MANUSCRIPT of *Mes Pontons* no longer exists and it is not possible to say whether each example of plagiarism it contains was actually included by Garneray or inserted by an editor or ghost-writer. However, Garneray took full credit for the completed book and it is reasonable to assume that he was personally responsible for the entire text including the passages taken from other authors.

A uniform regime applied to all the British hulks, and memoirs by different prisoners are often remarkably similar in descriptions of daily life, rations and activities on board. However, in Garneray's case, entire passages which set the scene for *Mes Pontons* are not only similar but virtually identical to parts of Lieutenant Mesonant's *Coup d'œuil rapide sur les Pontons de Chatam,* which appeared in the *Revue Rétrospective* in 1837. For example:

Mesonant: Les prisonniers sont divisés par plats de six personnes, recevant leur pain, leur viande et leur soupe ensemble. Tous les ustensiles qu'on recoit pour prendre sa nourriture consistent en un simple bidon en fer-blanc, et rien de plus; ni cuillers, ni couteaux ni plats.

Quand les fournisseurs ont approvisionné

Garneray: Nous etions divisés par plats de six personnes, recevant notre ration en commun. Tous les ustensiles que l'on nous donnait pour prendre nos repas se résumaient en un simple bidon en fer-blanc, une gamelle; les cuillers, les fourchettes et les couteaux nous étaient inconnus.

le ponton pour un jour, ce qui se fait la veille de chaque jour, ou le jour même, ils ne se mêlent de rien, pas même la distribution des vivres...	Quand les fournisseurs anglais avaient approvisionné le ponton pour un jour, ils ne se mêlaient plus de la distribution des vivres...

Similar examples of passages lifted from Mesonant could be multiplied.[135]

Garneray's plagiarisms were not confined to accounts of life in the British hulks. In Chapter XIX of *Mes Pontons* he inserted the text of a letter allegedly addressed by French officers on board the *Vengeance* to the Council of the Regency. The letter was first published in 1823 in de Méry's '*Mémoires d'un officier français prisonnier en Espagne*' in which it appears as a protest sent from the hulks of Cadiz to the Spanish government. Plagiarism from this source draws attention to the fact that details of the genuine horrors suffered by prisoners in Spain would have been available from at least a dozen French authors to heighten Garneray's descriptions of life in the Portsmouth hulks.

Another writer, whose book must have been read and used by Garneray, was Maréchal-de-Camp René Pillet (1762-1816). His *Views of England, During a Residence of Ten Years; six of them as a Prisoner of War*, one of the earliest popular accounts of life as a prisoner of war in England, was first published in France in 1815. Pillet's Anglophobia was boundless and he ransacked the newspapers with demented enthusiasm for reports of crimes and depravities to help him depict an England in which drunkenness, adultery, incest, infanticide, parricide and the sale of wives were common adjuncts of domestic life, whilst children playing 'à la *criquette*' bashed out one another's brains with their bats. Pillet had had first-hand experience of life on parole and in the hulks at Chatham and his vague and unsubstantiated allegations that the British attempted to exterminate thousands of their captives by a deliberate 'system of murder and cruelty'[136] seem to have influenced Garneray's unfair description of the treatment of the sick. Pillet appears also to be the source of Garneray's story of the eating of the English Colonel's dog by the prisoners after the prize-fight on board the *Crown*.[137]

Alexandre Lardier's *Histoire des pontons et prisons d'Angleterre pendant la guerre du Consulat et de l'Empire*, published in 1845, has some resemblances to *Mes Pontons*. Lardier (1785-1857), a purser in the Imperial Navy, had been a parole prisoner at Abergavenny and was later a journalist. His book, which purports to be partially autobiographical, contains convincing circumstantial details, covers similar topics to Garneray in respect of the hulks, introduces many named but unidentifiable characters and has some obvious elements of fiction.

Lardier includes the horrific story of a traitor who betrayed an escape plot and was tattooed on the forehead by his fellow-prisoners, with words describing his crime. Garneray has a similar tale and Édouard Corbière (1793-1875), himself a former prisoner of war, included one in his novel *Le Négrier*, which was published in 1832. Francis Abell in his *Prisoners of War in Britain, 1756-1814,* appears to treat Corbière's story as a real historical incident and it has to be said in defence of Abell's judgement that Chapter IV of *Le Négrier* gives an account of prison life that is wholly convincing, including a remarkably frank description of homosexuality amongst the men at Mill Prison at Plymouth. A prisoner was actually punished by tattooing on board the *Sampson* hulk at Chatham in 1811 and the details were given by Mesonant in his *Coup d'oeuil rapide*. Garneray undoubtedly took the story from Mesonant. Was the tattooing of the man on board the *Sampson* a single act of ingenious savagery or did such events occur regularly? In this and other matters it is difficult to know when the various authors are copying one another and when they are giving independent corroboration about common practices.

Bonnefoux's *Mémoires*, detailing his life in the hulks at Chatham, were not published until 1900 but his depiction of Lieutenant Milne of the *Bahama* hulk is that of a savage martinet like Lieutenant Rose of the *Crown*, as described by Garneray Milne is alleged to have left the body of a drowned prisoner exposed on a mud-flat until it began to rot and stories of this type may have been part of a stock of hulk anecdotes circulating orally which Garneray drew upon to describe his second alleged attempt to escape from the *Prothee* and Bertaud's fate on that occasion.[138] However the source is more probably a literary one.

Lardier briefly covers the story of Tom Souville, the privateer of Calais. Henri Chevalier's *Vie et Aventures du Capitaine de Corsaire Tom Souville, Ses Combats – Ses Évasions 1777-1839,* was not published until 1895 but the whole of Chapter 17 in that book is a reprint of an interview, which first appeared about 1840, between the naval historian and popular novelist, Eugène Sue, and Souville in the latter's old age. This would have been available to Garneray when he wrote *Mes Pontons*. Souville recounted his imprisonment in the *Crown* hulk in 1812 and introduced its commander, Lieutenant Rose, under the name of 'Rosa', though he gives him a more rounded and human character than that of the grotesque described by Garneray. As a warning of what to expect if he attempted to escape, Rosa displayed to Souville the corpse of Dubreuil – *l'homme aux yeux mangés* – an escaped prisoner who had perished on a mud-flat and like Bertaud had become carrion for birds of prey.[139]

Other sources that Garneray used or which influenced him could doubtless be identified, but it is plain that at this period a very limited number of French popular authors wrote about the British hulks and were not too particular about historical accuracy or where their material came from. Many years later Garneray's derivative account, grown respectable with age, was treated as a primary source of information concerning the hulks by Francis Abell who also relied on Chevalier's *Tom Souville*, a vague late work, for additional material. W. Branch Johnson in his *The English Prison Hulks* (1970), the only book so far in English devoted exclusively to hulks both for criminals and prisoners of war, follows Abell and is similarly uncritical in his chapters dealing with Garneray and French prisoners.

The modern scholar of the prisoner of war system in the British Isles needs to be very wary in trusting even the earliest printed authorities. Most of such early sources appear to be more or less tainted with fiction but the literature is not large enough for the researcher to be able to discard any book on mere suspicion that it is not entirely true. In the end one must keep a cautiously open mind when judging authors such as Corbière, Lardier and Garneray who present valuable facts from their own experience mingled with fiction.

APPENDIX D

THE *RAFALÉS*

GARNERAY ended the description of his first day on board the hulks with a dramatic reference to Dante's *Inferno*. Life in the hulks was indeed severe and unpleasant by any standards, but it can be argued that in some ways it was not significantly worse than that endured by men on board contemporary warships at sea or in port in the navies of either France or Great Britain. Flogging or any direct physical punishment of prisoners of war was forbidden, the only legally permitted means of coercion for infringement of prison rules being confinement in the Black Hole and the reduction of rations.

Given the many examples of men who not only survived, but worked and even prospered in the hulks and prisons it is clear that the system under which they lived was not intrinsically bad when applied to prisoners who conformed to the rules and behaved rationally. The *rafalés* did not conform, their behaviour was irrational and the parts of the hulks and prisons where they were present took on an infernal character to a greater or lesser extent, much against the will of the British authorities who struggled with little success throughout the wars to check the *rafalés*, segregate them from normal prisoners and suppress the practices that caused them to arise.

As Garneray indicates, the root of *rafaléism* lay in the insatiable mania for gambling which afflicted many prisoners and led them when they had lost their money and personal possessions to part with their clothes, their bedding and their present and future rations. *Rafalés* subject to this madness were capable of acts that defied comprehension, such as gambling away money or food that might have relieved their immediate starvation.

There was a voluntary element to becoming a *rafalé,* though inherent lack of character or physical weakness brought on by the poor diet must have predisposed many to become easy prey to their neighbours. And here lies the obvious fact, not developed by Garneray, but made plain by Mesonant, that a *rafaleur* was needed to create a *rafalé*. No *rafalé* ever wrote an account of his prison life but it is clear that extortion and oppression, backed by violence from the *rafaleurs* with whom the *rafalé* had gambled, traded or pledged his rations, were commonplace in an existence of perpetual hunger aggravated by cold and exposure except in the mildest seasons.

Garneray adapted Mesonant's account of life at Chatham to describe the lives led by the *rafalés* on board the *Prothee*, through the words of Bertaud and Captain Thomas. The Chatham *rafalés* may have been more numerous than any Garneray encountered at Portsmouth, but wherever *rafalés* existed they formed a desperate class in prison society, individually preyed upon by other prisoners yet collectively menacing, a tribe of sub-humans but with superhuman traits. All contemporary descriptions of them are tempered with awe, though there are obvious inconsistencies in many accounts, since it is clear that a starving *rafalé* was usually in no condition to do any desperate physical acts.

The *rafalés* were widespread throughout the hulks and shore prisons and went under a variety of other names, including *Le Peuple Souverain, Misérables, Romains* and *Manteaux Impériaux,* the last two being allusions to the blankets, worn like togas by those fortunate enough to have some covering and supposed when lice-infested to resemble Napoleon's imperial robes dotted with emblems of bees.

Mesonant describes the *rafalés'* existence. 'When they have eaten nothing for several days they sell their entire rations for a month, two months or three months, for two or three shillings cash to the men called *rafaleurs*. They then return to their gambling and if they win some money they lay it out on a lavish meal of bread, meat and beer... On the other hand, if they lose, they return cursing their fate, and are forced to rely on their labour. In a place where everyone has just enough rations to prevent himself from dying of hunger, this labour is limited to roaming the decks and the places where rubbish is thrown, to pick up potato peelings, leaves of leeks, cabbage stalks and the heads of red herrings, with which they sustain their feeble existence. Hunger drives them even further; some have snatched the food from the pigs belonging to the commander of the hulk, which are kept in sties on the forecastle, and the commander has been obliged to station a sentry there to frustrate these prodigal sons and drive them away... Their labour also includes the theft of English property or, very rarely, taking their comrades' belongings. Their expedients sometimes lead them to prostitute themselves for the modest sum of two sous which they carry away to gamble with, after spending the night in the hammock of their obscene lover...'

When *rafalés* collapsed from hunger they were taken to the hospital and stayed for a few days where the *rafaleurs* could no longer seize their rations. If the hospital was full, they would insult the hulk's guards and officers and do anything to get themselves committed to the Black Hole, which they called the *Grand-Restaurant,* where their rations would be equally untouchable by the *rafaleurs.* If both these expedients failed and there was nothing left to scavenge, the starving *rafalés* as a whole would occasionally pour up into the *Parc,* beating mess tins and other vessels, and declare a *Banqueroute Générale,* a repudiation of all their obligations to the *rafaleurs.* They would then be attacked by the *rafaleurs* and usually forced to capitulate.

Mesonant describes how after deaths from hunger had occurred the surviving *rafalés* were sometimes forced by their companions to eat their rations. The urge to gamble was so overpowering that despite being watched over by *forts à bras,* armed with ropes to lash them, to ensure that they actually consumed their food, the *rafalés* still attempted to hide fragments of bread and meat between their naked thighs for later sale to finance their gaming. According to Mesonant they found buyers, whose hunger exceeded their disgust, for these loathsome morsels.

The agents at the prisons and the commanders of the hulks sent weekly reports of prisoners' deaths to the Board of Transport. The reports were effectively death certificates, but the amount of detail concerning the causes of death varied with the sources from which it came. Deaths attributed to 'debility' from the Portsmouth hulks and the prison system generally may indicate in many cases the starvation and weakness that were the attributes of the *rafalés.* Occasionally this is specifically stated; the word 'debility' is crossed through on a certificate relating to a prisoner who died in Portchester Hospital in January 1813 and another hand has written, 'Raffalie – From Nakedness & cold.'[140] In the reports that came from the prison at Valleyfield in Scotland there emerges the starkest and plainest picture of how the *rafalés* died. 'Debility from selling his Rations', 'Debility from the effect of selling Provisions and Clothes', 'From the effect of Cold having repeatedly Sold their Cloths & Hammocks' (this last example relating to four men who died in the same week in April 1812), and 'From the effect of want of due sustenance having Gambled away his rations for 14 days', all appear amongst similar entries.[141]

APPENDIX E

WOMEN ON BOARD THE HULKS

CONTEMPORARY RECORDS show that the wives of British officers frequently lived on board the hulks, as did the wives of soldiers and militia guarding the prisoners. There were also a few British women with official duties, such as Elizabeth Arnold, the matron of the *Pegase* hospital ship at Portsmouth in 1810, and a sempstress in the same ship.[142]

So far as women living amongst the prisoners are concerned, it is surprising that Garneray did not mention their existence before he came to describe the theatricals on board the *Vengeance* in Chapter XVIII. Their presence is a detail which (so far as I am aware) is not mentioned in any near-contemporary printed account of the hulks, and the fact that a few women can be identified on the registers of some vessels lends authenticity to Garneray's general account of prison life, if not to his narrative of particular events.

Garneray's description of the women living with their men in little screened-off enclosures sounds like the arrangements made by carpenters, gunners and other warrant officers who took their wives to sea in the Royal Navy. Such women in Royal Navy ships were very seldom named in muster rolls unless officially victualled on board and knowledge of their presence and occasional heroism in battle depends largely on unofficial accounts and memoirs.[143] The registers of the hulks provide a similarly small amount of official information about women and occasionally children associated with prisoners. Physical descriptions are sometimes given but this is exceptional. So far as can be deduced from the details of when and where persons were captured, most women in the hulks seem to have been the wives or followers of soldiers, rather than sailors, and were generally taken prisoner with their men, often during some large-scale action or surrender of troops. Wellington's successes in Spain appear to have swept up a number of Spanish women who passed through the hulks.

Garneray says, 'These women lived with the men whose lot they had sought permission to share…' This might be taken as meaning that the wives of ordinary prisoners could apply to come from France and join their husbands in the close confinement of the hulks. It was relatively common for the wives of French officers in England and of English officers in France to join their husbands on parole, but it seems improbable that the Board of Transport allowed women from abroad to enter the British hulks or shore prisons to join common soldiers and sailors who were already there. If such applications were ever made they must have been so infrequent that no general rule on the subject was necessary. It is much more likely that women captured with their men were merely permitted to remain with them in the hulks. An example from Chatham, though whether from the hulks or the shore prison is unclear, is the case of Margrett Hendricks who 'Accompanied her Husband to Prison' and died of 'Difficult Parturition' on 25th February 1813.[144]

The hulk registers show various examples of women leaving their men to return to France after varying times spent on board and they may have been encouraged to go when space was available in a cartel vessel.[145]

I have only seen one application by a wife to join her husband on a hulk. On 7th September 1813 Sir Thomas Thompson sought to intercede with the Board of Transport on behalf of the wife of Captain Daudett, a French prisoner at Chatham. Mrs Daudett wished 'to be allowed to live on board the Prison ship with her Husband'. The response was initially favourable; 'if the Board have no objection I think the Lady may be indulged'. However, a note on the back of the Board's letter reads, 'Inform Sir Thos. Thompson that being a British Subject this cannot possibly be allowed'. Mrs Daudett was clearly an Englishwoman who had married a prisoner, and not one of the humble women mentioned by Garneray; her case may be unique.[146]

Occasionally one knows how various women came to be in the hulks. Two officers and two privates of the little French force that landed near Fishguard in South Wales in February 1797 brought their wives with them. These women must have been prepared to endure the hardships and uncertainties of a campaign with their husbands and all later appeared as prisoners in the register of the *Royal Oak* hulk at Portsmouth.[147] One of them, Madame Grillère, later gave birth to a child either on board, or in one of the shore prisons.

In his *Relation de captivité,* Captain Charles-Rémi Beaujot, who was imprisoned on board the *Vigilant* at Portsmouth in 1811, mentions Sergeant-Major Barreau who was accompanied on board the hulk by his wife, an *'ancienne vivandière'*. When she was to be repatriated to France, Madame Barreau proposed taking her husband with her in 'an uncommonly large trunk' in which she had pierced a few holes for him to breathe through. He declined to go and she is said to have liberated a more enterprising privateer captain in this uncomfortable way. It is a good story.[148]

How many women were there on board the hulks? Some vessels had none, others a handful, but where women can be identified amongst hundreds or even thousands of persons who passed through individual hulks their numbers are insignificant. The wives of two soldiers can be found in the *Crown* out of about 1,200 prisoners shown on her register between 1806 and 1813. Some 2,400 prisoners passed through Garneray's hulk, the *Vengeance,* between 1806 and 1814; amongst these Therese Chapelle, the wife of a drummer, Annette Paquet, a corporal's wife, and Catherine Chaumay, described as 'Girl' in the register, are the only females named. The two women were both captured with their husbands in the Mediterranean on 24th August 1807 and sent with them on board the *Vengeance* on 5th April 1808. Both were discharged on 25th April 1810 'To the Nancy Cartel for France', leaving their husbands behind.[149] These women endured a total of two and a half years' captivity, including two years in the *Vengeance.* The date of the girl's entry on board the hulk or where she was captured are not clear but she was released on 25th March 1809.

Appendix F

Mortality of Prisoners of War

FRANCIS ABELL comments in his *Prisoners of War in Britain, 1756 to 1815* (pp. 40–44) on the statistics produced by Charles Dupin in 1816 to show that it was the policy of the British government to destroy prisoners by neglect or ill-treatment. The number of prisoners brought to Great Britain from 1803 to 1814 was said to be 122, 440.

Dupin's figures were:

Died in English prisons	12,845
Sent to France in a dying state	12,787
Returned to France since 1814, their health more or less debilitated	70,041
Balance (of healthy men)	26,767
	Total 122,440

The British government claimed the following:

Died in English prisons 10,341
Sent home sick, or on parole or exchanged, those under the last two categories
for the most part perfectly sound men 17,607
Balance (of healthy men) 94,492

Total 122,440

Dupin was in effect asserting that imprisonment resulted in the death of about 10 per cent of all prisoners, that a further 10 per cent were likely to die when sent home and that 57 per cent more had their health impaired. The British government's figures suggest a far more plausible mortality rate of about 8.4 per cent and that the majority of prisoners were reasonably healthy. Dupin's ideas were widely believed in France and similar exaggerations were assiduously promoted by Maréchal-de-Camp Pillet in his *Views of England, During a Residence of Ten Years*.

Garneray seems to follow Dupin and Pillet in passages he wrote relating to medical care and adds his own exaggerations. Of mortality on board the *Vengeance* he says, '*Twenty wretches would die every evening...*' To calculate the death rate relating to any particular hulk is to some extent a meaningless exercise since the population of the hulks was transitory, with many individuals passing briefly through to other hulks and the shore prisons or to go on parole. With this caveat it can be said that the true death rate on board the *Vengeance* was under twenty *a year*. Approximately 2,400 prisoners passed through the *Vengeance* between 1806 and May 1814, a period of about 8½ years, of whom 120 died and had their names marked with the letters 'DD', 'Discharged Dead', in the registers. Some died on board the hulk, but the majority were sent either to the Hospital at Forton Prison or to the *Pegase* hospital ship where they died. The average number of deaths was about 15 a year and the real mortality rate was approximately 5 per cent of the total number of prisoners.

APPENDIX G

PERSONS CONNECTED WITH THE HULKS

Pierre-Marie-Joseph, Baron de Bonnefoux, 1782-1855

Bonnefoux's *Mémoires* were published in 1900 and are one of the best and most reliable accounts of life as a prisoner of war both on parole and on board the hulks. In some details they contain distinct echoes of *Mes Pontons*.

After being captured with Garneray on the *Belle-Poule*, Bonnefoux was initially sent on parole to Thame in Oxfordshire and then to Odiham in Hampshire. There he broke his parole in June 1807 by taking a trip for the day to Windsor, where he visited the Castle and saw George III, Queen Charlotte and various members of the royal family walking on the terrace. This breach was not immediately discovered but Bonnefoux later talked about his adventure in the hearing of a lady who understood French and betrayed him, with the result that he was ordered to be sent from Odiham to the hulks. He then went on the run but was eventually taken and imprisoned in the *Bahama* hulk at Chatham, from which he made three attempts to escape. He succeeded once in getting ashore but was recaptured.

Early in 1811 he was readmitted to parole and sent to Lichfield where he lived for eight months. His final and successful attempt to escape, organised through a smuggler, took place in November 1811. His subsequent career was outstanding and he retired as *capitaine de vaisseau* in 1848, distinguished for his work in hydrography and naval training. His *Dictionnaire de Marine à Voiles*, on which he collaborated with his son-in-law Captain François-Edmond Pâris (1806-93), is still in print.

Duclos-Legris

The name of this man is given as Ducros-Legris in the National Maritime Museum's catalogue but the name as written in his Journal seems to be Duclos-Legris. He was a *timonier* in the *Marengo* and a prisoner in the *Prothee* from 1806 until 1814. The text of his *Journal du voyage fait dans L'inde sur le V[aisse]au Le Marengo de 74 canons*, (NMM, Ref LOG/F/2) is written on British paper watermarked 1811 and the last note in it records his release at the end of May 1814. Unfortunately the text is impersonal and Duclos-Legris gave no written details of his imprisonment, although he did paint the interesting view of the *Prothee* reproduced in this present book. There is no watermark on the paper used for the paintings and it is impossible to say precisely when and where they were done, but they may well have been produced on board the *Prothee* over a long period and later bound up with the written Journal.

I have been unable to discover any personal information about Duclos-Legris, not even his Christian name, since the list of prisoners on board the *Prothee* under the initial D is missing from the Board of Transport's register in PRO ADM 103/529.

Lieut. John Edwards, 1776?-1838

According to Garneray 'the Captain commanding the *Vengeance* was retired on account of his age and replaced by a very young lieutenant named Edwards'. Captain Hugh Downman is said by O'Byrne in his *Naval Biographical Dictionary* to have 'superintended the prison-ships at Portsmouth' from September 1807 till January 1811 and his name appears in Steel's *List of the Royal Navy* as Captain of the *Vengeance* with Alexander Gilmour below him as Lieutenant. Gilmour was replaced as Lieutenant by John Edwards in 1810 and went on to command the *Suffolk* prison ship until 1812. Since Gilmour lived until 1853 and Downman died as an Admiral in 1858, neither of these officers can have retired on account of age, but Garneray is correct in naming Edwards as their successor.

John Edwards served in the *Gibraltar* at the battle of the Glorious First of June, 1794, and was 3rd lieutenant of the 98-gun *Prince* at Trafalgar. He was in the *Vanguard* at the siege of Copenhagen and next became commander of the *Vengeance* prison hulk. Edwards expressed his wish to be relieved of command of the *Vengeance* in September 1811 and was succeeded by Lieut. John Francis Wharton. Edwards got married on 2nd October 1811.

The Board of Transport appears to have been displeased with Edwards at this time because he left business outstanding with Captain Woodriff and did not clear up his accounts for the benefit of his successor. Edwards next served in the *Royal William* and the *Barham*. He was promoted to Commander on 4th December 1813 and his name appears as such in Steel's *Navy List* until the end of 1837. He died of heart disease at Torpoint near Plymouth on 25th February 1838 at the age of sixty-two. PRO ADM 98/263, John Marshall, *Royal Naval Biography*, Vol. IV, Part I, pp. 143-144.

General Louis-François Lejeune, 1775-1848

Lejeune rose from the ranks and had a long and distinguished military career through the

Revolution, the Empire and the Restoration, and was wounded many times. He was a Colonel and a Baron of the Empire at the time he was captured by guerrillas at Illiescar near Toledo on 5th April 1811. After narrowly escaping being hanged he was sent to Cadiz and onwards to Portugal from whence he was taken to England. I have searched without success for Lejeune's name in the surviving registers of the *Vengeance* and, if his meeting with Garneray ever took place, which is doubtful, it would have happened about the beginning of June 1811. Captain Woodriff, the agent at Portsmouth, was directed by the Transport Board on 8th June to 'send M. Le Baron Le Jeune on Parole to Ashby-dela-Zouche'.

Lejeune did not delay in escaping. He got away from Ashby on 15th July and arrived back in France on 30th July. He served in the Grande Armée in Russia and was frost-bitten on the retreat from Moscow. He was an artist, painted various portraits and historical subjects and eventually became Director of l'École des Beaux-Arts and l'École industrielle at Toulouse and Mayor of that city.

It should be noted that Lejeune's autobiography, *Souvenirs d'un officier de l'Empire*, was published in 1851 and may have been available to Garneray when he was writing *Mes Pontons*. PRO ADM 98/263 & ADM 103 439 & 440. See also Lejeune's entry in Georges Six's *Histoire Biographique des Généraux & Amiraux Français de la Révolution et de l'Empire*.

Lieut. James Rose, 17__?-1841

Garneray says in Chapter VIII that 'to avoid reviving old enmities, I shall simply call [him] by his initial Lieutenant R___' and does so throughout the French text. The *Crown*'s commander can, however, be easily identified as Lieutenant James Rose and accordingly I have named him in the translation. Since Garneray was never on board the *Crown* it is likely that his portrait of Rose is largely fiction, though details, such as the fact that Rose had lost a hand as a consequence of a duel, are correct.

The real James Rose probably had Scottish origins.[150] He became a lieutenant in September 1796, fought and was wounded at Camperdown in the *Ardent* in 1797, and was appointed to the command of the *Growler* gun-brig in 1804. In February 1805 he captured the French national gun-brig No. 163 after a fight of an hour and a half and brought her into Falmouth. The next month the *Growler* captured two gun-boats.

On 19th November 1805 Rose fought a duel at Falmouth with his sub-lieutenant Thomas Simpson which resulted in the amputation of one of Rose's hands on board the *Tromp* prison ship and the arrest of the principals and their seconds. This episode suggests that 'the intolerable irritability' of Rose's character as described by Garneray might have had some real basis.

On 1st July 1807 the *Growler* helped in the capture and destruction of two armed chasse-marées and twenty coasting vessels. Rose commanded the *Crown* Prison Ship from 1808.

Rose's first wife, whom he had married whilst still a midshipman, died in January 1810. She had the distinction of being the subject of three notices in *The Naval Chronicle*; the first announced her death, whilst the second regretted that the previous notice was an error, stating that 'the Lady is alive, and in perfect health.' The third, grovellingly apologetic, confirmed that 'Mrs Rose it appears, is really dead; and was buried on the 9th day of January.'

According to Garneray, Rose was disgraced and dismissed because of his conduct towards the prisoners on board the *Crown*. This is fiction; Rose exchanged the command of the *Crown* for that of the *Hearty* gun-brig in April 1812 and Lieutenant Wickham of the *Hearty* took over the *Crown*.

Rose was promoted to Commander on 9th August 1813 and was present in the *Hearty* at the surrender of Gluckstadt in January 1814, the Royal Swedish Order of the Sword being conferred on him for his conduct there. At some time he married again to a lady named Euphemia Bremner and they lived at Nairn in Scotland for at least the last few years of his life. His name appears as a Commander in Steel's *Navy List* until the end of 1840 and he died at Nairn early in 1841. John Marshall, *Royal Naval Biography*, Vol. IV, Part I, pp. 119-120, *The Times* 25th February and 25th November 1805, *The Naval Chronicle*, Vol. 23, pp. 88, 176 & 264.

Dr John Weir, 1759?-1841

In Garneray's text this man is called Dr Weiss, but his real name was John Weir, which name I have substituted throughout the translation. There is no reason to suppose that Garneray's grotesque caricature in any way resembles the real man. Weir was born in Scotland, studied at Edinburgh University from 1776 to 1778 and then entered the Royal Navy where he had a distinguished career. He was promoted to be Physician to the fleet by Lord St Vincent in 1798. In 1802 he was appointed a Junior Commissioner of the Sick and Hurt Board (which merged with the Transport Board in 1806) and subsequently became an Inspector of Naval Hospitals.

Weir visited the *Prothee* in June 1806 only a few weeks after Garneray was sent on board, so it is possible that Garneray actually saw him. Weir's Letter Book and his notes on hygiene in the hulks and hospitals reveal him to have been a conscientious man of considerable ability. He was intolerant of failings on the part of certain surgeons in the hulks, for example castigating Mr J. A. Madden, surgeon of the *Suffolk* in 1809, as being 'from professional ignorance, and an eccentricity bordering on derangement, totally unfit for holding any medical situation in His Majesty's Navy.'

Several references exist to Dr Weir's selection in March 1812 of incurables to be returned to France and he certainly attended the prisoners on board *Vengeance*, e.g. Auguste Grange, 'Invalided by Dr Weir for France.' Weir became a Medical Commissioner of the Victualling Board in 1817.

He died of 'Influenza and Decay of Nature' in London on 24th February 1841 at the age of eighty-two and left the bulk of his estate to his son John Charles Weir, a surgeon at the Royal Hospital at Haslar.

See also William Nisbet, *Authentic Memoirs Biographical, Critical and Literary of the Most Eminent Physicians and Surgeons of Great Britain*, 2nd ed., London 1818, pp. 541-544.

Captain Daniel Woodriff, 1756?-1842

Woodriff entered the Royal Navy as a gunner's mate on 12th August 1762, when he cannot have been more than an infant if the age given in his obituary in *The Times* is correct. He became a lieutenant in 1782, commander in 1795 and was the agent at the Depôt for prisoners of war at Norman Cross in Huntingdonshire from 1799 to 1802.

He returned to sea as Captain of the *Calcutta* in 1802 and himself became a prisoner of war when he was forced to surrender his ship to the French near the Isles of Scilly on 26th September 1805. He was landed at La Rochelle and in January and February 1806 travelled

600 miles to Verdun where he was imprisoned. He was released on Napoleon's personal orders in June 1807 and sent home at the expense of the French government. In exchange the British government immediately repatriated a French officer of similar rank.

Woodriff succeeded Lieutenant William Miller as agent for prisoners of war at Forton in July 1808 where he stayed until he was appointed as a Commissioner of the Navy at Jamaica in December 1813. He was appointed C. B. in 1831 and died at Greenwich Hospital on 24th February 1842 at the age of eighty-six.

T. J. Walker, *The Depôt for Prisoners of War at Norman Cross, Huntingdonshire, 1796 to 1816,* pp. 265-7, O'Byrne, *Naval Biographical Dictionary,* p. 1321, *The Times,* 26th February 1842.

APPENDIX H

GARNERAY'S VIEWS OF THE PORTSMOUTH HULKS

GARNERAY DID NOT SIGN or date his early work and it is possible that pictures of subjects other than the hulks which were painted during his captivity may survive unrecognised. However his views of the hulks are a very distinct aspect of his art and examples can be seen in the National Maritime Museum at Greenwich and in Portsmouth City Art Gallery. In addition as many as fourteen more may exist in private collections, of which I have been fortunate enough to inspect several by the kind permission of various owners.

The pictures are usually about three feet nine inches long by two feet high. The back of one of them clearly shows the artist's lack of materials on board the hulks since two pieces of canvas have been carefully sewn together to bring the surface up to the proper size.

The hulks are shown from the same general point of view, with a line of vessels receding away from the left hand side of the canvas, but nothing about these paintings suggests the work of an artist content to turn out a succession of near-duplicates. Each painting is individual in its composition, details, colouring, shore features and treatment of the sky. Oddly enough, none of the pictures shows the floating platforms that Garneray described as surrounding the hulks at sea level.

Some of the details Garneray gives in *Mes Pontons* about the production of his early paintings may be misleading or adapted to suit his narrative, but the hulk pictures survive in sufficient numbers for them to be tentatively regarded as a series whose remaining examples offer glimpses of stages in the artist's mastery of the techniques which supported his long career as a marine painter. The quality is generally very high and particular paintings can be characterised without exaggeration as superb. That such work could have been produced by a man in even the most favourable conditions on board a prison ship is some indication of Garneray's determination and his stature as a painter.

A little caution is advisable against identifying every picture of the hulks as having been painted whilst Garneray was actually a prisoner. In 1824 Garneray exhibited at the Salon a picture entitled *The English Hulks,* with the following catalogue note, 'In the winter of 1810 the chains holding one of the hulks in the line at Portchester broke in bad weather and the violence of the wind having driven it against the one anchored alongside, the French prisoners therein were placed in the gravest danger.' This canvas, if it depicted the incident described, is probably now lost.

NOTES

ABBREVIATIONS

NMM, National Maritime Museum.

PRO, Public Record Office.

1   **The Garneray or Garnerey family.** For all of his adult life Louis Garneray spelt his surname with an 'a' in the final syllable. His father, Jean-François Garnerey (1755-1837), his brothers Auguste-Simon (1785-1824) and Hippolyte-Jean-Baptiste (1787-1858) and his sister Pauline, about whom little is known, generally used the spelling 'Garnerey'. All of Jean-François Garnerey's children became artists.

2   '**...to ask me once more for your brushes.**' *Voyages, aventures et combats,* Chapter I.

3   **Vice-Admiral Linois.** Charles-Alexandre-Léon Durand, Comte de Linois, 1761-1848.

4   '**Superb had brought the news...**' *Mémoires du Baron de Bonnefoux, Capitaine de Vaisseau, 1782-1855,* p.189.

5   '**...entered their floating prison.**' Log of HMS *Ramillies,* PRO ADM 51/1632. For details of *Prothee* and the other hulks, see Appendix A, Prisoner of War Hulks at Portsmouth.

6   **Admiral Linois at Bath and Cheltenham.** PRO ADM 98/266.

7   **The Rafalés.** See Appendix D.

8   **Theatricals on the Crown.** The poster is NMM M. 154.

9   **Masonic Lodge on the Guildford.** A. Lardier, *Histoire des Pontons et Prisons d'Angleterre,* 1845, pp.53-55.

10 **Registers of Prisoners.** It should be noted that the ledgers in which the registers were kept are often not organised chronologically as one would expect. A register may begin, for example, with a batch of prisoners received on board a hulk in 1809 and immediately afterwards contain details of prisoners received several years before. This may add substantial difficulties to the search for a particular prisoner, even if one knows exactly when he was captured.

11 '**...the hulks were Royal Navy ships...**' See, however, Appendix A concerning the transfer of authority over the hulks from the Admiralty to the Board of Transport in 1810.

12 **Prisoners in the Prothee.** Log of HMS *Prothee,* PRO ADM 51/1708.

13 **Garneray's Description.** As a child Garneray's portrait was painted by his father. The eyes in this picture, now at Versailles, seem to be light blue. See colour plate 1.

14 **Registers of Prisoners.** The alphabetical entries are in PRO ADM 103/532 and 541.

15 '**...transported to England in HMS Superb.**' Priol would certainly have been on one of the vessels of Duckworth's fleet and *Superb* is named in the register as the ship that captured him.

16 **Terpsichore's log.** PRO ADM 51/1574.

17 '**...a vessel named the Turlurette.**' Laurent Manœuvre, *Louis Garneray, 1783-1857, Peintre, Ecrivain, Aventurier,* pp.174, 185-6 & 200.

18 '**...no records of certain events...**' Laurent Manœuvre, *Louis Garneray,* pp.42 & 44.

19 **Registers of Prisoners.** The Board of Transport's alphabetical register, PRO ADM 103 524-548.

20 **Entitlement to Parole.** A limited number of men from the lower ranks were, however, admitted to parole as servants to superior officers in parole towns.

21 '**...by Coach this Day...**' PRO ADM 98/263.

22 **Duclos-Legris.** See the note in Appendix G.

23 **See Appendix H,** Garneray's Views of the Hulks.

24 **Sergeant Flavigny.** Auguste-François Chomel, *Histoire du sergent Flavigny ou dix années de ma captivité sur les pontons anglais; avec notes de M. Louis Garneray, qui a fait le dessin des deux gravures* (Paris, 1821) 2 vols.

25 **Garneray's ghost writer.** In his preface to *Abordages d'un Marin de la République,* a shortened

version of *Voyages, aventures et combats* published in 1912, Albert Savine suggested that 'a veteran of maritime literature, probably Édouard Corbière, undertook to amend the manuscript…'. This seems unlikely since Corbière's style is very different from Garneray's.

26 '…to treat them with caution.' See Appendix C, Garneray's Sources.

27 '…a singularly doubtful document.' Auguste Toussaint, *Les Frères Surcouf*, pp.14 & 15, Philippe Masson, *Les Sépulcres Flottants*, p.9.

28 '…fellow-prisoner from the *Belle-Poule*…' *Mémoires du Baron de Bonnefoux, Capitaine de Vaisseau, 1782-1855.*

29 '…one particularly prejudiced author…' Maréchal-de-Camp René-Martin Pillet, *Views of England, During a Residence of Ten Years; six of them as a Prisoner of War*, 1815. See Appendix C, Garneray's Sources.

30 Île de France is now Mauritius, whilst St Denis is the capital of Réunion, formerly Île de Bourbon. Garneray's rank was that of *aide-timonier*, literally helmsman's assistant.

31 'One night an English frigate, the *Terpsichore*…' This happened on 15th August 1805. See Foreword, p. xvi.

32 '…the three-decker *London*, carrying 104.' Actually 90. D. Lyon, *The Sailing Navy List*, p.64.

33 HMS *Prothee*. This ship was a French third rate of 64 guns, launched at Brest as *Le Protée* in 1772. She was captured in 1780 and served in the Royal Navy under the name *Prothee*. She became a prison hulk at Portsmouth in 1795 and was broken up in 1815. D. Lyon, *The Sailing Navy List*, p. 215.

34 'This access…' was in fact on board the *Crown* hulk. See Chapter IX.

35 Hulks' officers. The Commander of the *Prothee* when Garneray went on board was William Todman who became a lieutenant on 8th July 1795. Up to April 1808 the garrison consisted of Royal Marines and thereafter until December 1809, after which no logs survive, detachments from various militia regiments did duty, including the Ayrshire Militia, the West Essex Militia, the Leicestershire Militia, the Oxford Militia and the Shropshire Militia. The numbers stated by Garneray appear roughly correct; 38 men of the Ayrshire Militia were received on board on 11th April 1808. Logs of HMS *Prothee*, PRO ADM 51 1708/4489/2708 & 1964. From about 1811 it became the practice to have another lieutenant as second in command of each hulk.

36 'Complete equality in suffering was the rule…' See Appendix B, French Officers on board the Hulks and on Parole.

37 Meat days and meatless days. Fr., *'en jours gras et en jours maigres.'*

38 '…an English pound contains fourteen and not sixteen ounces.' The 'seaman's pound' in the Royal Navy was of fourteen ounces; the other two were kept by the purser to allow for notional waste or leakage. See James, *The Naval History of Great Britain*, 1837, Vol. II, p. 24.

39 '…to provide some money for escapers.' Garneray equates food with money since rations, clothing, hammocks and every object that came on board had a value in the hulk's economy.

40 '…spoons, forks and knives were unknown to us.' An exaggeration since the prisoners were well able to make or procure wooden spoons and other implements.

41 *Rabiot.* Bonnefoux and Pâris in their *Dictionnaire de Marine à Voiles* give the noun as *rabieau* with the verb *rabiauter*, 'To pick up leavings, to take advantage of abandoned trifles.'

42 Delivery of rations to the *Prothee*. Garneray is very accurate. It is astonishing to note from the *Prothee*'s log that bread, beef, potatoes, herrings and sometimes cabbages were delivered *separately* by the various contractors at differing times in the day. The bread usually arrived at 8 a.m. but it could be as late as 4 p.m. The cooks and distributors of the food must have despaired. The log shows that there were particular problems in March 1807.
Friday, 13th March, *'The whole of this Day the Prisoners had no Herrings'.*
Saturday, 21st March, *'Received Prisoners Beef at 10 came alongside their Bread the[y] refused at 11 Received their Herrings…at 5 oClock Prisoners Bread came along side being as before they Refused*

Prisioners only [had] one Loaf for 12 men the whole of this Day…'
Friday, 27th March, *'…at 11 Received Prisioners Bread P. M. at 3 Received Prisioners pease at 4 their Potatoes…'* Log of HMS *Prothee*, PRO ADM 51/4489.

43 **Water Tanks.** The first mention of water tanks on board the Portsmouth hulks actually occurs in 1811. The Board of Transport wrote to Captain Daniel Woodriff, the agent at Portsmouth, on 9th August 1811 asking him to consider the practicalities of fitting cisterns similar to those installed on three hulks at Plymouth, where two had been fitted in each ship, capable of holding twenty tons each. As well as saving 'a Great Expence for Casks' the Board had in mind that the prisoners would be 'deprived of the opportunity of converting the Iron Hoops belonging to the Casks into Saws, and other Instruments of Mischief…' PRO ADM 98/263.

44 **Tobacco.** Presumably the prisoner who ground (*triturait*) the tobacco was preparing snuff. According to Captain Beaujot, who was imprisoned in the *Vigilant* hulk, tobacco was so exorbitantly expensive that prisoners got as much use out of it as possible by first chewing it, then drying what remained and smoking it. Charles-Rémi Beaujot, *Relation de captivité*, p. 78.

45 **'…I'll get back to my shoes.'** Garneray paid the shoemaker about 1s. 8d. (9p) for his help and gave Picot £3 for the place by the gun-port.

46 **'…have you been long on this hulk?'** Garneray begins *tutoyer* Bertaud.

47 *Pare à virer.* Prepare to tack, ready about.

48 **'…these degraded creatures…'** See Appendix D, The *Rafalés*.

49 **Body snatcher.** Fr., *'croque-mort'* an undertaker's man, hence a hospital orderly.

50 **Serpent.** The musical instrument.

51 **Exchanges at Sea.** An exchange at sea might be arranged, for example, when a British subject was captured by a French privateer. The captive would be allowed to return to England in consideration of a written promise given to the captor to procure the release of a named prisoner in British hands. The captive would be under an obligation to notify the arrangement to the Board of Transport and not to serve as a combatant against France until the exchange was actually carried out. Such an arrangement was in effect a private contract that required the co-operation of the British government for its completion. The uncertainties of this procedure, compared to the regular exchanges arranged between governments, are plain. Neither party would have known if the prisoner to be exchanged was still alive or, if alive, whether or not his status, perhaps as a 'Broke Parole,' would prevent the British government co-operating in the arrangement. An example of an exchange at sea relating to a prisoner on board a hulk occurred in 1812. On 21st January the *Industria* bound from Greenock for Belfast was taken by the *Amelia* privateer of St Malo. Robert Gleen, a passenger in the *Industria*, was exchanged for Jean Merven, a privateer officer of St Malo who had been in British hands since 1804 and was then on board the *Crown Prince Frederick* hulk at Chatham. PRO ADM 105/44.

52 **Escapes in Water Casks.** A similar escape by two prisoners from the *Crown* hulk using empty water casks is mentioned by the anonymous author of *Les Souvenirs d'un Prisonnier de Guerre*. The prisoners were retaken on the Isle of Wight. *Les Souvenirs*, p. 39.

53 **The Black Hole.** This was the official term in the hulks and contemporary prisons for punishment cells, though British officials frequently used the French word *'cachot'* in correspondence. The name is generally used in the singular, suggesting a sort of communal dungeon, but a Black Hole was in fact a small cell for one prisoner. De Bonnefoux, who was taken prisoner on the *Belle-Poule*, knew the insides of various Black Holes intimately and describes them as being six foot square and six foot high with a few round ventilation holes through which a mouse could not have passed. They were below the water-line in the hulks' holds. De Bonnefoux *Mémoires*, pp. 226-227. Forms recording imprisonment in the Black Holes were kept on board the hulks and though a blank example exists in the Public Record Office, no completed forms appear to have survived. A letter from the Board of Transport dated 30th January 1809 to Captain Daniel

Woodriff, the agent for prisoners of war at Portsmouth, requests him to furnish 'Sick Tickets & Black Hole Returns'. PRO ADM 98/259.

54 *'Navire'*. 'Ship ahoy,' the look-out's cry when sighting a strange ship.

55 *Armateur*. A shipowner in the specific sense of one who at his own expense sent out armed vessels in wartime as privateers by authority of Letters of Marque issued by the state.

56 **Letters from Prisoners**. Assuming that Garneray really tried to write direct to Surcouf it is scarcely surprising that his letters were never forwarded. There were strict rules relating to correspondence passing to and from prisoners and letters had to be sent by local agents for examination by the Transport Board before they went into the postal system. PRO ADM 97/129.

57 '...my captain's examination.' *'...mon examen de capitaine au long cours.'* The captain's examination for deep-water sailing on distant voyages.

58 *Pied de cheval*. 'The name of the largest known type of oyster.' Garneray's footnote.

59 *Chouans*. Bands of irregular fighters of royalist sympathies who operated in Normandy, Brittany and La Vendée during the Revolution.

60 **Punishment of Escapers**. In reality a recaptured escaper would probably have got at least ten days in the Black Hole and the prisoners on the deck from which he came would have had their rations reduced to compensate for the damage caused by cutting the hole in the hull.

61 **Bertaud's body**. See Appendix C, Garneray's Sources, for the origin of the story of Bertaud's corpse being attacked by the crows.

62 '...as in the fable...' La Fontaine's fable of *La fortune et le jeune enfant*. La Fontaine, *Fables*, Book V, Fable XI.

63 **Newspapers** could only be obtained and read illicitly, one of the reasons for the embargo on them being to prevent disturbances amongst prisoners if rumours of invasion were reported. They could, however, be easily smuggled on board and the reading aloud of newspapers by a prisoner capable of simultaneous translation seems to have been a common feature of hulk life. Captain Beaujot records that the better-off prisoners in the *Vigilant* at Portsmouth took out an *abonnement*, a subscription, to the *Morningcronick*, as he called it, and it was read aloud, though the reader was not always heard with avid attention since the older prisoners 'knew by experience that newspaper articles were seldom words of holy writ...' Beaujot, *Relation de captivité*, pp.79–80.

64 **Augustin Grisier**, a celebrated fencer and author of *Les Armes et le Duel*, for which Alexandre Dumas, *père,* wrote a preface.

65 '...the surrender of Santo Domingo...'. In 1803.

66 **Duels**. In the anonymous *Les Souvenirs d'un Prisonnier de Guerre*, first published from the original manuscript in 1903 and therefore not available for Garneray to have pillaged, there is a very similar story of a fatal duel fought with sticks, each tipped with half of a pair of scissors. To get rid of the evidence and save the winner of the duel from being hanged, the loser's dead body was cut up and the pieces dropped through the latrines into the sea. *Les Souvenirs, &c,* p.21.

67 **Lieutenant Rose**. See James Rose, Appendix G.

68 **Sent to Coventry**. Fr., *'mis en quarantaine'*.

69 **The gauntlet**. Fr., *La savate*, the slipper.

70 '...next to my gun-port...' At this point Garneray seems to be thinking of the *Prothee*.

71 **Compensation paid by Escapers**. This is an accurate account of what regularly happened. The Board of Transport wrote to Captain Woodriff at Forton on 20th December 1811. 'Monsr Jean Mésuer who absconded from Bishops Waltham, having been apprehended and lodged in Winchester Goal; we have directed his being sent to Forton Prison. He is to be kept on short Allowance to make good the Sum of 10 Guineas, the Reward paid for his Recapture.' PRO ADM 98/264.

72 **Duvert** is almost certainly a fictitious character.

73 '...slung their hook.' Fr., *Ils ont filé leur câble*. Édouard Corbière uses this expression in *Le Négrier* to mean dying and 'to slip one's cable' in English sailors' slang means to die. See Cdr J. Irving,

Royal Navalese, Edward Arnold & Co, London, 1946, p. 159.

74 **'God damn you!'** *'God bless me!'* according to Garneray.

75 **Officer of Police.** Garneray normally uses the word *police* in the French sense to cover English authorities such as constables and Justices of the Peace. Here he may literally mean a man such as 'David Lazarus the Police officer' who is recorded as having sent Claude Chesson, the surgeon of a privateer, on board the *Vengeance* hulk on 20th December 1811. Chesson had broken his parole at Moreton Hampstead, had been retaken and had again escaped from the shore prison at Forton. Lazarus was allowed only a guinea reward, rather than the usual ten, because the information that enabled him to capture Chesson had originated with the Board of Transport. PRO ADM 103/439, ADM 98/264 & ADM 103/165.

76 **Commodore of the Blue Squadron.** The *'Flotte-Pontonnière-Bleue'* and its Commodore on his throne seem to come from Garneray's imagination, but for details of Captain Daniel Woodriff, see Appendix G.

77 **Duvert's trial**, with witnesses summoned *en masse* from the hulks, is clearly fictitious and Garneray's understanding of English criminal procedure is confused. He makes haphazard mention of juries, coroners, magistrates and judges, which I have simplified to refer only to the magistrates. If a trial had in fact taken place Duvert would have been committed by the magistrates to the Hampshire Assizes at Winchester.

78 **The latrines.** Coyly described, in Garneray's or the interpreter's words, as *'cette petite cabane réservée, que je ne veux pas désigner par son vrai nom'*.

79 **The Interpreter's Pay.** The figure is correct. '…as there is one Prisoner already allowed Six Pence per Diem for acting as French Clerk and Interpreter in each Prison Ship, we cannot allow another to be borne as such.' Transport Office to Captain R. Mends, Portsmouth, 29th November 1811. PRO ADM 98/263.

80 **'…our wrestlers and strong-arm men…'** Fr., *forts-à-bras*. Although Garneray does not say so, the *forts-à-bras* were not just ordinary men of superior strength. The anonymous author of *Les Souvenirs d'un Prisonnier Guerre* characterises them as trouble-makers who 'attacked the weak and levied blackmail from the various tradesmen in the prisons, knocking over their stalls and beating them if they refused to satisfy their demands.' *Les Souvenirs, &c*, p. 23. In Chapter IV of Edouard Corbière's novel *Le Négrier* a description is given of the *forts-à-bras* in Mill Prison at Plymouth who 'reigned by terror over the weak…'

81 **'…the Bretons' corner…'** Fr., *carré armoricain*, the Breton mess or quarters.

82 **A *pardon*** is an annual pilgrimage and procession in honour of the patron saint of a Breton parish. In mediaeval times the faithful who participated were believed to be pardoned from suffering in purgatory for a specific period.

83 **Tattooing as a Punishment on board the Hulks.** The wording of the tattoo inscription and the placard are taken from Lieutenant Mesonant's *Coup d'œil rapide sur les Pontons de Chatam*. A soldier named Joseph Le Roux in the *Sampson* hulk at Chatham had betrayed a plan to escape through holes cut in the hull on the orlop deck. He in turn was betrayed when his comrades bribed one of the British guards with a guinea to reveal Le Roux's name. Le Roux was given fifty lashes by the prisoners, tattooed on his face with words identical, except for the date, to those inscribed on Duvert, and paraded on deck wearing the placard. The date of his punishment was 25th May 1811. Le Roux was afterwards protected by the British and according to Mesonant entered the Royal Navy. The reprisals by the British for cutting holes in the hulk took the legally permitted form of a reduction to two-thirds rations for those on the deck where the offence occurred. This led to a riot on 31st May in which six prisoners were shot dead and six were seriously wounded. This was the worst conflict between prisoners and guards that occurred on board the hulks and was always called a massacre by the French, the numbers involved being frequently multiplied by different writers. Garneray's freedom in adopting real episodes for his

narrative and adjusting their dates is well displayed here. See also Appendix C, Garneray's Sources.

84 **Protection of Informers.** The Board of Transport's records contain a number of references to protection and rewards given to French informers. In certain cases this could result in the informer's release, as in June 1811 when the Board of Transport wrote to Captain Woodriff, 'Jean Lacaster, a French Prisoner at Stapleton who has given Information of the Prisoners at that Depot intending to escape by Means of Excavation has been ordered to proceed to Forton; and we direct you to embark him onboard [sic] the first Cartel for France.' PRO ADM 98/263. Irregular releases of this type and the arrival in France of men claiming to have purchased the right to be exchanged from a fellow-prisoner were suspicious to the French authorities. The Abbé Robidou in *Les Derniers Corsaires Malouins* (p. 338) quotes a direction by Fouché, the Minister of Police, dated Pluviose Year VIII (January 1800) in which orders are given for the detention and interrogation of suspicious prisoners who might have been spies or émigrés.

85 *Drogue.* De Bonnefoux and Pâris, *Dictionnaire de Marine à Voiles,* define *Drogue* as 'A card game for four persons commonly played by sailors. Two players are opposed by another pair and the losers are condemned to wear a little wooden peg on their noses so as to pinch their nostrils until they are allowed to remove it by winning another trick; during this time they are said to be *Droguing.* (…on dit qu'ils Droguent.)*

86 '**Who are your** *parrains*?' Fr., *Parrain*, a Godfather, and also a second in a fight.

87 '**If the time exceeds half a minute…**' Garneray says five minutes, but half a minute seems more likely from contemporary accounts of prize-fights.

88 **The Great Dane.** Garneray may have lifted the story of the Great Dane from Maréchal-de-Camp René Pillet's *Views of England, During a Residence of Ten Years; six of them as a Prisoner of War,* in which there occurs a similar tale, probably equally fictitious. 'Milord Cordower [Lord Cawdor] Colonel of the Carmarthen regiment, on guard at Porchester Prison, having one day entered the prison, left his horse fastened to one of the rails, and in ten minutes it was cut up and eaten… An enormous butcher's dog, or rather every dog that entered the prison shared a similar fate.' Pillet, 1815 edition, pp. 388-9.

89 '**…once our gaoler was gone.**' The whole story of James Rose's humiliation and dismissal is an invention. See Appendix G.

90 **HMS** *Vengeance,* a 74 launched in 1774.

91 **Abraham Curtis.** Garneray must have had an intermediary for the sale of his pictures but Abraham Curtis cannot be found in contemporary local directories and is almost certainly a fictional character.

92 *Haemoptysis,* a spitting of blood 'characterised by coughing up florid or frothy blood' and *Marasmus,* 'a wasting away of the flesh, without fever or apparent disease.' Robert Hooper, *Lexicon Medicum or Medical Dictionary*, London, 1825.

93 '**…the victims of as many murders.**' See Appendix F, Mortality of Prisoners of War.

94 '**The surgeon…was called Weir…**' He is disguised as Weiss in Garneray's text. See Dr John Weir, Appendix G.

95 **The** *Éclair.* No privateer of this name was taken in the period 1808-1814.

96 '**…Twenty wretches would die every evening…**' See Appendix F, Mortality of Prisoners of War.

97 '**…a very young lieutenant named Edwards.**' See Lieut. John Edwards, Appendix G.

98 **Women on board the Hulks.** See Appendix E.

99 **Denis Decrès,** 1761-1820, Ministre de la Marine from 1801 to 1814 and during the Hundred Days.

100 '**This regulation, which had just been promulgated…**'No such arbitrary and illegal regulation was ever issued by the British government, but in March 1810 it seems that the Spanish government may have threatened to hang Frenchmen who escaped from the Spanish hulks at Cadiz. The letter of protest was shamelessly copied by Garneray from *'Mémoires d'un officier français prisonnier en Espagne'* by C. de Méry (possibly a pseudonym of Vantal de Carrère or Carrère-Vantal)

which was published in 1823. The letter may be a copy of a genuine historic document addressed by French officers to the Spanish government but in his *Geôles et Pontons d'Espagne*, (p.447) Geisendorf-Des Gouttes noted in 1932 that although the text is given in French by de Méry and a German version exists by a Swiss officer called Johannes Landolt, no Spanish version could be found in the National Archives at Madrid or at Cadiz. See also Philippe Masson, *Les Sépulcres Flottants*, pp. 157 & 159-160.

101 '...the English had just seized the Danish fleet at Copenhagen.' In fact the seizure of the Danish fleet took place in October 1807.

102 '...Captain Edwards left our hulk...' See Lieut. John Edwards, Appendix G.

103 Lieutenant T___ of Garneray's narrative appears to be a fictitious character. Lieut. John Francis Wharton assumed command of the *Vengeance* in September 1811. The details of his life in O'Byrne's *Naval Biographical Dictionary* show that he had a long and active career in the Royal Navy and died as a retired Commander in 1848.

104 James Smith, like his rival Abraham Curtis, cannot be traced in contemporary local directories and appears to be a fictional character.

105 *Passe-dix* and *Biribi*. The players of *passe-dix* used three dice and bet on getting more than ten on the throw of the dice; *biribi* was played with hollow numbered balls that corresponded to numbers on a cloth or table.

106 Gambling for Linch's life. Garneray was not exaggerating the callousness of the *rafalés* and he probably had in mind an episode on board the *Sampson* at Chatham in 1813 when three prisoners conspired to kill the master's mate, a sergeant of Marines and seven prisoners. They intended to kill each victim separately and drew lots as to who should do the first murder. The choice fell on Charles Manseraux whose conscience, or so he alleged, did not allow him to kill the sergeant, because he was a married man with a family. Instead Manseraux stabbed Thomas King, a Marine private, in the back and killed him. Manseraux and his accomplices were executed. *The Times*, 19th July 1813.

107 '...the deplorable surrender by General Dupont at Baylen.' General Pierre Dupont, Comte de L'Étang, surrendered his entire corps of 18,000 men to the Spanish army under General Castanos at Baylen in Andalusia on 22nd July 1808. The terms of the surrender required the repatriation of the French army and the men endured a terrible march to Cadiz through a violently hostile country. The Generals of the French army were sent home, but thousands of the men were imprisoned at Cadiz on hulks in atrocious conditions. By 1809 half of them were dead and in that year more than five thousand survivors were transported to the inhospitable Balearic island of Cabrera where the greater part perished from hunger, thirst and disease. Several hundred were removed in August 1810 and brought to England and for these unfortunates the prospect of life in the British hulks must, as Garneray states, have been heavenly by comparison with the horrors they had endured.

108 *Pégase* was in fact a 74, taken off Ushant on 21st April 1794. She became a prison hulk in 1794 and a hospital ship in 1801. Her commander from 1809 to 1812 was George Lacey Decœurdoux who had seved at Trafalgar in HMS *Mars*.

109 '...in the lowest terms...' Fr., '... *je le traitai en employant le tutoiement...*'.

110 Louis-François Lejeune (1775-1848). See Appendix G.

111 Queen Hortense. Hortense de Beauharnais (1783-1837), the daughter of the Empress Josephine. She married Napoleon's brother, Louis, who became King of Holland in 1806.

112 '...Lejeune was sent to Odiham.' He was actually sent to Ashby-de-la-Zouche in June 1811.

113 Fignolet appeared in *Voyages, aventures et combats* as a young man with a hearty appetite.

114 '...nearly a hundred francs...', i.e. about £4.

115 '...as sailing-master...' Fr., *officier de manœuvre*. See Bonnefoux's entry in Appendix G.

116 '...the same place in which Colonel Lejeune was living...' Lejeune had of course been sent

to Ashby-de-la-Zouche. Garneray's meeting with him at Bishop's Waltham is an obvious fiction and the same description almost undoubtedly applies to the rest of Garneray's narrative of his experiences on parole and on the run, until his supposed recapture near the coast of France.

117 '…at least two thousand Frenchmen have been killed…' A complete untruth. See Appendix B, French Officers on board the Hulks and on Parole.

118 'They hang you.' In fact the crime of helping a prisoner of war to escape was only a misdemeanour and very mildly punished until 1811. In that year the offence was made a felony punishable by transportation for seven or fourteen years or for life at the court's discretion. 52 Geo. III, c. 156.

119 '…the corvette, the *Victory*…' In his *Voyages, aventures et combats* Garneray recounts how in 1802 he and the crew of the *Petite Caroline* were attacked by pirates in the Indian Ocean and saved by 'the English corvette *Victory*, of twenty carronades and two cannons, commanded by Captain Colliers.' No corvette named the *Victory* appears to have existed.

120 '…I was put back on board the *Vengeance*.' The adventures recounted by Garneray in this chapter are fiction but the involvement of smugglers in the lucrative business of transporting prisoners back to France is accurate enough. In 1811 a smuggler called Thomas Moore, a man with several aliases and notorious for his activity in helping prisoners escape, was captured and held in the Tothill Fields Bridewell. He was persuaded by the Board of Transport to give information about 'persons in several seaport towns in Kent…in the practice of carrying on a Communication with the french Coast…' Moore produced a list of picturesque names of persons who might have been real life counterparts of Jeffries and his ruffians, including Old Stanley, Kite and Hornet of Folkestone, Tom Scraggs of Whitstable, and Old Jarvis and Hell Fire Jack of Deal. PRO ADM 97/108. Escaped Frenchmen were not always the helpless prey of English boatmen. François Retif and two other prisoners disguised themselves and succeeded in walking out of Forton Prison at Portsmouth in September 1813. They hired a boat from an old man named George Brothers and told him that they wanted to go to the Isle of Wight. When they were at sea and Brothers was informed that France was the real destination, he resisted the prisoners, was stabbed and thrown overboard. The crime was noticed from the shore, and the fugitives were pursued, retaken and hanged at Winchester. PRO ADM 103 491 & Beaujot, *Relation de captivité*, pp. 90–91.

121 'On 16th April I embarked for France.' Pierre Priol, alias Garneray, was discharged from the *Vengeance* to Forton Prison on 15th May 1814. According to the Archives de la Marine quoted by Laurent Manœuvre, Louis Garneray arrived at Cherbourg on 18th May.

122 **Garneray's scientific curiosity.** Garneray was the inventor of an 'imputrescible canvas' which was commended by contemporary artists and scientists. A solution of *caoutchouc* was used in the manufacture of the fabric. Laurent Manœuvre, *Louis Garneray*, pp. 148-9.

123 '…with a truly documentary care.' Laurent Manœuvre, *Louis Garneray*, p. 116.

124 'The French are the lads for painting action.' Herman Melville, *Moby Dick*, Chapter LV.

125 Laurent Manœuvre, *Louis Garneray*, p.179.

126 **Garneray's work for the Sèvres factory.** The service was intended to comprise 121 pieces. Four alone survive in the Musée national de Céramique at Sèvres.

127 '… an active Bonapartist agent.' See Laurent Manœuvre, *Louis Garneray*, p. 160.

128 Laurent Manœuvre, *Louis Garneray*, p. 162.

129 **Garneray's audience with Napoleon III.** See Laurent Manœuvre, *Louis Garneray*, p. 162.

130 **Murder of Garneray's widow.** Louis Garneray, *Abordages d'un Marin de la République*, edited by Albert Savine, biographical preface, p. 15.

131 **Vessels temporarily used for prisoners at Portsmouth.** For example PRO ADM 103/383 contains references to prisoners from the *Royal Oak* being moved to the *Fortitude* and *Ariel* and back again in 1798.

132 PRO ADM 98/263.

133 **Transfer of control of hulks to the Board of Transport.** See *The Naval Chronicle*, Vol. XXIII, pp. 187-8.

134 PRO ADM 105/53.

135 **Lieutenant Mesonant.** I tentatively identify him as 'J. Mesonan', an army lieutenant named in a list of parole-breakers, in PRO ADM 105/61. He was recaptured and sent to the hulks at Chatham on 13th October 1809.

136 **'... system of murder and cruelty.'** Pillet, *Views of England*, 1815 ed., pp. 267 & 387.

137 **Pillet's style and subject-matter** are equally startling; his revelation that the English were addicted to sexual intercourse in churchyards was suppressed by his American publisher who in 1818 delicately refrained from translating, 'C'est là que plus d'une fille, par suite de son libertinage, est devenue mère, à son tour, sur la tombe de celle qui lui avait donné le jour.' Pillet, *Views of England*, 1815 ed., p. 236.

138 **Lieutenant Milne of the *Bahama* hulk.** Bonnefoux, *Mémoires*, p. 230.

139 **Tom Souville.** Chevalier, *Vie et Aventures*, pp. 319-357.

140 PRO ADM 103/645.

141 PRO ADM 103/648.

142 PRO ADM 105/61.

143 **Women on Royal Navy ships.** See *The Life and Adventures of John Nicol, Mariner*, 1828, in which Nicol mentions the women who carried powder to the guns on board HMS *Goliath* at the battle of the Nile.

144 PRO ADM 103/639.

145 **A cartel** was an agreement for the exchange of prisoners. The word was also used to mean a ship carrying prisoners home under a flag of truce. British cartel vessels sailed from Portsmouth, Dartmouth, Plymouth and King's Lynn, but Morlaix in Brittany was the sole French port to which Napoleon allowed them access.

146 PRO ADM 105/44.

147 PRO ADM 103/383.

148 **Sergeant-Major Barreau.** Beaujot, *Relation de captivité*, pp.80-81.

149 PRO ADM 103/439.

150 **James Rose** was living at Nairn in Scotland at the date of his death, where his unmarried sister also resided. He mentioned in his will, dated 20th December 1837, that his late brother Alexander Rose was also known as Ross.

BIBLIOGRAPHY

Anonymous, *Les Souvenirs d'un Prisonnier de Guerre*, printed in Carnet de la Sabretache, Paris, 1903.

Francis Abell, *Prisoners of War in Britain, 1756-1815,* Oxford University Press, 1914.

Charles-Rémi Beaujot, *Relation de captivité*, Éditions Historiques Teissèdre, Paris, 2001.

Pierre-Marie-Joseph, Baron de Bonnefoux, *Mémoires du Baron de Bonnefoux, Capitaine de Vaisseau, 1782-1855*, ed. E. Jobbé-Duval, Plon-Nourrit & Cie, Paris, 1900.

Pierre-Marie-Joseph, Baron de Bonnefoux, & Capitaine de Vaisseau F. E. Pâris, *Dictionnaire de Marine à Voiles*, Éditions du Layeur, 1999.

Henri Chevalier, *Vie et Aventures du Capitaine de Corsaire Tom Souville, Ses Combats – Ses*

Évasions 1777-1839, Librairie Plon, Paris, 1895.

Édouard Corbière, *Le Négrier,* Éditions l'Ancre de la Marine, St Malo, 2002.

Louis Garneray, *Voyages de Garneray, Peintre de Marine, Premiere Partie, Voyages, Aventures et Combats, Deuxième Partie, Mes Pontons.* Gustave Barba, Paris, n.d. [1851].

Louis Garneray, *Scènes Maritimes faisant suite aux Pontons et aux Mémoires du même auteur,* Dupray de la Maherie, Paris, 1863.

Louis Garneray, *Abordages d'un Marin de la République,* edited by Albert Savine, Société des Éditions Louis-Michaud, Paris, 1912. A shortened version of *Voyages, aventures et combats,* valuable for Savine's biographical preface.

Geisendorf-Des Gouttes, *Les Prisonniers de Guerre sous le Premier Empire, Geôles et Pontons d'Espagne, L'Expédition et la Captivité d'Andalousie.* Les Éditions Labor, Geneva & Nlles Éditions Latines, Paris, 1932.

William James, *The Naval History of Great Britain,* Richard Bentley, 1837.

W. Branch Johnson, *The English Prison Hulks,* Revised ed., Phillimore & Co, Chichester, 1970.

Alexandre Lardier, *Histoire des pontons et prisons d'Angleterre pendant la guerre du Consulat et de l'Empire,* Paris, 1845.

David Lyon, *The Sailing Navy List,* Conway Maritime Press, London, 1993.

Laurent Manœuvre, *Louis Garneray, 1783-1857, Peintre, Écrivain, Aventurier,* Bibliothèque de l'Image, Paris, 2002.

John Marshall, *Royal Naval Biography,* London, 1833.

Philippe Masson, *Les Sépulcres Flottants, Prisonniers Français en Angleterre sous l'Empire,* Éditions Ouest-France, 1987.

Lieutenant J. [?] Mesonant, *Coup d'œuil rapide sur les Pontons de Chatam* [sic] in *Pontons et Prisons sous le Premier Empire,* Librairie Historique F. Teissèdre, Paris, 1998.

W. J. O'Byrne, *A Naval Biographical Dictionary,* John Murray, London, 1849.

Maréchal-de-Camp René-Martin Pillet, *L'Angleterre vue à Londres et dans ses provinces pendant un séjour de dix années, dont six comme prisonnier de guerre,* Alexis Eymery, Paris, 1815, translated as *Views of England, During a Residence of Ten Years; six of them as a Prisoner of War,* Parmenter & Newton, Boston, 1818.

L'Abbé F. Robidou, *Les Derniers Corsaires Malouins,* Imprimerie Oberthur, Rennes-Paris, 1919.

Georges Six, *Histoire Biographique des Généraux et Amiraux Français de la Revolution et de l'Empire,* Librairie Historique et Nobiliaire Georges Saffroy, Paris, 1934.

J. T. Thorp, *French Prisoners' Lodges,* The Lodge of Research, No. 2429, Leicester, 1935.

Auguste Toussaint, *Les Frères Surcouf,* Flammarion, Paris, 1979.

T. J. Walker, *The Depôt for Prisoners of War at Norman Cross, Huntingdonshire, 1796 to 1816,* London, Constable & Co. Ltd, 1913.

INDEX

Names marked with an asterisk are probably fictitious characters invented by Garneray.